THE HEALING POWER OF THE
SANTUARIO DE CHIMAYÓ

RELIGION, RACE, AND ETHNICITY
General Editor: Peter J. Paris

Beyond Christianity: African Americans in a New Thought Church
Darnise C. Martin

Deeper Shades of Purple: Womanism in Religion and Society
Edited by Stacey M. Floyd-Thomas

Daddy Grace: A Celebrity Preacher and His House of Prayer
Marie W. Dallam

The Methodist Unification: Christianity and the Politics of Race in the Jim Crow Era
Morris L. Davis

Watch This! The Ethics and Aesthetics of Black Televangelism
Jonathan L. Walton

American Muslim Women: Negotiating Race, Class, and Gender within the Ummah
Jamillah Karim

Embodiment and the New Shape of Black Theological Thought
Anthony B. Pinn

From Africa to America: Religion and Adaptation among Ghanaian Immigrants in New York
Moses O. Biney

Afro-Pentecostalism: Black Pentecostal and Charismatic Christianity in History and Culture
Edited by Amos Yong and Estrelda Y. Alexander

Creole Religions of the Caribbean: An Introduction from Vodou and Santería to Obeah and Espiritismo
Margarite Fernández Olmos and Lizabeth Paravisini-Gebert

The Divided Mind of the Black Church: Theology, Piety, and Public Witness
Raphael Gamaliel Warnock

Preaching on Wax: The Phonograph and the Shaping of Modern African American Religion
Lerone A. Martin

The Ground Has Shifted: The Future of the Black Church in Post-Racial America
Walter Earl Fluker

The Healing Power of the Santuario de Chimayó: America's Miraculous Church
Brett Hendrickson

For a complete list of titles in the series, please visit the New York University Press website at www.nyupress.org.

The Healing Power of the Santuario de Chimayó

America's Miraculous Church

Brett Hendrickson

NEW YORK UNIVERSITY PRESS

New York

NEW YORK UNIVERSITY PRESS
New York
www.nyupress.org

© 2017 by New York University
All rights reserved

References to Internet websites (URLs) were accurate at the time of writing. Neither the author nor New York University Press is responsible for URLs that may have expired or changed since the manuscript was prepared.

ISBN: 978-1-4798-1550-0 (hardback)
ISBN: 978-1-4798-8427-8 (paperback)

For Library of Congress Cataloging-in-Publication data, please contact the Library of Congress.

New York University Press books are printed on acid-free paper, and their binding materials are chosen for strength and durability. We strive to use environmentally responsible suppliers and materials to the greatest extent possible in publishing our books.

Manufactured in the United States of America

10 9 8 7 6 5 4 3 2 1

Also available as an ebook

For Alex, Tom, Lily, and David
In memory of Wanda Brisco

CONTENTS

Acknowledgments ix

Introduction 1

1. Catholic Settlement of Río Arriba 14

2. The Origin of the Santuario 39

3. New Mexican Catholicism in Transition 68

4. The Santo Niño de Atocha 101

5. Selling the Santuario 122

6. The Pilgrims and Pilgrimage 139

7. The Holy Family and the Santuario Today 169

Conclusion 195

Notes 203

Bibliography 221

Index 233

About the Author 245

ACKNOWLEDGMENTS

What a pleasure to thank friends for their help! Many people and institutions aided me in the writing of this book, and I am so grateful to them all.

During my various research trips to New Mexico, numerous people made time to meet with me, give me access to their notes and archives, and generally guide me in this project. My sincerest thanks go to the people who agreed to talk with me and share their personal stories during their visits to the Santuario. In Chimayó itself, I thank Joanne Dupont Sandoval, the now-retired co-manager of the Santuario, for her time and generosity. I also thank Raymond Bal and Vicki Bal Tejada of El Potrero Trading Post for helpful conversations. New Mexico boasts many excellent archives and archivists. Tomas Jaehn at the Fray Angélico Chávez History Library at the Palace of the Governors was very supportive of this project. Thank you to the staff at the New Mexico State Records Center and Archives for opening so many exciting documents to me. Many thanks to all the archivists at the University of New Mexico's Center for Southwest Research, especially Nancy Brown-Martinez and Claire-Lise Bénaud. Robin Farwell Gavin at the Museum of the Spanish Colonial Arts Society kindly made her files on the Santuario available to me. At Santa Fe's Laboratory of Anthropology, I received helpful information and advice from Diane Bird, Dedie Snow, and Tony Chavarria. The librarian at the School for Advanced Research, Laura Holt, shared her time as well as documents with me. The staff at the Archives of the Archdiocese of Santa Fe provided assistance. I would also like to thank Thomas Guthrie and Andrea McComb Sanchez for helping me with proper terms for New Mexico's people. I thank Gala Chamberlain, a trustee of the Ann Baumann Trust, for permission to use the beautiful woodcut by the artist Gustave Baumann on the cover of this book.

At Lafayette College, I work with a talented and generous bunch of people. My thanks go to the entire Religious Studies Department for their collegiality, and I especially thank Jessica Carr and Steve Lammers for their specific feedback. I owe a great debt to the members of my writing group: Laurie Caslake, John McKnight, Mary Roth, and Angelika von Wahl. John T. Clark crafted the maps in this book, for which I am grateful. My research was funded in part by grants from Lafayette's Academic Research Committee and a Richard King Mellon Summer Research Fellowship; I am thankful for Lafayette's commitment to faculty research.

I am particularly grateful for my Young Scholars in American Religion cohort, who helped me through the preparation of this book: Kate Bowler, Heath Carter, Kathryn Gin Lum, Josh Guthman, Lerone Martin, Kate Moran, Angela Tarango, Steve Taysom, T. J. Tomlin, David Walker, Grace Yukich, Laurie Maffly-Kipp, and Doug Winiarski. Thanks go also to Katie Holscher, Kristy Nabhan-Warren, Brandi Denison, and Tom Bremer for talking me through parts of this project. As always, the staff at New York University Press have been phenomenal; special thanks to my editor, Jennifer Hammer, and to the Religion, Race, and Ethnicity series editor, Peter Paris. Thank you, also, to Amy Klopfenstein and Rosalie Morales Kearns for their work on this book.

I have been blessed with friends and family who were at my side during the research and writing of this book. Thank you to Ken McAllister and Rachel Srubas for listening to me think out loud and for sharing popsicles in front of the Santuario. A huge thank you to Drew Henry and Tamara Hudson for allowing me extensive use of their *casita* while I was doing research and for their friendship. David Gambrell was a true companion on the road. I am so glad that we were able to share the pilgrimage together. My deepest love goes to my children, who continue to be my best supporters: Tom, Lily, and David. My whole heart is devoted to my wife, Alex, who believes in me. This book is dedicated to my wife and children and also to the memory of my mother, who taught me to love going up to the house of the Lord.

NOTE ON ETHNIC TERMS

Just as race and ethnicity are socially constructed, so are the terms we use to refer to people of different racial and ethnic heritages. In New Mexico, the way that people talk about groups of other people is not simple, has often been fraught with prejudice, and has changed frequently, often to meet the social and political needs of one or more groups. In this book, I have tried to be as careful and clear as possible when using words that signify ethnic background. I have also tried to the best of my ability to use terms that people use for themselves and find acceptable. For people in New Mexico who trace their ancestry to parts of the Americas that were once part of the Spanish Empire I have mostly opted not to use "Hispanic" or "Latino/a" because these blanket terms have not been specific enough for the story of the Santuario de Chimayó that is recounted in these pages. I have instead used the terms "Hispano" and "Nuevomexicano" to refer to the people of New Mexico who, in their stories about themselves and their families, remember their ancestry as a continuation of Spanish settlement in the region from before the U.S. takeover during the Mexican-American War. I have avoided "Mexican American." Even though this term is common and strongly preferred in many contexts, in New Mexico it often signifies more newly arrived citizens of Mexican descent (that is, since New Mexico became part of the United States). This latter population, although quite important in the state today, plays a comparatively small role in the history of the Santuario de Chimayó and therefore is not much mentioned in this book. In the instances when I do use the terms "Hispanics" or "Latinos," I am generally referring not only to Nuevomexicanos but to people across North America who trace their ancestry to Latin America. When referring to English-speaking people with non-Spanish European roots, I follow the longtime convention in New Mexico and use "Anglo Americans" or simply "Anglos." None of these terms is perfect, and with time, other terms may grow in popularity and preference. I ask the reader for forbearance and humbly submit that this is but one vexing aspect of New Mexico's complex and incredible history.

Introduction

Dirt—the holy dirt—is what the people go to see, to touch, to gather. Inside the adobe church, past the altar and sideways into a low-ceilinged little room, lies the *pocito*, the hole in the floor that goes down into New Mexico's soil, source of the famous healing dirt at the heart of the Santuario de Chimayó.[1] Some people go to get the dirt because they have always done so, since childhood, walking alongside their families. The familiar church in the familiar landscape remains a lodestone of faith, healing, and togetherness, generation after generation. Other people go because they are sightseers, tourists, or first-time visitors, but they too find themselves reaching into the *pocito*, letting the sandy earth trickle through their fingers, smelling the mineral richness of the ground, and wondering about the possibility of miracles. People go to experience the dirt, to pray in the Santuario, and to make a connection. Their aches and pains, the suffering they feel in their joints, the despair in their hearts, their hope against hope for recovery, and their memories of their beloved dead—all draw them to the dirt, the holy dirt.

Why dirt? Why does the Santuario de Chimayó, the most popular site of Catholic pilgrimage in the United States, feature a hole in the ground? As one popular version of the story goes, Bernardo Abeyta, a community leader and landowner in El Potrero, which is an area of the village of Chimayó, was in his fields near the Santa Cruz River sometime in the first decade of the 1800s. Noticing a glowing light shimmering in the ground, he discovered a large crucifix buried in the earth. Awed by the miraculous apparition of the crucifix, the devout Abeyta carried the object to the parish church in Santa Cruz, some eight miles distant. With the cooperation of the Franciscan priest, he placed the crucifix on the altar and returned home. The next day, he again found the artifact buried in his field, right where he had discovered it the day before. After he repeated the journey to Santa Cruz, this time with mystified townspeople alongside, only to have the cross return to its original position in El Potrero, it dawned on Abeyta that the Crucified Lord himself had chosen the spot where he wanted to be venerated. Construction began in 1813 on the Santuario and was completed in 1816. Almost immediately, people began to come to the shrine to venerate the miraculous Christ, to pray, and to gather dirt from the hole from which the crucifix had emerged. Abeyta identified the miraculous object as the Lord of Esquipulas, a popular image of Jesus in New Spain that had first originated centuries before in Guatemala.[2] The dirt in this hole, according to multitudes, has the power to heal.

These days, the Santuario de Chimayó receives hundreds of thousands of visitors every year, tens of thousands on Good Friday alone. Indeed, it is the largest site of Catholic pilgrimage in the United States. Many of these visitors are the descendants of those first Nuevomexicano devotees and health seekers. The Santuario is not only a pilgrimage destination and a site of worship for these people but also a tangible expression of their northern New Mexican Hispano heritage. But the Santuario de Chimayó is also important to others, who, in this peaceful and beautiful church, find that their own spiritual needs are met. The Tewa Pueblo people, who long predate the Hispanic population in the land, speak of Tsi Mayoh hill, rising behind the present-day church, and remember stories of openings in the earth and healing mud. More recent immigrants from Mexico, other Latin American lands, and even parts of Asia—especially Vietnam and the Philippines—come to the church in remembrance of similar shrines in their places of origin. Anglo Americans likewise come; they run the gamut from devout Catholics in practice of their faith, to New Age spiritual seekers in search of energy and the perceived wisdom of so-called traditional peoples, to buses and cars full of tourists who snap photographs of the picturesque church and who gather dirt as a souvenir. New Mexico, especially this part of the state just within the orbit of Santa Fe, is justly known for both its arresting physical beauty and its veritable glut of alternative and complementary medicine and religious experimentation. The Santuario, in this context, acts as a centerpiece both in New Mexico's Hispano Catholic heritage and in the state's seemingly endless offerings of healing, inner peace, and authentic experiences.

This book, a history of the Santuario de Chimayó, tells the story of this remarkable church, one of the most important religious sites in

North America. And since the church is nestled in northern New Mexico, this book is also the story of the people who have made their lives in this place that is or has been the Tewa homeland, the northernmost province of the Spanish Empire, the fraying edge of an independent Mexico, and a unique region of the United States known as the Southwest. The village of Chimayó, in which the church is located, is important to the history of the state. It has been at the forefront of rebellion and self-determination against the several imperial and national powers that have laid claim to it over the centuries, from the Spanish, to Mexicans, to Americans. The Santuario thus serves as a linchpin of sorts, focusing the desires and needs of the Hispanic majority of the region even while highlighting the ongoing influence of the native Pueblo people, of Anglos and tourists, and of the Catholic Church.

In one sense, then, the history of the Santuario grapples with the waves of conquest and new regimes even as it navigates long eras of relative peace and seclusion, and even periods of de facto autonomy. But unlike a mere parcel to be bought, sold, or stolen, the Santuario is a place of worship, a place rich with symbolism. As the noted historian Robert Orsi has argued, religions are the stuff of relationships between heaven and earth, between humans and sacred figures.[3] At Chimayó, where the holy itself wells up out of the ground, people forge relationships with each other and with Jesus, both his suffering adult form on the crucifix and his boyish persona known in the guise of the Santo Niño de Atocha. The Santuario is also a feature of a village, a political community with economic needs and desires. It is a meeting place, a marker of heritage, and a source of revenue because of its popularity. And the Santuario is a church, specifically a Catholic church, which carries its own host of meanings and associations. Of late, it is a destination of thousands—pilgrims and tourists alike—who come to make a connection with the place, to appreciate it, to interact with it, to *feel* what it feels like to be there. Because of this mass appeal, this book carries the subtitle *America's Miraculous Church*; however, it is worth noting that the bulk of the Santuario's story is rooted in the history of Nuevomexicano Catholics. To recognize the Santuario as part of the patrimony of the entire United States, then, requires that we carefully consider the historical claims that many groups have made to the church, its miracles, and the land it sits on.

Religious Ownership

To help understand this church that attracts so many people, to make sense of its miraculousness, and to interpret its impact in New Mexico and beyond, we may find it helpful to use the metaphor of *religious ownership*. Like any metaphor, this one has its limits—the word "ownership" can often simply mean the legal right of possession. But here, despite the limitations of the metaphor, the words "religious ownership" are used as a term for the multifaceted and complex relationships, collaborations, and sometimes competitions between the groups and individuals who make use of religious places, rituals, narratives, and sense of belonging. While these features of religious places can intertwine in an infinite number of ways, in regard to the Santuario, this book focuses on two broad types of claims concerning religious ownership.

First, we can speak of legal claims to church property, as well as to religious functions within that property. For instance, Bernardo Abeyta was the original owner of the Santuario as a religious building on his property. But it is less clear that he owned the rituals and movement of the pilgrims who had begun to come to his church to seek the holy, healing dirt adjacent to the Santa Cruz River. Later, in the twentieth century, when Abeyta's descendants sold the Santuario and it became the property of the Catholic Archdiocese of Santa Fe, the legal right to the land and building was transferred, but religious ownership is not so easily transacted. It took decades for the Catholic Church to exercise its authority of legal ownership, and even today, much of what happens at the Santuario remains insistently outside the control of Church oversight or even interpretation.

The second broad type of claim at play with the metaphor of religious ownership has to do with belonging, meaning making, and a sense of connection. Here, the claims made on a place like the Santuario emerge from the subjective experiences of individuals or groups that feel that they belong at the Santuario and that, in turn, it belongs in some way to them. Like lovers who may speak of "our song," religious sites, because of their emotional and spiritual connections between people and sacred figures, can become "our place," the place where our lives were made more essential, where we were healed, where we experienced the ineffable. In short, then, one of the main arguments this book makes is that the Santuario de Chimayó is a place that, through its history, has been the object of many competing claims of religious ownership; these claims have been based in legal possession, community usage, and a sense of connection or personal belonging. A careful examination of these claims can tell us much about political or ecclesiastical regime change; racial and ethnic dynamics and conflicts, especially between Hispanics and Anglos; tensions between institutional and popular forms of U.S. Catholicism; the impact of faith on healing and health; and the role of commerce at religious sites.

Indeed, the history of the Santuario and the people who have made various kinds of claims on it has long merited more scholarly attention. While the Santuario has been mentioned in hundreds—if not thousands—of feature stories in newspapers and magazines that play up its picturesque qualities, it has rarely been the focus of the historian, and until this volume, its history has never been the subject of an entire book.[4] Before now, the most comprehensive coverage of its history was an article written by a Hungarian American anthropologist named Stephan F. de Borhegyi. First published in 1956 for the Spanish Colonial Arts Society in Santa Fe, Borhegyi's article has been reprinted several times in booklet format to meet the needs of a public who wants to know more about the Santuario's past.[5]

This lack of attention is regrettable for a number of reasons, two of which I would like to mention. First, the history of the Catholic Church in the United States has often been overlooked or under-told, given its sheer numbers of adherents and obvious importance in the life of this country. This is especially the case when we consider American Catholics who trace the roots of their faith to the Spanish evangelization of what we now think of as Latin America and the Caribbean. Histories of sites like the Santuario that are, at least in part, the legacy of Spanish Catholicism need to be told so that we can better understand the complexity of the United States' largest Christian body. This leads to the second reason why the Santuario's history is so important: the largest racial/ethnic minority population in the United States today (and for the foreseeable future) is Latinos and Latinas, people who trace their ancestry, recent or ancient, to the Spanish-speaking countries of the Americas. As with the history of the Catholic Church, the history of Latinos/as requires much more robust consideration. The religious

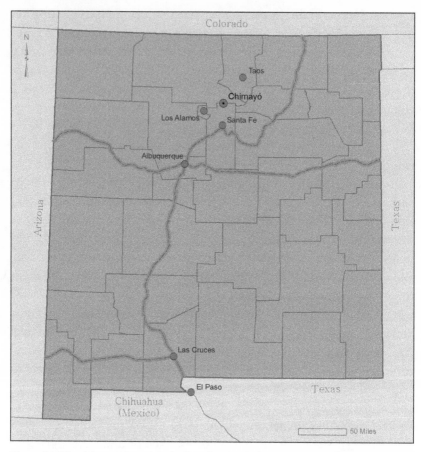

Figure I.1. New Mexico. Cartography by John H. Clark, Data Visualization and GIS Librarian, Digital Scholarship Services, David B. Skillman Library, Lafayette College.

history of Latinos/as is, of course, a significant piece of the story, and the history of the Santuario provides exciting insights into the religious experiences, beliefs, and heritage of one segment of the Latino/a population of the United States. While both Catholics and Latinos/as deserve more historical attention, I would like to say this in the clearest possible terms: the history of the Santuario de Chimayó is not only important for Catholics and Hispanics; it is one of the United States' most distinctive and visited religious sites and as such has the potential to educate all of us about essential national issues of religious identity, race, and the healing and peace we hope to eke out of holy ground. To begin to tell this story, I now turn to an introduction of the setting of the Santuario de Chimayó and a summary of some of the important events and periods in the famous church's life.

The Place

One way to think about the location of the Santuario de Chimayó is to start at the place itself and zoom out. The Santuario lies along the bank of the Santa Cruz River and is surrounded with buildings, some of which are historic, others new. Surprisingly, the church is adjacent to another chapel; this other church belonged historically to the Medina family but now, like the Santuario, belongs to the Archdiocese of Santa Fe and is known as the Santo Niño Chapel. Other old buildings in the immediate vicinity of the Santuario include an old house repurposed as a gift shop, the old El Potrero Trading Post, the ruins of Bernardo Abeyta's house, and a few other older adobe structures. New buildings include a large visitors' center, additional gift shops, and a number of ramadas near an outdoor gathering area. Just south of the Santuario, across Route 98, there is a low hill with a cross at the summit. North of the Santuario, across the river, is a lovely pasture that runs up to the foot of Tsi Mayoh hill, from which the town takes its name. Up the road, near the intersection with Highway 76, lies the "center" of Chimayó, the Plaza del Cerro, though Chimayó, like many northern New Mexican villages, is less of a cohesive unit than a line of settlements, each with its own chapel.

Chimayó is one of the cities or towns in what is now referred to as the Española Valley. Española, through which runs the Río Grande, is a relatively new city founded in the late nineteenth century around the railroad. The much older settlement, now nearly encircled by the city of Española, is what Diego de Vargas named in 1696 the Villa Nueva de Santa Cruz de la Cañada. For centuries the ancient Catholic church at Santa Cruz was the center of Catholic administration in the region, and the Santuario, when it received the services of a priest, was served by Santa Cruz. "La Cañada" refers to the Santa Cruz River valley, a relatively well-irrigated and verdant area of northern New Mexico. No doubt, the agricultural viability of La Cañada made it attractive to the Spaniards who returned to the region after their reconquest of the territory subsequent to the Pueblo Revolt (1680–1692), which had driven the

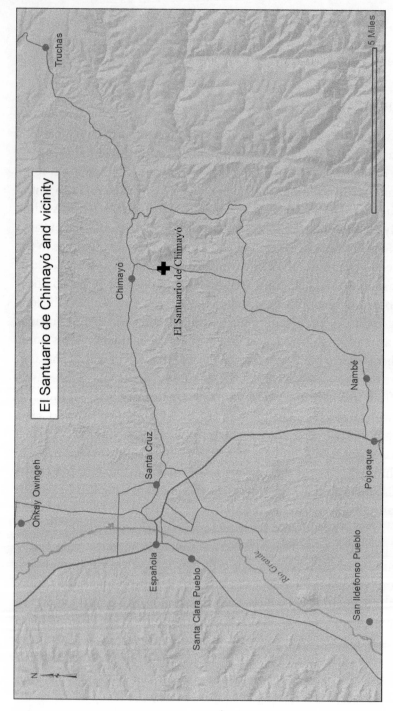

Figure I.2. Cartography by John H. Clark, Data Visualization and GIS Librarian, Digital Scholarship Services, David B. Skillman Library, Lafayette College.

colonizers back for a time to El Paso and out of Pueblo territory. Along with Santa Fe, and later Albuquerque, Santa Cruz de la Cañada was one of the major Spanish population centers of Spanish New Mexico. Chimayó, although in the orbit of Santa Cruz, lies at the eastern end of the valley before the terrain again rises toward the Sangre de Cristo range. According to the 2010 census, Española's population was over 85 percent Hispanic or Latino/a, making it the city with the highest percentage of Hispanics in northern New Mexico, a demographic trait common to La Cañada overall.[6]

The entire region, stretching along the Río Grande from Santa Fe north to Colorado, is often referred to as Río Arriba, or the upper part of the river. (Río Abajo correspondingly refers to the settlements south of Santa Fe down to Albuquerque and beyond.) The northern area, which was the original focus of Spanish settlement and Franciscan evangelization, is the heartland of several Pueblo peoples and their settlements, including Ohkay Owingeh, Nambé, and Santa Clara. There is no mystery as to why both the Pueblos and the Spanish settled along the river and its tributaries; aerial views show the stark difference in the green irrigated landscapes of the agriculturally rich river valleys and the arid and semi-arid high desert and mountain peaks that surround them. Ohkay Owingeh, long known as San Juan Pueblo, just north of Española, is the principal Pueblo of the Tewa-speaking Pueblo people and was Juan de Oñate's first capital in the territory. Other nearby Tewa Pueblos include San Ildefonso, Tesuque, Pojoaque, Santa Clara, and nearest to the Santuario, Nambé. Farther up the Río Grande are the related Tiwa-speaking Pueblos of Picuris and Taos. Santa Fe, Los Alamos, Española, and Taos are the largest non-Pueblo cities in the Río Arriba area. Residents of Chimayó often work in one of these cities and commute back and forth to their homes in the village.

The Action

A brief outline of important events and breakdown of time periods can help to orient us to the main characters and occurrences in the Santuario's past. Histories of New Mexico are often broadly divided into eras based on the governing regime: pre-Hispanic times, the centuries of the Spanish Empire (interrupted by the interregnum of the Pueblo Revolt), the Mexican period, and the contemporary era as part of the

United States. The religious history of New Mexico likewise corresponds to New Mexico's various governmental jurisdictions. Spanish conquest and Spanish evangelization went hand in hand. The Franciscan order was the most important ecclesiastical presence in early New Mexico and left an indelible imprint on the Catholicism all throughout the northern missions of the Spanish Empire from Texas to California. In the years leading up to Mexican independence, the Franciscans had begun to decline and were eventually replaced, for the most part, with diocesan clergy, first under the Diocese of Durango and later the Diocese, then Archdiocese of Santa Fe. The Santuario's history is inextricably intertwined with the political and ecclesiastical histories of New Mexico, and therefore, in some ways, this book also offers a history of New Mexico with particular emphasis on the Catholic Church.

With that said, the Santuario de Chimayó is hardly one of the oldest churches in New Mexico. It was built between 1813 and 1816 in what would soon be acknowledged as the final years of the Spanish Empire in Mexico. Nonetheless, at the time of its construction, the Santuario lay almost at the very northern end of a vast political, religious, and economic network. It is no coincidence that the miraculous crucifix of the Santuario is named for a similar crucifix in distant Guatemala, for north-south trade routes united the empire up and down the continent. Northern New Mexico was distant from the metropolitan centers of the empire, but it is not quite correct to think of the region as isolated. Businesspeople and clergy members alike operated within international organizational structures and markets.

But the writing was on the wall for the Spanish throughout the Americas as, one by one, Latin American countries gained their independence. Mexico's own successful bid for self-rule in 1821 did not have an immediate effect on Bernardo Abeyta's Santuario, though new measures to centralize authority in Mexico did incite a spate of rebellions in northern New Mexico to maintain the relative autonomy the region was accustomed to, including one in 1837 that arose in Chimayó itself. One important feature of the sometimes rebellious autonomy of the region was the famous lay order that oversaw Catholic life in many New Mexican villages, the Fraternidad Piadosa de Nuestro Padre Jesús Nazareno, popularly known as the Penitentes. Abeyta himself was a leader in this brotherhood, and it is more than likely that the Santuario was a bastion of this independent-minded religious confraternity. In fact, the years under Mexican rule were a time of great vitality for the lay leadership of the Penitentes as other forms of oversight, in terms of both church and state, lacked continuity and did not always extend into more rural areas.

For the most part, however, religious practices in the Mexican period (1821–1847) in the Río Arriba region were in continuity with those of the latter years of the Spanish Empire. This cannot be said for the next big change in government, when in 1847, during the Mexican-American War, U.S. forces swept in and seized power in a mostly bloodless takeover. Not long afterward, the Vatican transferred the Catholic churches of New Mexico from the Diocese of Durango, Mexico, to a newly formed ecclesiastical administrative unit in the new U.S. Southwest. This unit would soon become its own diocese (1853) and then archdiocese (1875) under the decisive guidance of Jean Baptiste Lamy, a French-born priest, whose administration was much more "hands-on" than what New Mexican Catholics were accustomed to. The Santuario is relatively unmentioned in the historical record during the territorial period, which is to say, the decades after the U.S. takeover but before New Mexico attained statehood in 1912. It persisted as it had for many years as a mission outpost of the Santa Cruz de la Cañada parish, and it also continued to receive health-seeking pilgrims from the surrounding villages and Pueblos. Abeyta died in 1856, but the Santuario stayed in the family, now owned by one of his daughters, Carmen Chávez. Throughout the territorial period, the church belonged to the Chávez family, who made it available to pilgrims as well as to local clergy for celebration of Mass and other religious services.

The railroad spread around northern New Mexico in the latter half of the nineteenth century, and the economics of village life began to change as more and more people began to seek work away from home. Chimayó's local employments, such as agriculture and weaving, waned even as the village's population thinned. Along with the passing of the years, these changes took their toll on the Santuario. Even as it became more difficult economically to maintain the art and physical structure of the church, greater numbers of Anglo settlers were making their way to the Southwest. In 1929, on the eve of the Great Depression, the Chávez family had reached the point where they needed to sell the Santuario. The newly formed Spanish Colonial Arts Society, a group of Anglo artists and upper-class Nuevomexicanos dedicated to the preservation of New Mexico's folk arts, arranged to purchase the Santuario and immediately transferred the deed to the Archdiocese of Santa Fe. Since the sale in 1929, Abeyta's chapel has belonged to the Catholic Church, but it would be some decades until the church placed a full-time priest at the Santuario. In the interim, it remained a much-visited focus of popular devotions and unorganized, small-scale pilgrimages.

It was not until the postwar years of the twentieth century that the massive Holy Week pilgrimage first began. Its genesis was with a group of Nuevomexicano World War II veterans who had survived the Bataan Death March. In the 1950s the Santuario also received its first permanently assigned priest in its history, a Catalonian named Casimiro Roca. Roca would go on to serve the Santuario and other nearby parishes for most of the rest of his career. Under his tenure, the Santuario's appeal to both pilgrims and tourists grew exponentially, making Chimayó one of the largest pilgrimage destinations in North America. Rising devotion to the Santo Niño and recognition of the holy dirt are part of the story; the other part has to do with New Mexico's growing importance in terms of tourism as well as alternative healing and health care.

* * *

The contemporary state of the Santuario is prosperous and promising, if not totally free from conflict. With half a million visitors a year, the current clergy have felt the need to greatly expand the infrastructure around the Santuario to serve the needs of the crowds. The presence of nearby gift shops to fund these projects is more notable than in the past. Critics find that these new levels of commercialization at the shrine detract from the church's peaceful and rustic ambience as well as its purported religious mission. Supporters answer that continued growth is probable and that administrators must be pragmatic and even have a vision for new development to accommodate still higher numbers of pilgrims and other visitors.

As a history of the Santuario, this book cannot pretend to make predictions for the future other than to note simply that the Santuario has long existed as a place of healing and peace in a context of competing claims not only on its sacred precincts but on the entire region. The objective of this book is to tell this story and to reflect on these competing claims of ownership and belonging. As will become clear, the Santuario—as a key part of New Mexican history and experience—is a useful case through which to understand developments in the contemporary U.S. Catholic Church as well as current demographic trends in the United States. Contestations over space, meaning, religious devotion, and ethnic identity markers serve as fruitful points of departure in further studies of how Hispanics and Hispanic religiosity are integral parts of the national religious experience. Despite these very real contestations and occasional conflicts, the Santuario remains a generous and welcoming gathering place for many different varieties of people. Perhaps the best word for the Santuario's future is a familiar *dicho*, or saying, common in Chimayó: *El pan partido, Dios lo aumenta* (God multiplies bread that is shared).[7]

1

Catholic Settlement of Río Arriba

Where the Santuario de Chimayó now sits has been a place of nearly continuous human habitation for centuries if not millennia. The reasons for this have largely to do with the fertile nature of the Santa Cruz River valley, referred to in the Spanish of the people of the area as La Cañada. Today, various villages, towns, and cities lie along the approximately ten-mile length of La Cañada, from Chimayó and its constituent parts at the eastern end to the midsize city of Española at the west, where the Santa Cruz River empties into the Río Grande. Along the banks of the Santa Cruz, crops and woodlands flourish; the area is known for its relative verdancy in New Mexico and its towering and ancient cottonwoods. In short, while La Cañada cannot boast the mineral wealth of Zacatecas or the agricultural abundance of Mexico's central valley, it has nevertheless been coveted land in the desert and mountain reaches of the northern watershed of the mighty Río Grande. It is no wonder that Pueblos long made the valley their home before the arrival of the Spanish, who likewise identified the place as good for settlement. The very *goodness* of the place, in all senses of the word, has made it the site of ongoing declarations of ownership and control. Before the first adobes of the Santuario were first laid down in the mud, people have been claiming a place for themselves here, using all the power and strategies at their disposal to enjoy this valley and to sanction the kind of religious practice that can take place therein. In the earliest years of Spanish settlement in the area, sometimes these competing claims found ways to coexist, while in other cases, they came into violent opposition.

First Spanish Settlement, 1598–1680

Of course, several Tewa Pueblos still surround the mostly Hispano village of Chimayó. Archaeologists have uncovered evidence of Pueblo occupation of La Cañada as early as 1000 CE by people who were likely ancestors of the present-day Tewa people. Initial settlement appears to be in scattered, small gatherings of dwellings located in lowlands near the river, with approximately eight hundred to a thousand inhabitants throughout the valley. Archaeological evidence suggests that, around 1250, the population gathered into large Pueblos located on the hilltops, perhaps to better defend their growing agricultural enterprises. For unknown reasons, although possibly related to soil erosion, these early Pueblos had left the immediate vicinity of La Cañada by 1400; however, thousands of Pueblo people lived at that time throughout what would eventually become northern New Mexico.[1]

The growing Spanish Empire spread slowly northward from Mexico City, conquered in 1521. Initial European forays into the Pueblo home-lands occurred haphazardly between 1540 and 1598, but during this period, little changed in terms of the Pueblo way of life. Albert T. Schro-eder, the noted archaeologist of the Southwest, somewhat innocently notes that these decades were "nothing more than a time of contact be-tween two vastly different cultures."[2] While this may have been true in the short term, the "time of contact" sowed the seeds for the cataclysmic changes that would follow Spain's eventual move to settle permanently in Pueblo territory.

As mentioned, former Pueblo settlements—likely Tewa-speaking—had either been abandoned or had shrunk to the size that they made no archaeological impact in the century prior to Spanish entry into the area. However, this does not necessarily mean that the Santa Cruz River valley and its cluster of hills and small mountains had lost all signifi-cance for the Tewas. Specific Tewa myths and religious practices relat-ing to Chimayó are discussed in chapter 2, but it is helpful to mention here that the hill called Tsi Mayoh, which is directly northeast of the Santuario, constitutes an important part of in Tewa cosmology, and it is certainly not a coincidence that the Spanish village founded in the valley would take its moniker from a Pueblo place-name. The Tewas, in these early years of European encroachment, were not universally allied with the Spanish but did frequently find themselves in close, sometimes mutually beneficial, associations with them. They were also some of the first Indians in the upper Río Grande valley to experience the full evan-gelistic attention of the Franciscans who accompanied the first perma-nent wave of Spanish settlers.

Don Juan de Oñate was the man at the head of this wave of conquest in 1598. The story of his invasion and its infamous brutality has been told elsewhere, and his expedition's forces almost immediately made their way to the center of the Tewa world at Ohkay Owingeh Pueblo, the site of Oñate's first headquarters, which they renamed San Juan.[3] Already in 1598, the Santa Cruz valley had been named La Cañada by the Spaniards, and at the time had been reinhabited by a Tewa settlement, which Oñate himself visited and mentioned in his voluminous writings. Within three years, a small Spanish settlement had been established in La Cañada, although in these earliest years of Spanish occupation, the region represented the bleeding edge of relative safety against Indian attacks. In 1601 a Spaniard named Juan Luxán reported to Oñate that the local Indians had warned him in no uncertain terms that the Spanish should proceed no farther to the north and east of La Cañada lest they be outnumbered and killed.[4] Much later, the archaeologist and explorer Adolph Bandelier came to the same conclusion in his own investigation of the region and its history, identifying "the gorges of Chimayo" as the eastern point of early settlement and a kind of lookout.[5]

Oñate and his men had relatively peaceful relations with the Tewas in and around San Juan and La Cañada. At this historical distance, it is impossible to know why the Tewa people chose to accommodate Oñate's forces, but it is possible that annual agricultural rhythms required the Pueblos to remain dedicated to their crops at the stage of the year when Oñate and his men arrived on the scene. To be sure, food production was essential to both Pueblos and the Spanish, and Tewa work crews assisted the Spanish to enlarge irrigation canals to ensure larger crop yields. In addition to the demands of agricultural life on the Tewas, the *realpolitik* of their situation also may have convinced the Pueblos that military resistance against the Spanish was futile. In any case, this early détente between the Tewas and the Spanish gave Oñate the opportunity to begin to communicate Christian stories to the native people. Oñate and his men soon organized the performance of one of the folk religious dramas that were popular in the Iberian Peninsula, in Oñate's own words, "a good sham battle between Moors and Christians, the latter on foot with harquebuses, the former on horseback with lances and shields." The pageantry of the battle culminated in the Moors' epic defeat, no doubt communicating a sufficiently clear message to Pueblos.[6]

In terrible contrast to the heavy-handed but peaceful occupation of San Juan, the Spaniards' brutality at Acoma Pueblo had long-lasting effects on all the New Mexican Pueblos. Late in 1598, the fortress Pueblo atop a nearly impregnable mesa received demands from Oñate for provisions. When a small group of Spanish soldiers scaled to the Pueblo to gather the goods, the Acomans divided the invaders into small groups and attacked, killing many of them; other Spaniards escaped only by leaping off the mesa. In response, Oñate's sergeant, Vicente de Zaldívar, led a siege and attack on Acoma in the cold January of 1599 that ultimately resulted in the Pueblos' bloody defeat five days later. More important than the Acomans' defeat were the consequences of the trial held shortly thereafter to punish the survivors. The now notorious sentence for all men over twenty-five years of age was to have one of their feet amputated and to spend twenty years in bondage. All girls and women over twelve and all boys and young men from twelve to twenty-four years were, like the older mutilated men, enslaved to the Spanish for twenty years. The fear inspired by these harsh acts would prove to be effective in the short term as Oñate and his forces continued their occupation of the Pueblos' territories, but this brutality—which was often accompanied by religious scripts concerning the conquest of evil and the conversion of infidels—would set the scene for rebellion and long-lasting conflict with the Pueblos.[7]

Even before Oñate's arrival, Franciscan friars, accompanied by soldiers, had made their way to many of the Pueblos in the Río Arriba region with hopes of both converting them to the Catholic faith and discovering new sources of mineral wealth for the Spanish crown. Their first explorations included several Pueblos in the area of present-day Albuquerque as well as the Sandia mountains. They also learned of the line of Pueblo towns stretching up the Río Grande to Taos and of the presence of hostile people who lived even farther away to the northeast, on the plains. This intelligence would eventually be amply confirmed by decades of conflict between the Spanish and Pueblos allied against marauding Comanches and other plains peoples on the northern and eastern edges of New Mexico. Groups of friars and soldiers made their way as far as Zuni, northwest of Acoma, and Jemez, west and southwest of Oñate's eventual settlement at San Juan. Another unsanctioned expeditionary force traveled through Taos and on toward the plains, possibly reaching what is now Nebraska before perishing. While no permanent missions or settlements were established prior to 1598, these initial forays convinced the friars that the Pueblos represented a promising mission field. Their well-organized dwellings and stable agricultural economies made them excellent prospects for proselytization, education in Catholic doctrine, and participation in the folk dramas and devotions of Iberian Catholicism.[8]

Before Oñate and the six hundred permanent settlers who accompanied him, the earlier Spanish expeditions had come initially in search of mineral wealth. Once it was generally acknowledged that New Mexico would not immediately produce gold or other precious resources, the Spanish crown refocused its support to emphasize Christianization of the natives. To this end, the government in New Spain equipped northern-bound Franciscans with a "building kit" to aid their efforts in converting the Pueblos. Each kit contained tools and construction materials as well as some religious objects for the administration of the sacrament of baptism and the celebration of the Mass. After Oñate's successor, Pedro de Peralta, moved the territory's headquarters from the San Juan area to the newly formed city of Santa Fe around 1610, the friars could count on infrequent but regular shipments of other necessary goods to construct and maintain their mission churches and outposts. There is no doubt that the Tewa-speaking Pueblos around Ohkay Owingeh/San Juan, including the scattered Pueblo settlements in La Cañada, were some of the first Indians in the new province to experience sustained interaction with the Franciscan missioners and witness the impact of their fervor for building and baptizing.[9]

Although the relationship between the Spanish settlement party, the Franciscans, and the Tewas was relatively peaceful, the threat of violence hung perpetually over the region. Even in distant New Mexico, the imperatives of the Patronato Real—the complex balance of power achieved between the Spanish crown and the Catholic Church concerning settlement and evangelization of the Americas—still dictated much of the Spaniards' behavior. For example, upon contact, Oñate read to the Pueblos the *Requerimiento*, a document that outlined Spain's legal and ecclesiastical right to conquest and that admonished the listeners to submit to both the crown's authority and the dogmas of the Catholic faith. After Oñate had experienced some semblance of success with various Pueblos, whose leaders seemed to accept the new authorities, he planned a dedicatory celebration in September 1598. An assemblage of Pueblo leaders met with Oñate and the upper echelons of his command, and the Pueblos were made to swear that they would assist the friars and accept Spanish rule. A witness to the event reported, "The governor repeated this three times, warning them that, if they failed to obey any of the padres or caused them the slightest harm, they and their cities and pueblos would be put to the sword and destroyed by fire." Tragically, the battle and subsequent punishments meted out against Acoma would soon prove the sincerity of Oñate's threats.[10] It was in this threatening atmosphere that conversions began to be recorded.

The nascent Franciscan missions soon began to make claims of astonishing success. By 1604, only six years after Oñate's arrival, the collection of missions in New Mexico had already been named a commissary, or the basic ecclesiastical unit of organization. By 1616, they had made sufficient inroads to advance to the level of *custodia*, the next rung of the organizational ladder, and by 1625, there were twenty-six missionaries laboring principally among the various Pueblos. Some areas could boast new church buildings as well as mission compounds where the friars taught the Indians weaving, carpentry, blacksmithing, and other skills that the padres deemed essential for Christian civilization. The custodian in charge of all these missions, Fray Alonso de Benavides, reported in 1630 that sixty thousand Pueblo individuals in ninety villages had been converted to the Catholic faith:

> All the Indians are now converted, baptized and well ministered to, with 33 convents and churches in the principal pueblos and more than 150 churches throughout the other pueblos. . . . Here where scarcely 30 years earlier all was idolatry and worship of the devil, without any vestige of civilization, today they worship our true God and Lord.[11]

The Tewas, of all the Pueblos, experienced some of the Franciscans' most intense missionary activity. By the 1620s, all the main Tewa Pueblos had their own resident priest, and the mission training programs introduced significant changes to Tewa life and culture that extended well beyond religious instruction to include music, gardening, the tend-ing of livestock, leather working, and Spanish-style construction. The Tewas, in addition to being the first Pueblos to be baptized Christians, were the Spaniards' closest allies throughout most of the seventeenth century. Fray Benavides lauded their cooperativeness and willingness to support Spain's efforts in conversion as well as in military pacification of the other Pueblos. He wrote in the early 1630s that the Tewa "nation is very attached to the Spaniards, and when a war breaks out they are the first to join and accompany them."[12] Again, at this historical remove it is perhaps impossible to know for certain what motivated the Tewas to ally with the Spanish, but reasonable explanations point out ongoing congruencies between Tewa values and traditions and those being forcibly imported by the Spanish. The archaeologist Albert Schroeder suggests that Tewa conversion to Christianity was greatly facilitated by similar elements in Tewa religious life: both included "the use of altars, singing, specialized instruction for neophytes, ornamentation and painting, formalized ceremonies and rituals, care of religious objects, and a religious calendar."[13] Another explanation suggests that Tewa conflicts with the other Pueblos made the Spanish attractive allies and that Spanish calls-to-arms to the Tewa often appealed to the latter's ongoing wars and skirmishes with the surrounding peoples, both Pueblos and other peoples such as the Apaches.[14]

All, however, was not well. The padres freely expressed their animus toward the religious practices of the Pueblos, including their use of kivas and their katsina dances, often referring to the Pueblo sacred figures as devils and their ritual life as the darkest idolatry. This meant that the reported statistics concerning baptisms and conversions often obscured the fact that, rather than being eliminated, many Pueblo ceremonies moved into the realms of secrecy where they were able to continue to flourish and affect the overt practices of Pueblo Christianity for years to come. The Tewas of San Juan and the surrounding region were the group most committed to Christianity, but even with that qualifier, by the middle of the seventeenth century, it became clear that the ostensible conversions of thousands of Pueblo people throughout New Mexico had not stopped widespread practice of their ancestral ceremonies and observances, sometimes in tandem with the new European religion and sometimes in conflict with it.[15]

Revolt

By the 1670s, suppression of Pueblo ritual practices and traditions had become part and parcel of both the Franciscans' missionary efforts and the Spanish governors' strategy of control from their seat in Santa Fe over the various Río Grande Pueblos. The friars had long forbidden the katsina dances, so essential to Pueblo cosmology and maintenance of proper living conditions. Their heavy-handed corporal punishments of Indians as well as widespread reports of the missionaries' sexual impropriety in various locales only exacerbated growing Pueblo displeasure with the missions. In the decades after Oñate's original settlement, his successors sometimes tangled with the friars over questions of authority over the new province, which meant that sometimes the political leaders, as a bargaining strategy, showed more leniency toward the Pueblos in terms of their religious rituals. For the most part, however, the governors moved firmly against the natives' ritual activity. A late and important instance occurred in 1675, when Governor Treviño organized a bloody campaign against idolatry and "sorcerers." Several Pueblo leaders perished and many others were enslaved before an uneasy truce could be restored between the Spanish lords in Santa Fe and the surrounding Pueblo villages.[16]

The Pueblos who lived in closest proximity to the large Spanish presence at Santa Fe and the less populous settlements near San Juan and La Cañada were, as mentioned, the Tewas to the north of Santa Fe, and the Tanos, who made their homes in the Galisteo basin just to the south of the Spanish capital. The Tanos, sometimes referred to as the "southern Tewas," were natural allies of the Tewas, and both groups had experienced large rates of superficial Christianization and had likewise suffered some of the most sustained repression of their dances, healing ceremonies, and indigenous leadership. Due to this unique position among the New Mexican Pueblos, the Tewas and the Tanos produced both some of the Spaniards' most trusted allies and some of the most explosive rebels. Indeed, a Pueblo leader named Popé from San Juan— Oñate's first seat of power in New Mexico—relocated early in 1680 to Taos Pueblo to begin to plot rebellion. Choosing Taos for his headquarters to evade both the concentrated Spanish populations farther south and the possibility of pro-Spanish sentiment among some Tewas, Popé quickly did what had never been done before: he united the Río Grande Pueblos against their common enemy.[17]

With a precision achieved through the use of knotted cords that counted down the days to rebellion, the Pueblos arose en masse in August 1680. A force of Tanos besieged Santa Fe and quickly took it under their control even as other Pueblos throughout the villages attacked and killed the missionaries and destroyed churches. Spanish suppression of Pueblo religious life and ceremony was likely the principal flashpoint for the 1680 revolt, but other motives abounded. The massive die-off of indigenous populations throughout the Americas due to the spread of European diseases and the famines that often resulted from Spanish violence also took a heavy toll on the New Mexico Pueblos. Over the course of the seventeenth century, their collective population declined from an original number between sixty thousand and a hundred thousand in 130 Pueblos to fewer than seven thousand gathered in only 13 Pueblos by the end of the century. Another major factor that facilitated the union of the Pueblos was enslavement. Even though human captivity had been part of warfare and economic life both within and outside the Pueblos before Spanish arrival, the enslavement and detribalization of captives under Spanish rule motivated the rebels, who almost immediately made demands for the return of their captive family members as well as the release of several non-Pueblo captives.[18]

But if one considers just the numbers of people killed in the rebellion, the totalizing and destructive nature of the Franciscans' evangelism emerges as the primary focus of the Pueblos' wrath. In a matter of days, every single Catholic mission was destroyed, and twenty-one of the thirty-three missionaries in the province had been killed. Compare this rate of killing with that of the general nonreligious population, in which 375 of 2,350 colonists were killed. The objectives of the revolt, clearly, were to eliminate the friars and their program of forced Christianization and to push the Spaniards out of Pueblo territory. If the former was successful, so was the latter. In short order, Governor Otermín (who had assumed his position in 1678) marched southward with the surviving colonists, stopping briefly in Isleta Pueblo and then continuing on to El Paso. Otermín made a few feeble efforts to retake New Mexico, but ultimately the Spanish were forced to remain in El Paso for twelve years during which the various Pueblo peoples enjoyed a tense freedom from Spanish rule.[19]

Remaining Spanish documents from the period feature the testimony of Indians who had come to identify as Christians and had become so allied with the Spanish that they found it necessary to flee south with them. One such individual, a Tewa man named Gerónimo, joined Otermín's forces in Isleta in 1681 after deserting a group of "risen up apostates" from various Pueblos that had gathered at Jemez. His account reveals a considerable amount of detail about the nature of the rebellion as well as what the Spanish expected from Christian Pueblos. To save his own life, Gerónimo begins his testimony with positive information about himself. He claims the depth of his own faith and explains that he had tired of the "bad life" among the rebels, and he also says that he misses his wife, who at the time was in service to one of the surviving friars among Otermín's band in Isleta. To further burnish his commitment to the Spanish, he shares intelligence with the governor, warning him of a planned nighttime raid on their horses. He goes on to finger Popé as well as the others from San Juan and Taos Pueblos as ringleaders. Popé had commanded the Pueblos "to kill the Spanish religious, women, and children, and to burn churches and images." He told his followers to leave behind the wives that had been given them in Christian marriage and instead to go and get new wives. The people were happy to be out from under the friars, and Popé had encouraged them "to wash the baptism off their heads." Gerónimo also provides information about destruction in La Cañada and gives one of the only mentions in the documentary record of a pre-revolt Spanish settlement at Chimayó; he describes the destruction there, saying that "Zimayo, Jurisdiction of la Cañada" had been burned to the ground.[20]

Gerónimo's testimony, despite the fact that it is coming from a man who hoped to remain with the Spanish, cannot hide the depth of Pueblo rage against the impositions that had been made on their social and economic lives by the Catholic religious. The complete destruction of the early Franciscan missions and Popé's particular instructions to reverse the sacramental ministrations of the Catholic Church, including baptisms and marriages, speak volumes about how disruptive and hurtful the friars' plan for Pueblo conversion had been. The missions had challenged Pueblo lifeways at every level, from social relationships like marriage, to economic organization, to vast issues of cosmic balance and connection to the Pueblo deities. It was perhaps only this level of disruption in their communities that could have united the several Río Grande Pueblos, a feat that had never been accomplished before, a union that would soon disintegrate after the Spanish withdrawal.

During the twelve-year period when the Spanish were banished to El Paso, not all indigenous groups returned to inhabit their ancestral homelands; some divided up and took possession of places the Spanish had occupied. Many of the Tewas were able to remain in their places of origin, but the Tanos, or "southern Tewas," who had been residing in Galisteo moved to more agriculturally productive areas, with half of the people making homes in and around Santa Fe and the other half settling in various places in La Cañada, especially around Santa Cruz but also stretching eastward up the valley toward Chimayó.[21]

Governor Diego de Vargas, appointed to his position to recapture New Mexico, led a force of three hundred men out of El Paso in 1692, and by the fall of that year, a tenuous peace with the Pueblos was reestablished, with the Spanish once again in control. By the next year, de Vargas had orchestrated the move of a thousand returning and new Spanish settlers into the province, and towns and villages were retaken from the Indians, sometimes peacefully; more often, the Spanish had to squelch small rebellions from Santa Fe to Taos before they could lay full claim to the territory. Fourteen of the northern Pueblos organized a more significant rebellion in 1696, which de Vargas also defeated. The governor needed to act quickly to dampen the explosive environment up and down the Río Grande. One step was to unite with the Pueblos against common enemies: Apache and Comanche raiders from the plains to the east of the Sangre de Cristo range. Another tactic was demographic change through the creation and settlement of several Spanish towns. A final move for pacification involved reinstating the missions, but with significant reforms.[22]

In the Chimayó area, permanent Spanish settlement became a reality in the first decades of the eighteenth century. This was made possible by Spanish population increases as a protective strategy against Plains Indians combined with the removal of many of the Pueblos who had settled there in the 1680s. The Spanish passion for record keeping allows us to chart the development of Spanish reentry into La Cañada. As mentioned, around half of the Tanos, previously from Galisteo, had occupied the area after the Pueblo Revolt. With some Tewa allies from San Juan, the Tanos built two new Pueblo villages in La Cañada on farms that had previously been inhabited by Spaniards; these Pueblo settlements were called San Lazaro and San Cristoval. In 1695 de Vargas made Spanish claim to the land based on the prior Spanish agricultural settlement in the area, and granted the land to Spanish farmers, at least some of whom claimed to have lived in the place before the 1680 revolt. In the same document, de Vargas orders the Tanos off the land and out of San Lazaro and San Cristoval and to resettle among the San Juan Pueblos. Some of the Tanos from both villages, especially those in the more easterly San Cristoval Pueblo, refused to move to San Juan and so were allowed to move farther east in the Santa Cruz valley to a site named the Cañada of Chimayó to provide something of a defensive buffer in the easternmost foothills of the Santa Cruz River valley, a new settlement some sixty-eight houses in strength. To the west, near or on the site of the newly emptied Pueblos, de Vargas established Villa Nueva de Santa Cruz, which would long be the primary Spanish settlement in the area north of Santa Fe.[23]

The missionary ethos of the Franciscans continued to motivate their activities in New Mexico, which meant in practice that they spent the majority of their efforts on re-creating the mission churches that had been destroyed in 1680 and endeavoring to reestablish the tenuous Christianity of the Pueblos. By 1740, the number of missionaries in New Mexico had risen to forty men, but, at least to some extent, they had to adopt new approaches and attitudes. To begin with, their claims of success were immensely curtailed. Where Fray Benavides once claimed sixty thousand Christians among the Pueblos, the eighteenth-century friars never counted more than fifteen thousand. Likewise, the attacks on Pueblo religious ceremonies and civil organizations that had so precipitated the 1680 revolt were replaced with more modest efforts to provide religious education and to promote more gradual changes in belief and practice. The former raids on kivas and destruction of katsinas were no more, and attendance at Mass was no longer strictly enforced.[24] In addition to these evangelistic ministrations to the Pueblos, the Franciscans also met the needs of the Spanish colonists in New Mexico, since for most of the eighteenth century, there were no secular (that is, diocesan) clergy in the province.

Santa Cruz would become the religious and political hub of La Cañada for the remainder of Spanish colonial rule. At least some sort of church building existed in the Tano Pueblo of San Lazaro before de Vargas created the new Spanish settlement there in 1695. The colonial-era adobe church that still stands in Santa Cruz today was slowly built through the 1730s and 1740s under the close supervision of the Franciscans and with the full support of the New Spanish government. In 1776 the Franciscan order sent an official Visitor and Custos (the overseer of a "custody," a subdivision of the Franciscan province) north to inspect and make an inventory of the order's missions in New Mexico. The Visitor, Fray Francisco Anastasio Domínguez, was a realist and not given to exaggeration, and the account of his visit remains one of the clearest records of New Mexican churches in the colonial period. Unlike his sixteenth-century predecessors, who were often too quick to trumpet their successes, Domínguez does not embroider: "In view of the fact that the Villa of Santa Fe is not as golden as the glitter of its name, in spite of the circumstances mentioned that it is the capital, etc., it will be apparent that this Villa of La Cañada, which does not have such an ostentatious aspect, is probably tinsel." Despite this low view of Santa Cruz's charms, his description of the church there depicts a thriving mission church that, unlike many of the churches in the area, existed to meet the needs of Spanish villagers rather than those of Pueblo converts. Padre Domínguez takes an inventory of Santa Cruz's religious appurtenances and altars, its various confraternities, and its income. He likewise notes the wide-ranging reach of the church, naming the various districts the friars there had to cover, including Chimayó, Quemado, and Truchas. By 1776, the population for the whole region, according to Domínguez's census, was 1,389 people, 367 of these residing in Chimayó.[25]

Looking back from this point, we can see that the success and growth of the Spanish settlement at Santa Cruz and its environs depended on the earlier relocation of the Tanos to Chimayó at the time of de Vargas's reconquest, and, not surprisingly, the Tanos themselves appear to have been unhappy with the arrangement. In 1696, on the heels of the founding of the "new town" of Santa Cruz, the Chimayó Tanos rose up in one of the several small rebellions that punctuated the reestablishment of Spanish rule in New Mexico. Joined at first by co-revolutionists from Taos Pueblo and later by additional forces from Picuris, Santo Domingo, and Cochiti, the Tanos and their allies killed six missionaries and twenty-one other Spaniards. A simultaneous rebellion at San Ildefonso

Pueblo also claimed the life of the two missionaries who had been newly assigned there. As with all of these scattered rebellions, de Vargas's reaction was swift and violent. The Pueblo rebels who were not destroyed were enslaved to the new Spanish colonists up and down the Río Grande from Santa Fe to Taos. The Tanos who had so recently been relocated to Chimayó, excepting slaves who remained in the area, relocated once again, this time all the way to the outskirts of the Hopi Pueblos far to the northwest and, for the moment, relatively protected from Spanish influence.[26]

After these violent episodes and ongoing strife with the Pueblos, the documentary record reveals that Spanish families began to settle Chimayó very early in the eighteenth century. De Vargas's dealings with the Tanos in La Cañada were predicated on claims that some of his men made concerning preexisting properties and farms in the Santa Cruz and Chimayó areas, and mention of their ruined pre-revolt homesteads dots the legal documents that de Vargas compiled to remove the Tanos. Other claims can be found in land grant records. A typical example is that of Luis López, one of the soldier/settlers who had accompanied de Vargas northward in 1693. López requests lands for himself in the "unpopulated area above the Cañada de Chimayo," lands that he claims have never been planted or used profitably, though in the same claim he reports that Tanos had helpfully already dug an irrigation ditch (*acequia*) on the land he desired. Catholic Church records also show that the Spanish were active in Chimayó very quickly after the reconquest. For instance, Fray Joan de Fagle records that "Josepha Lujan, citizen of the Cañada de Sta. Cruz in the village of Tzimayo," had established her desire to get married to a Clemente Montoya in 1701. In other words, in less than five years since Spanish resettlement, enough people had settled in Chimayó for it to be considered an outlying village of Santa Cruz that one could claim as a place of origin.[27]

With Santa Cruz as the western anchor for the whole valley, Spanish settlement of La Cañada was greatly furthered when de Vargas created a permanent land grant of forty-four thousand acres—the Santa Cruz grant—to accommodate the growing number of Spanish inhabitants. In a short time, several defensive plazas were built and occupied up and down the Santa Cruz River valley, with the Plaza del Cerro in Chimayó, constructed around 1730, being the most prominent outside

Santa Cruz itself. In the first decades of the eighteenth century, relationships with the various Pueblos remained tense, and attacks from Plains Indians constituted a real threat for both the Spanish and the Pueblos. To some degree, all Spanish settlements were vulnerable to attack, but Chimayó's position at the eastern edge of the province left it especially open to raids. This meant that the defensive plazas along the Santa Cruz River, including Plaza del Cerro in Chimayó and, to the west, La Puebla and Santa Cruz, served as central housing and headquarters for farming families in the valley. During the summer months, male members of the families would stay in small ranch houses up and down the river and along irrigation ditches in order to be near their crops, but they would leave behind these *rancherías* in times of violence or during fallow periods of the year and rejoin their families in the more heavily fortified plazas.[28]

Eventually, as the Spanish territories became more secure and the Spanish population grew in proportion to the Indians, many of these *rancherías* became places of permanent residence with their own names and identities. The village of Chimayó, with the exception of Plaza del Cerro, never organized centrally but has always consisted of a collection of these smaller population centers. Some of these *placitas* are El Llano, La Centinela, Dolores, Ranchito, Plaza Abajo, and of greatest interest for the Santuario, El Potrero, a collection of houses to the south of the Plaza del Cerro. In the early days of Chimayó, however, the Santuario had not yet come into existence, and the religious life of the Chimayosos found expression in other places.[29]

The Plaza del Cerro in Chimayó, sometimes referred to as San Buenaventura de Chimayó after the village's patron saint, included an *oratorio*, a small room on the southwest side of the fortress-plaza set aside for prayer and religious functions.[30] Until well into the twentieth century, priests from Santa Cruz would visit the *oratorio* on occasion to celebrate Mass, although the regularity of their visits waned over the course of the colonial period.

Popular Religion

The daily religious experiences of the people in Chimayó and the rest of La Cañada during the colonial period are difficult to nail down due to the lack of documentary evidence. However, we can be certain that religious activities were taking place in ways that both cohere with and depart from the Catholicism promoted by the Franciscan friars. By the final decades of the eighteenth century, the Hermanos de la Fraternidad Piadosa de Nuestro Padre Jesús Nazareno (Brothers of the Pious Fraternity of Our Father Jesus the Nazarene), more commonly known as the Penitentes, had formed orders throughout northern New Mexico and were especially active in Santa Cruz and Chimayó. In addition to the lay leadership provided by the Penitentes, other types of popular religious devotion surely marked the quotidian struggles, illnesses, and joys of the villagers, even if evidence about these devotions is sometimes speculative.

Based on the experiences of other villages in northern New Mexico in the middle of the eighteenth century, we can envision a day-to-day Catholicism in Chimayó that expressed itself most saliently in practical ways. This practical religion emerged from the continuous contestation and negotiation that occurred between the various actors, which included lower-class Spanish farmers, Pueblos, Franciscan missionaries, a smattering of enslaved Plains Indians, and a not insignificant population of *genízaros*. The latter group, which made up an important sector of colonial New Mexico, consisted of Native Americans who, through Spanish violence and captivity, had been stripped of tribal connections and lumped into a new social and racial category. Although some *genízaros* took on an ethnic identity of their own and lived in stand-alone communities, most worked as servants who eventually related to their Spanish masters through *compadrazgo* (godparent/godchild kinships created at baptism) and gradually integrated into Hispano communities.[31]

In Chimayó, where the padre from Santa Cruz visited only occasionally to celebrate Mass and pray for the sick, the folk traditions, medical knowledge, and religious worldviews of farmers, Pueblos, and *genízaros* came together into popular practices and religious logics of health and healing. Since popular healing had long been part of Spanish health care both in the Iberian Peninsula and throughout the Spanish Empire, the medical connections and exchanges that occurred between Spanish citizens and indigenous Americans often permitted much more freedom than more doctrinal or ritual religious expressions. Village healers, known as *curanderos*, walked a fine line between religiously sanctioned

care providers and religiously suspect dabblers in witchcraft and the occult. Even in this fraught position, priests, when they were present, tolerated and even utilized popular religious and folk healing.[32]

An outsized example of these kinds of negotiations between priests
and healers began in the village of Abiquiu in the 1760s. Fray Juan José
Toledo was the Franciscan in charge of the mission at the village, which
contained a large population of *genízaros*, and like Chimayó, existed on
the edge of Spanish territory. Over the course of his tenure in Abiquiu,
Toledo became more and more convinced that the ceremonies and healing arts of the village *genízaros* were devilish witchcraft that stood in opposition to his own evangelistic and educational efforts. Moreover, these
genízaro practices had made inroads with the folk arts of the Spanish,
and it had become difficult to disentangle the different healing and practical arts used by the villagers. The records that remain from the inquisi-
torial witchcraft trials Toledo carried out in Abiquiu provide perspective
on the often tense relationship that continued to exist between daily village religious life and the overarching aims of Catholic officials. In Toledo's case, he accused various healers in the Abiquiu area and beyond
of bewitching and even killing fellow villagers with demonic curses.
Ironically, when Toledo himself was struck ill by these supposed curses,
he went to a trusted *curandera* for relief, which he experienced. Before
the largely failed witchcraft trials were complete, Toledo had accused
dozens of villagers in the Río Arriba area of occult behavior, including
an exceptionally large contingent from Chimayó: twenty *genízaros* and
thirty-five Spaniards.[33]

The various New Mexican witchcraft trials that Franciscans carried
out in the eighteenth century are, in some ways, the last-ditch attempt
in their missionization efforts to stamp out lingering public traces of
Pueblo and folk religious rituals, ceremonies, and healing arts. Memory
of the 1680 Pueblo Revolt and the colossal challenge to Catholic advances that it had posed compelled the friars to tread a fine line between
promoting Catholic orthodoxy and allowing Spanish political aims to
be achieved in the province. The latter consideration often meant that
friars, already overextended over huge areas, could do little to stop Spanish, Pueblo, and *genízaro* combinatory and creative religious expression,
especially since these combinations did so much to strengthen and sta-
bilize Hispano settlements. In Padre Toledo's case in Abiquiu, the gov-

ernor at the time, Tomás Vélez Capuchín, was unwilling to destabilize the restive northern reaches of New Mexico with sharp punishments against accused witches, healers, and sorcerers. Toledo's failure to make many accusations stick and Vélez Capuchín's reluctance to impose harsh sentences indicate the importance of northern towns like Abiquiu and Chimayó as political buffer zones and as spaces where folk religion could flourish even against the desires of zealous clergy. Ultimately, as the historians Malcolm Ebright and Rick Hendricks argue, this relatively free space—in terms of religious and cultural exchange—eventually allowed *genízaros* to blend completely with the Spanish population, and in so doing, create the unique Hispano culture and folk religion that has so typified northern New Mexico.[34]

Franciscan Decline and the Rise of the Penitente Order

By the end of the eighteenth century, most villages, *ranchos*, and remote plazas around northern New Mexico could hope to see one of the few aging Franciscan padres only rarely. The friars had left their mark on New Mexico, principally in their mission to the Pueblos, but also in the role they played in maintaining the Catholic faith of Spanish colonists. In addition to being the face of the Church for more than a century, the Franciscans promoted popular devotionalism in various *cofradías*, sodalities of laypeople who provided mutual aid and celebrated the seasons and saints of the Catholic Church. For instance, in Santa Cruz alone, Visitor and Custos Fray Domínguez recorded at least three confraternities in the parish, including the Franciscan Third Order, a lay organization committed to Franciscan devotions and community support.[35]

However, in the waning years of the century, several factors came together that led to the Franciscans' decline. First, despite their less invasive missionization tactics and the eventual pacification of the Pueblos after de Vargas's reconquest, the friars had only modest successes in converting New Mexico's indigenous population in the eighteenth century. As evidenced by Padre Toledo's ongoing trials with supposed witches in Abiquiu and Chimayó, the Christianity of Pueblo converts and *genízaros* and the folk Catholicism of Spanish farm families hardly satisfied the doctrinal expectations of the priests. Second, as New Mexico's economy began to develop and thrive in this period, Nuevomexicanos came to rely less on the colonial metropolis and more on local trade with surrounding Plains Indians, sometimes in disobedience to royal decree. A peace accord with the Comanches in 1786 not only freed up informal trade with plains peoples but also allowed frontier communities like Chimayó to flourish economically and socially as never before due to the relative safety that accompanied the peace.[36] Finally, and most importantly, the reforms imposed by the Bourbon monarchs in Spain had a tremendous effect on religious orders like the Franciscans. In the monarchy's efforts to centralize control over its vast empire, the Bourbons curtailed the regular clergy of the mendicant orders and made attempts to replace them with the more tightly supervised diocesan clergy under the watchful eye of powerful and loyal bishops. The Franciscan missions were officially secularized (turned over to diocesan control) in New Mexico in 1767, though in practice, the churches and *oratorios* of the region continued to be served by the remaining Franciscans for some time. Nevertheless, the writing was on the wall for the friars, despite the fact that the northern dioceses of the late-colonial Catholic Church in New Spain could not immediately meet their obligations to their northernmost areas.[37]

Although the missions were secularized on paper in 1767, New Mexico did not receive any sort of diocesan clergy until thirty years later, in 1797, when the villa churches at the principal population centers at Santa Cruz, Santa Fe, Albuquerque, and El Paso were actually secularized. Even so, the new priests, under the distant bishop of Durango, comprised a definite minority for years, leaving most of the ecclesiastical labors to the dwindling and aging Franciscans. The bishop of Durango himself did not visit this portion of his diocese until 1833, but two of his representatives did make official visitations to the New Mexico churches in 1812 and 1826. Don Agustín Fernández de San Vicente, the second Visitor, was under pressure in 1826 to secularize all the missions after Mexican independence and found the area almost devoid of any clergy, with a mere nine Franciscans and five secular priests covering a vast territory. An 1832 report by Antonio Barreiro, a legal adviser to the independent Mexican government, is worth quoting at length regarding the dismal state of affairs:

Spiritual administration in New Mexico is in a truly doleful condition. Nothing is more common than to see an infinite number of sick die without confession or extreme unction. It is indeed unusual to see the eucharist administered to the sick. Corpses remain unburied for many days, and children are baptized at the cost of a thousand hardships. A great many unfortunate people spend most of the Sundays of the year without hearing mass. Churches are in a state of near ruin, and most of them are unworthy of being called the temple of God.[38]

It was into this context of flagging clergy leadership and thriving folk Catholic communities that the most famous expression of New Mexican popular piety was born: the Brothers of Our Father Jesus, popularly known as the Penitentes. While it is outside the scope of this book to retell the entire story of the Penitentes, their eventual importance to the Santuario de Chimayó requires our attention. No one as yet has been able to determine with any precision the origin of the Penitente Brotherhood, but we can be sure that by 1833 they were an active and important part of religious life throughout much of northern New Mexico and southern Colorado. It was that year that the bishop of Durango, Don José Laureano Antonio Zubiría y Escalante, first came to visit this portion of his diocese. At the church in Santa Cruz, the same church that supposedly covered the religious needs of the people of Chimayó, Zubiría found an active penitential order, perhaps related to the Third Order Franciscans, a lay *cofradía* that Fray Domínguez had recorded at Santa Cruz in 1776. Bishop Zubiría found the corporal penances of the group to be unacceptable not only for their excess but due to the lack of episcopal oversight. He issued an utterly ineffective statement forbidding further membership in the order, which "we annul[led] and which must remain forever abolished."[39]

His command, besides surely falling on unsympathetic ears, could not be enforced due to the chronic lack of clergy. Indeed, Penitentes offered a social structure and religious services to the community that were much stronger and more cohesive than those offered by the overextended and often decadent priesthood. Local chapterhouses, called *moradas*, served as gathering places for the Penitentes and occasionally as places of religious observance for the public.[40] The *hermano mayor* (local leader) oversaw the various activities of the Brotherhood and administered the various other officers, including the *celador* (warden and discipline keeper), *enfermero* (nurse and caretaker for both the order and members of the community), *picador* (bloodletter during corporal penitence), *rezador* (reader/recite of prayers), and *pitero* (liturgical flute player for processions). Tasks were thus delegated, but the *hermano mayor*, according to at least one nineteenth-century Penitente constitution, remained ultimately responsible not only for the proper functioning of his *morada* but also for the spiritual and temporal well-being of the community under his care.[41] With the general absence of ordained clergy and the scarcity of civil authorities, the *hermano mayor* and his brethren fulfilled various social and religious tasks in the villages. In addition to hosting religious festivals, especially during Holy Week, they also cared for the sick, watched over the recently deceased, dug graves, punished misconduct, and gave succor to the poor and needy.[42]

As mentioned, the precise origins of the Penitente Brotherhood are unknown, but historians have proposed several informed guesses, two of which are most common. The first is that the Penitentes evolved from Third Order Franciscans, a lay order with European origins that promoted Franciscan ideals of poverty, simplicity, and daily holiness. The famous priest Antonio José Martínez of Taos believed that this was the origin of the Brotherhood, a contention that the historian Richard Ahlborn suggests is the most sensible conclusion. Ahlborn cites Domínguez's 1776 visit to New Mexico and discovery of Third Order Franciscans at Santa Cruz as a likely point of connection.[43] The second theory comes from a Franciscan himself, the great New Mexican historian Fray Angélico Chávez, who posits that "the idea of the flagellant Penitentes was first introduced somehow from southern Mexico, initially at Santa Cruz and its villages," sometime in the early nineteenth century. Noting various differences between the Penitentes and Franciscan Tertiaries, including their dress, their heavy penitential exercises, and their all-male societies, Chávez ultimately finds "no connection at all between the two altogether dissimilar groups."[44]

Whether or not we accept the Third Order origin or Chávez's contention that the penitential rites came from southern Mexico, we can acknowledge that almost all commentators agree that one of the principal impetuses for the Penitentes—in addition to clergy scarcity—was the stress and power vacuum created in New Mexican Catholicism by the forced secularization of the Franciscan missions. What was at stake was not the lock-step continuation of Franciscan authority but the maintenance of Hispano village life, which included festivals, Masses, and saints' devotions. Of course, these elements were introduced long before by the Franciscans, but they had taken relatively stable and productive forms under the lay leadership of the *hermano mayor* and his Penitente brethren. However, it would be naïve and wrong to consider the early Penitentes as mere lay repeaters of Franciscan orthodoxy; the practical considerations of folk Catholicism, Pueblo worldviews, and *genízaro* communities all contributed to the ritual and social life of Hispano villages.[45]

This brings us to a theory of Penitente origins that has been frequently discounted: Indian influences. For the most part, recent scholars have rejected the notion that Pueblo rituals and religious customs somehow contributed to the advent of the Penitentes. A reason for this rejection is the explicit racism that was at the core of many early observers' arguments about Penitente origins. For example, in 1904 a reporter named Carl Taylor brought the Penitentes a level of national infamy with his flamboyant reporting:

> It is interesting to note that when the Spanish conquerors entered Mexico they found that among almost all the Indian nations there were professional penitents who made vicarious atonement for the sins of the whole tribe. The periods of penance occurred at regular intervals and a prescribed routine of torture was gone through. These facts, taken together with the barbarous cruelty, the indifference to suffering shown in the rites of the penitents, and the very nature of some of the torments, suggest that though the order remained Christian, it was influenced to a very marked degree by the religion of the native races.[46]

In short, according to Taylor and other like-minded critics, the barbaric practices of one group passed easily to another barbaric group. His concession that the Penitentes "remained Christian" pales before his accusations of religious adulteration. Likewise, the writer Charles Lummis noted in 1896 that the penitential rites of the New Mexicans seemed to echo ancient Pueblo practices in a "curious devolution" of Mexican Catholicism.[47]

The historian Marta Weigle, who wrote the premier history of the Brotherhood in 1976, responded particularly to earlier assertions like

Taylor's and Lummis's that linked Indian penitential practices to those of the Spanish villagers. "Neither the ethnocentric recourse to a subjective notion of the primitive nor the discovery of a single identical trait such as flagellation constitutes substantial evidence for Indian influence on Penitente rites," she wrote. Weigle's argument here—namely, that superficial similarities are not an indication of a causal relationship—is strong. Weigle makes a second argument against Indian origins that depends on the Spaniards' own sense of moral and religious superiority over the Pueblos. In short, a "significant religious influence of the subordinate over the dominant . . . is highly unlikely." In this calculus of influence, the Spanish would not take on the penitential rites of the Indians because they dismissed the ceremonies and rituals of the indigenous people as demonic, savage, and worthless. Moreover, as Weigle, Chávez, Ahlborn, and many others have noted, there were plenty of preexisting penitential orders and traditions in European Catholicism, which would obviate the need to borrow from the Indians.[48]

It is not that Weigle's arguments are incorrect, but her focus, ironically like that of Taylor in 1904, remains on the transfer of specific penitential acts like self-flagellation. However, as Ebright and Hendricks have shown in their history of witchcraft trials in colonial northern New Mexico, Abiquiu and Chimayó, two primary centers of eventual Penitente activities, were highly mixed societies where Pueblos, Spanish, and *genízaros* lived and worked side by side. Additionally, they at least shared common assumptions and practices concerning witchcraft, healing, and related practical aspects of folk religiosity. To be sure, the Spanish in these villages enjoyed social prestige and at least a claim to religious orthodoxy that the other two principal groups did not, but both geographical distance and shared economic challenges colluded in the late colonial era to create contexts in which practical religious exchanges and reformulations could and did take place. In such a context, a strict focus on causality concerning the transfer of specific ritual acts is less useful than an examination of broader flows and reconfigurations. If we refocus ourselves on a larger picture of exchange and discount the notion that ethnic identities remained constant throughout the eighteenth century, it becomes much more possible to posit that a combination of Pueblo, *genízaro*, and Spanish religious and social mores all contributed to the context in which the Penitentes were born. Thus, by the early 1800s, *genízaros* had slowly disappeared as they integrated with the Spanish. Likewise, although indigenous religions remained vital parts of Pueblo life, Pueblo Catholicism also strengthened throughout the period, especially among the Tewas, who had long been the group most closely associated with the Spanish. In fact, Ebright and Hendricks note that, as *genízaro* identity shifted to be more and more Hispano, the Penitentes were growing rapidly in Abiquiu, and they suggest that *genízaros* were an important part of that growth. Their argument can be extrapolated to Chimayó, which, like Abiquiu, was a buffer community with a large *genízaro* population.[49]

To be clear, I am not suggesting that the Penitentes positively have an indigenous origin, but it is undeniable that the Penitentes emerged from a cultural and religious context that included many, sometimes indefinable, Indian influences. In this sense, it would be more accurate to say that the Penitente Brotherhood originated in places that lacked regular access to clergy, that had undergone a century or more of ethnic reconfiguration on the borders of empire, that self-identified for the most part as Catholic, and that had developed autochthonous religious narratives, practices, and social functions in order to support their unique communities. The specific penitential practices and the particular hierarchy of leadership within the Brotherhood probably developed from some combination of the Franciscan Third Order and comparable Mexican penitential orders, but the entire complex of Penitente leadership and social functioning in New Mexico transcends these likely historical linkages.

Historical accounts of Hispano Catholicism in northern New Mexico, as the historian Michael Carroll has noted, often stress ostensible continuity with Spanish American Catholic traditions. Of course, this way of remembering the past bolsters the notion of Franciscan and Spanish heroism and victory during the colonization of the land. Indeed, this narrative is often related explicitly to the establishment of pure racial categories, especially over and against the Indians, as, for instance, when the Visitor and Custos Fray Domínguez writes in 1776 of the population around Chimayó that "most of them pass for Spaniards" and "speak the Spanish current and accepted here." His words betray his distaste for the quality of racial purity in La Cañada even as they illustrate the Hispanicizing process that was occurring in populations that contained large numbers of *genízaros*, Pueblos, and poor Spanish farmers. But, as

Carroll convincingly argues, it is not this supposed continuity but the immense religious creativity of northern New Mexicans that sets them apart. In the late eighteenth and early nineteenth centuries, for all of the historical reasons discussed above, the Río Arriba area enjoyed an outpouring of novel religious forms, including the *bultos* (statues) and *retablos* (altarpieces) of the great *santeros* (carvers of saints' images), the rise and flourishing of the Penitentes, and the construction of the Santuario de Chimayó as a center of miraculous healing and pilgrim devotion.[50]

In the next chapter, we turn decisively to the story of the Santuario. Central to this story is the figure of Don Bernardo Abeyta, a landowner in El Potrero, a small plaza within the district of Chimayó. Abeyta, as we shall see, forms a linchpin of sorts in this setting of fertile religious creativity: he is the *hermano mayor* of the local Penitente order, he has a reputedly miraculous connection to a pivotal piece of folk art (the crucifix of Our Lord of Esquipulas now displayed on the main altar of the Santuario), and, of course, he is the founder and builder of the Santuario itself. How the Santuario came to be the place that it is, and its relationship to both the hole of healing earth and its various depictions of Christ and the saints, is not a straightforward narrative of one fact leading to another and another. Rather, dozens of origin stories weave together in an intricate tapestry that variously highlights Catholic orthodoxy, emphasizes Pueblo lore, and challenges the power of the Church. This incredible site of devotion and restoration thus comes together as something of a living symbol of the unique confluence of actors and authorities that constitute New Mexico.

2

The Origin of the Santuario

Of the many so-called legends no two agree, consequently
any student of this Chimayo mythology who will undertake
their solution will have an impossible proposition if he tries
to harmonize them with the view of forming from them all
a presentable fib.
—Benjamin M. Read, historian and Speaker of the House,
New Mexico Territorial Legislature[1]

According to many stories, the spark of life for the Santuario de Chimayó emerged from the ground. The most common of these accounts
says that Don Bernardo Abeyta was doing penance in a field near his
home in the village of Chimayó on Good Friday, 1810, when he saw
something glowing in the dirt near the Santa Cruz River. He walked
over to the source of the light and discovered that a crucifix was buried
in a hole. Being a pious man, Abeyta immediately took the crucifix to
the priest at the closest parish church, eight miles away in Santa Cruz,
where the two men placed the holy object on the altar. The next morning, the crucifix had vanished—only to be rediscovered in the hole in
the ground back in Chimayó. Abeyta returned the cross to the church
in Santa Cruz, but in vain, because the peripatetic Christ returned once
more to the original spot in the ground. Understanding that God desired
for the crucifix to remain in Chimayó, Abeyta sought permission from
the Catholic Church to build a chapel around the site of the crucifix's
discovery, a project he began in 1813 after first housing a shrine to the
crucifix in his nearby home. Finished in 1816, the chapel was named the
Santuario de Nuestro Señor de Esquipulas, since Abeyta had identified
the Christ as a replica of a famous crucifix of the same name in Esquipulas, Guatemala. Soon, pilgrims were coming from miles around to pray
to Our Lord of Esquipulas and to draw the sacred and healing earth that
quickly became associated with the hole from which he had emerged.[2]

But this account of the Santuario's genesis is just the most frequently uttered among several others. Some are similar to this legend and differ in a few relatively minor details, while other origin narratives for the Santuario and its famous healing dirt depart significantly from it. This chapter collects the various etiologies of the Santuario. Stories about the sources of religious devotions can reveal several important insights. First, these kinds of narratives, when read across the grain, can help us understand the religious—and sometimes political—needs of the story-teller. Religious origin stories can privilege particular groups, or inform expectations about certain types of ritual practices. Second, these stories can shed light on the kinds of cultural and religious combinations that were taking place at the time of the origin as well as during the times in which the origin tale is retold. In this kind of analysis, we often look at the "ingredients" that went into creating the final product; in this case, we can examine what religious stories or devotional objects predate but ultimately lead to the Santuario. Finally, stories that smack of legend or myth can help us reflect on the project of history itself. How do these stories give us a window on the past in ways that also illumine the present? Religiously motivated memories or official accounts of the past are one way of remembering that must be put in conversation with other historiographical priorities.

There is something ultimately creative about religious origin stories, not in the sense that they describe the actual creation of a religious observance, but in a more generative, Durkheimian sense. One of the founders of sociology, Emile Durkheim, argued, in essence, that religious ideas and actions represent society in ways that create and re-create the unity of the collective.[3] Origin stories about Chimayó's Santuario and miraculous earth, then, do not function to explain how things came to be as they are; instead, they reinforce for the storytellers and the story hearers how they are to live and act at the time of the telling. They also function to create group solidarity, sometimes over and against other groups that are telling the same story in a different way. Of course, the latter group, likewise, is telling the story to achieve and maintain its own internal aims and group cohesion. To wit, Durkheim writes, "Believers—men, who, leading the religious life, know it through daily experience—know that its true function is not to enrich our knowledge . . . but to make us act and to help us live." Later he adds,

"There is something in religion . . . that is destined to outlast all particular symbols within which religious thought has successively enveloped itself. No society can exist without feeling the necessity of maintaining and confirming at regular intervals the collective feelings and ideas that constitute its unity."[4]

However, as the following will demonstrate, origin stories serve the purposes of the particular group doing the telling. And although the focus here is the Santuario de Chimayó, it is true of all contested and popular sites of religious devotion that different constituencies vie for what we may call "religious ownership." In this context of overlapping or competing narratives, at stake is who can make the most legitimate claim to the place and to the religious practices therein. As we shall see, the stories of the genesis of the Santuario, its pilgrimage, the earth in the *pocito*, and the various objects of adoration inside the building are all opportunities, à la Durkheim, to narrate a particular community, to knit that community together, and to establish claims. To complicate matters significantly, origin stories in a place as complex and full of signifiers as the Santuario overlap and become entangled such that the same story can accomplish different objectives for different groups. But let us turn now to the stories.

The Tewa Origin

The exact spot where the village of Chimayó now sits almost certainly was once inhabited by Tewa Pueblo people, and the landscape still constitutes part of their sacred geography.[5] The most reliable account of Tewa cosmology and social structure continues to be the Tewa anthropologist Alfonso Ortiz, who was born at San Juan Pueblo, now known as Ohkay Owingeh, only twenty miles from the Santuario. According to Ortiz, the Tewa world comprises various categories of existence that fall onto a conceptual grid oriented to the four cardinal points. Marking these cardinal points are several "tetrads," or geographically locatable places, that help set the bounds of Tewa life. At the heart of this world is the "earth navel," which is physically located in the center of the Pueblo at Ohkay Owingeh, and serves as a place of eternal emergence and return. However, other earth navels are likewise found at the tops of mountains and sacred hills and can also act as places of entrance to a vast, interconnected, and labyrinthine underworld. The outer ring of the Tewa world is marked by a tetrad of high mountains; an intermediate ring is made up of a foursome of lower hills. It is the eastern hill, called Tsi Mayoh, that rises directly to the north and east of the Santuario and that gives the village its name. To be sure, while this does not make Chimayó the most sacred spot of the Tewa, it clearly lies in an important place and has narrative significance as a site of activity of the Towa é, some of the both human and supernatural personages who are part of Tewa cosmology.[6]

Some of the earliest suggestions that the Santuario's healing dirt has Tewa origins come from explorers, curious health seekers, and the first wave of anthropologists to study the region. The proto-anthropologist and archaeologist Adolph Bandelier mentions in his own writings "the gorges of Chimayo" as early as 1892; he understood the place to be something of an eastern lookout for both the Tewa and Hispano villagers against marauders from the plains.[7] John Harrington wrote an ethno-geography of the Tewa world and published it in 1916. Known principally for his intense curiosity and classificatory passions, Harrington mostly collected place-names without much explanatory information. He notes that Chimayó, according to the Indians of the region, was once a Tewa Pueblo called Tsimajo'oŋwi, which was situated incredibly "where the church is now." At the site of this Pueblo—that is, where the Santuario currently sits—was a pool called Tsimajopokwi. The pool's mud had healing properties.[8]

The most colorful anthropological account, however, comes from Edgar Hewett, an anthropologist and archaeologist of sorts who came originally to New Mexico because of his wife's ill health. Fascinated with Native American culture and artifacts, he became involved with preservation as well as educational efforts to study and enshrine New Mexico's native peoples. His 1912 explanation of the healing shrine at Chimayó features several factual inaccuracies but is perhaps the clearest early exponent of the idea that the dirt has Pueblo origins:

Chimayo was originally an Indian pueblo, a pueblo of blanket weavers. There is a famous old shrine at the place. It was originally an Indian shrine. After the pueblo became Mexicanized a church was built by the shrine and pilgrimages were made to the shrine from all over the

Southwest. The church built at the shrine is in the custodianship of purest Indian descent. In a grotto is the curative earth. Boards in the floor are taken up in order to get at the earth. People used to carry the earth away with them. Articles of silver, brass and glass were deposited at the place. The earth was consecrated.[9]

From his description, it seems highly unlikely that Hewett had visited the Santuario, and he unfortunately does not provide his sources about the ancient Indian shrine. Moreover, he mistakenly remarks that the custodians of the shrine, which we know to be the Abeyta and Chavez families, were of "purest Indian descent." Other problems with his picture, of course, include that the dirt is in a grotto under boards, and that by 1912, the people seem to have ceased carrying away the earth, much evidence in other records to the contrary.[10]

If Hewett did not, in fact, have any reasonable familiarity with the Santuario, why then did he cobble together this particular story, with its marked emphasis on Indian origins? We cannot know the precise answer to this question, but it is more than reasonable to speculate that Hewett, Harrington, and others in the first corps of anthropologists to study New Mexico were taking their initial, if poorly informed, stabs at explaining the provenance of the healing earth in the Santuario. Identifying the Pueblos as the original source of the practice of using the dirt in the area for medicinal purposes was one of two natural hypotheses, the other being that the devotion originated with the Catholicism of the Spanish, an idea that is examined below. The reasons for the attractiveness of the "Indian hypothesis" for these Anglo explainers are twofold. First, these men desired to understand New Mexico as a place where Indian lore and tradition had left an indelible mark that could connect the new Anglo settlers to the land's ancient past without the unpleasant interlude of Spanish and then Mexican control. In this mindset, the healing mud had always been there but had only recently been "Mexicanized" with the trappings of a Catholic shrine. Conversely, the second plausible reason for the Indian hypothesis is the anthropologists' thinly veiled desire to see the unique and picturesque Catholicism of the Hispanos not as an acceptable counterpart to their own understandings of Christianity but rather as endlessly syncretized with the more creative and ultimately spiritual additions of the Indian. Charles Lummis, friend of Bandelier and fellow ethnographer and adventurer, provides us an example of this viewpoint when he wrote in his famed *Land of Poco Tiempo*, "With the superstitions dwells the simple folk-lore. That of the Mexicans is scant; but that of the Indians infinite and remarkably poetic."[11]

More recent versions of the Indian hypothesis tend to focus less on these romantic reconstructions of New Mexico's ancient folk life and more on the influence that Pueblo stories have on current understandings of the origins of the healing earth. The photographer and historian Don Usner recounts a Hispano legend in Chimayó that seems to have originated with the Tewa people of the area. In the story, a cave on the side of Tsi Mayoh—the above-mentioned hill that lies behind the Santuario—is an entrance to a warren of subterranean passageways in the Tewa underworld that connect Tsi Mayoh all the way to Black Mesa in San Ildefonso Pueblo.[12] Such a connection to the Tewa underworld maps the Santuario onto contemporary Tewa cosmology. Moreover, according to the folklorist Enrique Lamadrid, Tewa stories confirm the early ethnographic accounts mentioned above about Tewa use of healing mud in the Chimayó vicinity. They say that the place was where the twin sons of the Sun killed a dangerous and threatening giant. As a result of this act, fire came out of the ground and dried up what had been a sacred spring. The remaining mud became the source of the healing earth now enclosed inside the Santuario.[13]

Contemporary scholars mention the Pueblo origins of the place in order to demonstrate the Catholic Hispanos' canniness in locating their Santuario over a prior sacred place. The historian Ramón Gutiérrez has studied the Santuario and identifies the *pocito* as a *sipapu* upon which Abeyta built the chapel. A *sipapu* is the Hopi word used to describe the hole in the bottom of a kiva through which the Pueblo peoples entered into this world. The Tewas do not use the word *sipapu*, as it is not in their language, but there is a cognate word that is used in a similar origin story. Likewise, the Tewas do speak of "earth navels," one of which has long been associated with the hill of Tsi Mayoh.[14] Unfortunately, Gutiérrez does not cite his source when he quotes "Pueblo Indians" who claim that "the padres came and learned about the sipapu's power . . . so they built a church." But his analysis is clear and follows on the anthropologists Victor and Edith Turner's conclusions that Christian shrines

Figure 2.1. Procession at the Santuario de Chimayó with Tsi Mayoh hill rising behind the church, 1910. Jesse Nusbaum, courtesy of Palace of the Governors Photo Archives (NMHM/DCA), 014379.

around the world, and perhaps especially in Spanish America, have been built atop places once deemed sacred or vital by the preexisting people. In the Turners' words, the Christians "baptize the local customs."[15]

Of course, if the muds and earth of Chimayó were once important to the Tewa, and perhaps to other Pueblos as well, they still are. Groups of Pueblos continue to make pilgrimage to the Santuario, some as part of their Catholicism, and others for reasons known to them and to the religious societies of which they form part. Since Tsi Mayoh hill has long been an important site in Tewa cosmology, and the location of an earth navel, there is every reason to expect that the place continues to hold meaning for Pueblo people, even if the specifics of that meaning and related ritual practices are not publicly known, nor are they for public consumption.[16]

In balance, the Pueblo origin stories relating to the Santuario tend to emphasize the etiology of the healing earth. In this understanding, the *locus sanctus* in Chimayó can be tied directly to pre-European mythologies and cultural geographies. This implies, of course, that Hispanos and others who have believed in the power of the holy dirt are, in some measure, participating in Indian knowledge and ritual practice. One effect of this kind of origin story, then, is to push back the starting date for devotional practices at the Chimayó site into the relatively undocumented indigenous past. This interpretive move provides a historical depth to what could otherwise be considered a comparatively young church in northern New Mexico. It also connects the church in a predominantly Hispano area with the more ancient structures built specifically for the evangelization of the Indians.[17] Such a connection gives the Santuario a historical patina beyond its two hundred years.

But there are other implications involved in pointing out explicit connections with prior Indian traditions and customs. When Christian practices evince a history of mixing with indigenous non-Christian rituals, the loaded word that scholars have often used to describe the process and its outcomes is "syncretism." For some, syncretism is bemoaned as an adulteration of religious purity or European civilization. If the healing earth in the Santuario has Indian origins, this is proof that the local Hispano devotion to the earth is a sign of cultural declension and religious degradation. We can understand this type of analysis as one example of the *leyenda negra*, the Black Legend that paints the Spanish and their descendants in the Americas as hopelessly backwards, medieval, cruel, and superstitious—traits that left them open to the pernicious influences of the natives. On the other extreme are those who have romanticized American Indian cultures as profoundly spiritual, artistic, and natural. In this kind of analysis, syncretism with purported indigenous healing earth in the Santuario can only burnish the shrine's mystical connection to spiritual and miraculous power.

Our Lord of Esquipulas

If the Tewa origin story connects the Santuario de Chimayó with an ancient Native American past, the following origin story emphasizes continuity with older expressions of Spanish American Catholicism. The official name now and historically of the Santuario is El Santuario de Nuestro Señor de Esquipulas, the name ascribed to the Christ on the large crucifix on the main altar of the church as well as a smaller *bulto* now located in the room where the *pocito* is located.[18] Who or what is the Lord of Esquipulas? In brief, it is the name of a large crucifix in southeastern Guatemala that originated in the late sixteenth century, over two hundred years before the construction of the Santuario at Chimayó. How did a Guatemalan Christ almost 2,500 miles away from Chimayó come to be venerated in Abeyta's chapel? Is there a connection between the two Lords of Esquipulas?

The answers to these questions are not easy to come by and depend to some degree on speculation. The principal guide in this endeavor is a Hungarian anthropologist, archaeologist, curator, and immigrant to the United States named Stephan F. de Borhegyi. Borhegyi spent considerable time in the 1940s and 1950s doing fieldwork in Guatemala and also resided for stints in the Santa Fe area. His insightful writings about Esquipulas suggest several important points: First, like the Tewa mud stories, there is every likelihood that the Guatemalan Christ also was established like a palimpsest over miraculous healing earth known to pre-Hispanic indigenous Central Americans. Second, the physical features of the Esquipulas crucifix indicate further combinations between Spanish Catholicism and indigenous traditions. And finally, while there are no certain connections between Chimayó and Guatemala, the speculations that tie these two places together are well-founded. Let us examine Borhegyi's conclusions in turn.

First, we turn to Borhegyi's position that Esquipulas veneration has significant indigenous origins. At the time of the Spanish conquest of the eastern portion of Guatemala in the early years of the sixteenth century, the area was inhabited by peaceable Chorti Indians, a subgroup of the Maya who still reside in Guatemala, Honduras, and El Salvador. To avoid their own massacre, the Chortis, under a leader named Esquipulas, agreed to turn over custodianship of their territory to the Spaniards.[19] By the 1560s, they were resettled into a new town called Santiago de Esquipulas in present-day southeastern Guatemala; the town was felicitously located on a popular trade and pilgrimage route between points in Guatemala and the vaunted Maya religious center at Copán in Honduras. A small Christian church was built at Esquipulas in 1578, and the villagers commissioned and paid for a noted colonial artist, Quirio Cataño, to craft a large crucifix to adorn the altar. Significantly, the crucifix was made in such a way that the typical white skin of Spanish Christ images was replaced with a lustrous black such that the image has long been known as the Cristo Negro de Esquipulas.[20]

Despite this last detail, one might assume from the story so far that the Spanish had pacified and evangelized the Chortis with unusual dispatch, settling them in a well-administered village centered on a Catholic church. However, Borhegyi relates that the Esquipulas shrine was built atop an older indigenous sacred place known for its health-giving springs and curing earth. By the opening years of the seventeenth century, a pilgrimage to Esquipulas for the purpose of seeking healing was under way, and the indigenous roots of the place had already become entangled irreversibly with the image of the Black Christ. Pilgrims found relief by venerating the crucifix, and they also purchased and ingested tablets, called *benditos*, made out of the *tierra santa* of the surrounding area. Furthermore, such geophagy, or earth eating, was common from the central valley of Mexico and south throughout the Maya region. Eventually, due to the prominence of the Black Christ, whose image is often impressed on the earthen tablets, the practice of ingesting or using earth for healing became associated with the Lord of Esquipulas. The health-seeking pilgrims to Esquipulas were blessed and sanctioned by the Catholic Church in 1737, but, as Borhegyi makes clear, "It can safely be assumed that the cult of Esquipulas has its roots in the pre-Columbian past of this hemisphere."[21]

In addition to the common feature of the presence of healing earth, the artistic rendering of the Guatemalan Cristo Negro also relates to the Esquipulas crucifix in Chimayó. First, the dark aspect of the skin of the earlier image may signify a further indigenous connection to the Maya and other Mesoamerican peoples. Remaining art and codices as well as colonial-era episcopal reports suggest that several groups of Maya ranging from the Yucatan and throughout Guatemala venerated black-tinted deities, "the lord of black ones," and "the tall black lord." Borhegyi surmises that the immediate popularity of the Black Christ results from these prior and ongoing devotions.[22] Second, Quirio Cataño, the artist who crafted the crucifix, situated the Christ on a dark green cross carved with leaves and growing vines. Trees of life, or world trees, are a common motif in Maya art and may represent a graphic depiction of Maya cosmology. Whether or not the Esquipulas crucifix's green, leafy cross was intentionally carved to make this connection, it has been made by both academic and ecclesiastical observers.[23] One conclusion that can be drawn is that the speedy rise of the healing pilgrimage in Esquipulas relied on the not-so-subtle connections to Maya religious aesthetics and ideas that can be discerned in the crucifix's appearance. In this analysis, the Santuario does not only boast deep-seated ties to an ancient Pueblo past, it also is rooted in Mesoamerican cosmology.

However, not all commentators emphasize the indigenous aspects of this syncretic origin story; the Catholic administrators at Chimayó acknowledge the Guatemalan Maya influences on the image but interpret them with an emphasis on the Christian content. And it is true that the two crucifixes are not identical. The crucifix that Abeyta placed in the Santuario, unlike its Guatemalan namesake, does not have black skin, but rather has the creamy white color that is typical of other European-origin images of Christ. But, as in Esquipulas, the cross of the Chimayó crucifix is dark green and painted with leaves.[24] It is worth quoting at length the interpretive materials regarding this fact that are displayed prominently in the Church-operated visitor center adjacent to the Santuario:

> The most distinguishing characteristic of the crucifix is the green color of the wood on which Jesus has been crucified. Truncated stems on the cross signify that the wood is alive. For that reason, it is green and not brown.
>
> Tradition calls the cross *"the Tree of Life."* The Indians from Santiago de Esquipulas (Guatemala) revered the *"Tree of Life"* before the arrival of the Christian missionaries. This tree has the form of a cross and when the Indians saw the cross of Jesus for the first time, it was easy for them to accept that this was the God that they should worship.
>
> The Ceiba tree has been recognized in Guatemala as a sacred tree since pre-Columbian times. Mayan mythology holds that its main branches both point to the four directions and also embrace the entire universe.
>
> According to Mayan mythology "It is possible to be in touch with the gods through a being which reaches toward the sky while rooted in the sustaining earth, becoming divinized as it moves toward the sacred sphere."
>
> In this way, the Ceiba tree becomes a means of communication whenever a human being searches for the divine.

The Tree of Life or the Tree of the Knowledge of Good and Evil is also found in the Bible. Trees are often used as images of the strength and weakness of the human being.[25]

In this version of the arboreal cross, the leaves and tree motif facilitated the Indians' evangelization to "the God they should worship." And the Maya world tree that stretches up and down the axis mundi also becomes a meta-symbol shared across religious traditions that can be and is replaced with the cross of Jesus Christ, the mediator *par excellence* between the heavens and the earth.[26]

Art historians who have studied the various images, including the Lord of Esquipulas crucifix, in the Chimayó chapel have taken yet another tack in establishing the origins of the image. First, they note that the Franciscan coat of arms, the cross of Jerusalem, and other symbolic images commonly associated with the friars on the main altar screen (*retablo mayor*) in the Santuario suggest an ongoing Franciscan influence on New Mexican sacred art and architecture, despite the Santuario's relatively late date (1816) and the fact that it was not built as a Franciscan mission. It is in front of this altar screen that the Señor de Esquipulas, ostensibly the crucifix that Abeyta discovered in the ground, is located. Various art historians agree that both the *retablo mayor* and the crucifix are the work of a noted early nineteenth-century *santero* named Molleno. Molleno's extant work includes four altar screens, two in the Santuario and two others in churches in Ranchos de Taos and Talpa, New Mexico. The speculated dates for when Molleno carved the crucifix are 1816 to 1818, meaning that the crucifix—at least according to the art historians who have catalogued the chapel's artworks—has a later provenance than the building itself. A much smaller crucifix, also referred to as the Cristo de Esquipulas, is found in the small room where the *pocito* is located. This Christ also has an early nineteenth-century origin and is affixed to a plain cross, that is, without sprouting leaves and green wood.[27] Some insist that this smaller Christ was the one that Abeyta found in the hole in the dirt and that the larger crucifix upon the main altar of the Santuario was made later and based on the smaller Christ. While this cannot be verified in the documentary record, it seems unlikely, since the larger crucifix exhibits aesthetic similarities to its Guatemalan namesake, which the smaller *bulto* does not.

Figure 2.2. Señor de Esquipulas crucifix on the main altar of the Santuario. Author's photo.

To be sure, the Esquipulas crucifix in Chimayó is easily the most important replica of Esquipulas in New Mexico, and indeed in all of North America. However, in addition to the original in Guatemala, there are other images of Esquipulas in New Mexico. The noted contemporary *santero* and researcher Charles Carrillo has found that by the 1830s, an image of the Lord of Esquipulas was part of the typical repertoire of most *santeros* in New Mexico: "In New Mexico, the principal key in the identification of the colonial images of Our Lord of Esquipulas is not the color of his flesh; rather it is the identification of a Latin cross from which seven living branches emanate." Carrillo argues that the green, leafy crosses metaphorically suggest life and curing to the devotee, and possibly even the more specific idea of medicine.[28] In this reading of the Esquipulas devotion, the emphasis is again on healing. And while the Santuario and its healing dirt lead the pack among healing devotions in New Mexico, the fact that there are other Lords of Esquipulas around the state suggests that healing and recovery have been attractive themes in New Mexico Hispano Catholicism even outside the precincts of Chimayó.

If *santeros* were supplying *bultos* and images of Our Lord of Esquipulas to the New Mexican faithful in the early decades of the nineteenth century, then there must have been a demand for this image. The earliest specific mention of it occurs in 1803, when the vicar of Santa Cruz de la Cañada writes a letter to his friend Father Mariano Sanches Bergara (spelled elsewhere as Sánchez Vergara) and asks him to remember him in prayer with the "Sr. de Esquipula."[29] The vicar, Don José Vibián Ortega, was the first diocesan priest to serve Santa Cruz. The great New Mexican historian Fray Angélico Chávez speculates in one place that Vicar Ortega may have been the person responsible for introducing devotion to Esquipulas to New Mexico Hispanos, and most significantly, to the Penitentes. In another place, Chávez reverses this order of events and suggests that the Penitentes knew of Esquipulas from some immigrant from Guatemala and in turn spread the devotion to Vicar Ortega.[30] In either case, by the first decade of the nineteenth century, the veneration of the Guatemalan Christ was spreading among both clergy and laypeople in the Río Arriba area.

The connection to Bernardo Abeyta can be established shortly thereafter. In 1805 Abeyta's nephew was born and was christened Juan de Esquipulas. One of Abeyta's own children was born and given the name Tomás de Jesús de Esquipulas in 1813, and it was later in that same year that Abeyta, speaking on behalf of all the families in El Potrero—the area of Chimayó where the Santuario is now located—solicited approval from the priest in Santa Cruz to begin construction of a chapel named for the increasingly popular image of Christ:

> I declare [illegible] myself desirous of [illegible] tribute to our God and Redeemer [illegible] the corresponding worship in his form as Esquipulas, to be allowed to be built in the said place a chapel where people can congregate with the objective of [illegible] his mercies in all their needs.[31]

Fray Sebastián Álvarez, the priest in Santa Cruz who received this letter, was in full support and sent the request on to the diocesan authorities in Durango. Álvarez's explanation of the devotion to Esquipulas demonstrates the extent of its popularity by 1813:

> I affirm that the miraculous image of the Lord of Esquipulas, which for three years has been venerated in the shrine that is contiguous to his

[Abeyta's] house and dwelling, and supported at his own expense. . . . This place is frequented by many people and in pilgrimage they come from even twenty and more leagues away to give their intercessions (*votos*) to the Sovereign Redeemer, and to experience relief and healing of their ailments. From the constant fame of these portents has originated the laudable desire that comes from the faithful and other devotees of the Lord of Esquipulas to build him a chapel in the most decent and well-proportioned place that has been chosen in the same Plaza or Rancho of El Potrero, that they already have named the Santuario de Esquipulas, wherein they hope to offer to the Lord their reverent worship.[32]

It is clear, therefore, that it is not only Abeyta who is devoted to Esquipulas, but that the devotion had spread by this point to many in the region. It is also evident that some sort of story about the "miraculous image" and its "portents" had already become sufficiently well known to attract an extensive pilgrimage.

How the New Mexicans, including Abeyta, came to know of the Señor de Esquipulas in faraway Guatemala is not precisely known, although historians have ventured two reasonable hypotheses. The first is that Abeyta, as a relatively successful citizen and leader in his community, may have had business connections that led him to travel down the Camino Real and into southern reaches of New Spain. There is no reason to suppose that this is not the case, as commerce up and down the empire was common.[33] The other supposition is that, rather than a New Mexican visiting the south, the natural movement of goods, people, and ideas inevitably brought the Esquipulas devotion north all the way to Chimayó. Borhegyi considered this the likely scenario, as he had documented the spread of the veneration from Esquipulas throughout several other more northerly precincts of Mexico. Shrines to Esquipulas were established, often along with the practice of geophagy, or earth eating, in places as diverse as Oaxaca, Veracruz, and Guadalajara, as well as points south of Guatemala in many of the lands that would eventually become independent Central American nations.[34]

Another purported connection between Chimayó and Esquipulas, Guatemala, draws on popular legend, one that has been promoted by the Catholic Church, which claims that the "legend is based on fact." The story goes that a Guatemalan priest accompanied the first Spanish settlers to the Chimayó area; no date is given—this may refer to the poorly documented settlement of the area that occurred before the Pueblo Revolt or the later settlement in the 1690s. In any case, the padre was killed by Indians and buried along with a crucifix in El Potrero, the district of Chimayó where the Santuario now sits. When the Santa Cruz River flooded its banks in 1810, the legend tells that both the body of the priest and the crucifix were uncovered by the surging waters. According to the tale, there were still older people alive at the time of the flood who recognized the priest, and they shouted, "Miren, el Padre de Esquipulas" (Look, the Father from Esquipulas). The locals soon began referring to the crucifix that emerged from the ground as Our Lord of Esquipulas not after the namesake crucifix in Guatemala but due to its association with the Esquipulan priest.[35] This version of the Esquipulas connection (which perhaps invites skepticism, given the detail that personal familiarity with the alleged priest spans more than a century for some Chimayó residents) has the virtue of explaining both the Guatemalan connection and the persistent notion that the original Chimayó crucifix emerged from the ground. It also emphasizes the role of heroic Catholic clergy in spreading the faith and specific devotion to a powerful, healing image of Christ, which unsurprisingly has meant that this particular origin story has been endorsed in an Archdiocese of Santa Fe publication as historically grounded.

To summarize, the origin stories that focus on the Esquipulas crucifix tend to highlight associations with two interrelated historical forces. The first, of course, is the colonial Catholic Church and the complex reconfigurations of Christian symbols and narratives that emerged from the crucible of evangelization and colonization of Indian peoples. The ethnologist Borhegyi and later academics have focused their attention on the ways central Christian motifs—none more central than Christ himself—entangled themselves with preexisting Indian devotions and sacred places. Thus, the Lord of Esquipulas, the Black Christ of Guatemala on his budding tree of a cross, connotes the miraculous suffering and caregiving of Jesus *and* the long-standing geophagy in Mesoamerica *and* the black-skinned deities of the Maya as well as other indigenous groups in the region who worked in relationship to a great Tree of Life. Related to this intricate web of signifiers is the massive entwining of the Viceroyalty of New Spain, which allowed commercial goods, members of the clergy, and popular devotions to communicate and spread from the Isthmus of Panama to the upper Río Grande valley. In a word, if Esquipulas reigns in Chimayó, this tells us much about the scope and combinatory nature of Spanish political and religious colonialism.

The second interrelated force is the historical and ongoing interpretation of Esquipulas by official Catholic voices. Fray Álvarez of Santa Cruz approved of Abeyta's petition to build the Santuario because he understood the place as one where Catholic devotion to Christ could flourish. He insisted in 1813 that the Christ image, experienced by faithful pilgrims, brought upon the miraculous healing and excited faithful devotion among his flock. As we have seen, more contemporary Church interpretations have echoed this original sentiment: while the crucifix's qualities may remind the viewer of Indian world trees, and while the dirt in the *pocito* may be deeply attractive, it is ultimately the heroic evangelization of the Christian message by selfless padres and friars that ties the Lord's subjects together from colonial Guatemala all the way to twenty-first-century Chimayó. No doubt, the Esquipulas crucifix is evidence of astonishing processes of cultural and religious combination, but the Church has made consistent its message that Esquipulas is Christ, and Christ is Lord.

Miraculous Apparition Stories

To document and consider the Tewa Pueblo and Guatemalan Maya and Catholic origins of the holy dirt and the Esquipulas crucifix implicitly suggests that some kind of cultural and religious combination has occurred to produce the distinctive traits that make the Santuario de Chimayó so unique. However, for thousands of Nuevomexicano devotees, the Santuario is not the obvious result of Spanish and Catholic colonial entanglement with indigenous rituals and beliefs; rather, it was born from a miraculous apparition—most frequently, but not always, of the crucifix of the Lord of Esquipulas. Oral and occasional written histories of these apparitions give us a window onto the mindsets, the priorities, and the traditions of the group that has historically made the greatest use of the Santuario: Hispano pilgrims and visitors. Among that diverse group, we can recognize a continuum of sorts, with one end represented by those Hispanos most aligned with the Catholic Church, its clergy, and its role in the development of the Santuario, and the other end perhaps best characterized by fervent lay devotion, sometimes tied to the famous Penitente Brotherhood. In all of these stories, there is at least some creative tension between the faith (or lack thereof) of the people of Chimayó and the sanctioning power of the priest, the diocese, or other representative of the Catholic Church.

Neither oral tradition nor the historical record debates the centrality of Bernardo Abeyta in the origin, foundation, and building of the Santuario, and not surprisingly, the most common miraculous apparition stories feature Abeyta as the central character. Abeyta's property lay in El Potrero, one of the *placitas* that make up the village of Chimayó, and he was a well-known leader, the *hermano mayor*, of the local Penitente order. His granddaughter passed on the most frequently retold account that Abeyta was doing penance in El Potrero when he noticed a bright light emerging from the ground. He approached the source of the light, digging into the earth, and discovered the crucifix of Our Lord of Esquipulas. In most versions, a procession of people from El Potrero bring the crucifix right away to Fray Álvarez at the church in Santa Cruz, there being no church in Chimayó at the time. Over the course of the night, the crucifix miraculously returns to the hole in Abeyta's field. The people once again return the holy object to Santa Cruz, only to have to repeat the same journey the next day after the crucifix once more relocates to El Potrero. At this point, all involved, from the padre in Santa Cruz to Abeyta and the rest of the Chimayosos, realize that the Lord of Esquipulas himself has chosen where he wants to be, and Abeyta begins construction on the chapel around the original hole in the ground.[36]

Variations on this basic story also focus on Bernardo Abeyta. One of these versions accentuates Abeyta's important position within the Fraternidad Piadosa de Nuestro Señor Jesús Nazareno (Brotherhood of Our Lord Jesus the Nazarene). Chapter 3 goes into more detail about the role of the Penitentes in the religious history of northern New Mexico, but suffice it to say here that the order's commitment to veneration of Jesus is probably related to the emergence and apparition of the Esquipulas Christ instead of some other saint or popular Marian image. In this version of the origin story, approximately a dozen Penitentes were gathered on the cold evening of Good Friday in 1810 with Abeyta, their leader, to pray and do penance. In this telling, one of the men sees the light shining out of the ground, and they all rush together to unearth the large crucifix; the rest of the story unfolds in a similar fashion, with the crucifix returning repeatedly to El Potrero from Santa Cruz.[37] In another comparable story, Abeyta is alone, but instead of doing penance in his field, he is sitting outside his home wrapped in one of Chimayó's famous woolen blankets and almost too sick to walk. This time it is not a light that appears to the man but rather his patron saint, San Esquipula. The saint calls for Abeyta to come down from his house and follow him. With great effort, the sick man hobbles out toward San Esquipula. When he nears the apparition, the saint disappears, and Abeyta is immediately made well. The spot of the miraculous cure becomes the site around which the Santuario is built, and soon pilgrims are on the road to Chimayó to experience their own miraculous cures.[38] The latter account indicates that not all tellings of the origin of the Santuario rely on an accurate understanding of the Guatemalan devotion to the Black Christ. "San Esquipula," an invented saint, represents a folk etiology of the name of the Santuario that combines the commonplace of saint veneration with the genesis of sites of devotion and pilgrimage.

Another remarkable origin story that shares many of the "Abeyta-centric" features of the stories profiled above includes many of the same characters, with slightly different names or details, but this time with all Pueblo actors at different locations. Juan Abeita, a resident of Isleta Pueblo, told the anthropologist Elsie Clews Parsons in 1925 that an Isleta shepherd once found a "santu" named Escapula sticking out of the ground. The shepherd kept the little santu on his person when he was working and in the hole at other times. When he tried to move him, at a priest's request, to Santa Fe, the santu returned to his hole at Isleta. When the shepherd's wife threatened to burn up Escapula, she was disfigured and struck ill. Only after praying to Escapula for relief was she returned to health, an occurrence that eventuated widespread prayer to Escapula for favors and healing. The same Abeita told Parsons another version of this story, this time set in Chimayó. Abeita explained to Parsons that the origin of the hole in the side chapel of the Santuario was with a Picuris man named Shamnoag, who like the Isleta shepherd, found an statue of "Sant Istipula" in a hole in the ground that the Tewa had long appreciated for its healing power. Sant Istipula, as in the other stories, kept returning to his hole, despite Shamnoag's efforts to relocate him.

Eventually, he decided to just leave him in the hole, where the "Mexicans" later found him. In this story, Abeita even names the church on the spot the "Santurio de Shamno," in memory of the original discoverer of the holy image.[39] These stories at first seem to suggest that the entire pattern of finding a wandering *bulto* of a saint who is named something like Esquipulas predated Abeyta's establishment of the Esquipulas devotion at the Santuario. It is far more likely, however, that these stories demonstrate that "baptizing the customs" is not limited to the Spanish regarding Indian practices but can flow in the opposite direction as well.

The majority of apparition stories follow this same basic format, that is, with Abeyta (or a Pueblo proxy) finding a crucifix or "San Esquipula" in the dirt, the crucifix insistently returning to the place of its discovery, and the eventual erection of the Santuario on the site. In these stories, the miraculously appearing crucifix or saint is what ultimately confers the healing power on the dirt. Proximity to the sacred object imbues the dirt with salubrious holiness. But there are some miraculous apparition or miraculous discovery stories that do not follow this pattern. Rather than putting the emphasis on Abeyta's—and sometimes the Penitentes'—heroic role in the Santuario's origin, these stories tend to highlight divine or ecclesiastical intervention. The message in these stories is that the privately owned and operated Santuario was not truly rendered sacred and miraculous until symbols of the Church were properly installed inside its walls.

The first of these legends emerges from a memoir-type collection of lore written by Cleofas Jaramillo, a resident of Hondo Arroyo, a village north of Taos. She recounts an oral tradition that puts the origin of the Esquipulas crucifix well after the actual building of the Santuario: "One morning a mule came down the mountain at Chimayo and stood for hours before the door of the fabled church until someone called the sacristan's attention to it. The man came out to investigate and found that the mule carried across its saddle a long coffin-like box." As one might guess, when the sacristan opens the box, he finds inside the crucifix, which he names Nuestro Señor de Esquipula. In this version of the story, the pilgrimage to Chimayó is strengthened by the miraculous delivery of the crucifix, even though the Santuario had already been known for healing earth before the mule came down the mountain.[40] A unique feature of this story, in addition to the mule and the coffin, is the existence of a sacristan at the church. There is no historical record of a sacristan, who serves under the supervision of clergy, administering the Santuario; instead, a caretaker, often an Abeyta or Chavez family member, oversaw the day-to-day operations of the chapel. This legend, then, has the effect of making the Santuario seem more connected in its early years to the official oversight of the Church than it actually was.

A second tale accentuates even more the notion that the autonomous Santuario required ecclesiastical administration, and in so doing, departs even further from historical evidence. In this variation, the Santuario was never constructed in the 1810s, and Chimayó languished without a church. Some years after the 1837 Rebellion (see chapter 3), a priest arrived in the collection of settlements that make up the village and encouraged the local people to build a chapel for the purpose of proper Catholic worship. "But the people were too indifferent and refused the admonition." Soon afterward, the priest disappeared. Coinciding with his departure, a miraculous foot appeared, protruding from a great cottonwood tree on the spot where the priest had desired to build the church. This finally gets the people's attention, and they construct on the spot "the most beautiful church in all of New Mexico." Interestingly, in this version, the Lord of Esquipulas is not mentioned at all; instead, the miraculous curing that follows on the construction of the beautiful church is related to the statue of the Holy Child that the villagers carve. He is responsible for the healings and the village's good fortune due to his nightly sallies to watch over, protect, and minister to the local people. Only later is the dirt in the chapel found to be holy and miraculous as a result of the other miracles that occurred there with the foot and the Santo Niño.[41] This version noticeably emphasizes priestly intervention, downplays the idea of preexisting holy dirt, and does away with the Guatemalan connection. The hero in this tale is thus the mysterious and pious priest. Both this variation and the previous one about the mule, to various extents, underscore the idea that Chimayó needed or benefited from the official presence of Catholic clergy and administrative staff. The miraculous apparitions in these cases do not necessarily suggest the desire of a sacred object to be venerated in El Potrero but rather a divine wish that a functioning and well-administered Catholic church have a key presence in Chimayó. The miraculous healing and dirt are adjuncts to that original foundation.

Perhaps the most incredible apparition story is one that, to my knowledge, has not been published elsewhere. The source of this story is a letter that a woman named Ruth Barber mailed in 1972 to a resident of Chimayó named Martha E. Vigil. Enclosed with the letter is an alleged translation of the origin of the Santuario as remembered by the famous Padre Martínez of Taos. (The original Spanish document, if it ever existed, is not to be found.) Barber understandably states that she cannot verify the authenticity of the story, but she claims to have received the document from the wife of Lansing Bloom, a historian and former curator at the Museum of New Mexico. It is worth reproducing much of the translation of Martínez's supposed account here, but it should be noted that the original is rife with spelling and grammatical errors along with some questionable assertions. I have left all such errors intact:

> In 1617. [This is almost certainly a typographical error for "1817."] The Priests had all failed to interest the indians & mexicans at Santa Cruz to build a church. The Priest Ramon Peña being in charge, had a pion (workman) Whom was send for wood, in the month of Oct. Found a large pine log hollow inside, after chopping a hole in the log found to his surprise the feet of an Image: Which pruved to be 5 feet high. The pion brought the news to Father Peña at Santa Cruz. The Priest announced a mass at the spot Where the log was found. Hundreds of indians mexicans attended the mass. In presence of this large congregation "The Log" was split open carefully. And behold a biutifull Image life size, as perfect and natural as could be even in life. The Image was called "Nuestro Señor de Esquipula." The Image bore the open wounds in both hands and feet and a large wound on the brest by a spear from which real blood & water flood out at torrants. A cross was also found near by which corresponded to the size of the Image. The people assembled from all parts of the known country to witness the reality of this wonderfull appearing of the Image of Jesus of Esquipula. A number of Priests were summond to the spot. Bishop Zebidias from Santa come to see the great sight. After a long Series of meetings and masses, fasting offering of all discription.

To this point, the story appears to be a variation on some of the more well-known apparition stories in which priests and tree trunks produce miraculous images in such a way that excites Hispano devotion in officially sanctioned ways—namely, the increased celebration of Masses. However, the tale continues:

Father Peña had a revelation from Heaven, As follows.

"Ramon Peña Priest & Servant of the most High thou art blesst among the Priests of the Provices of New Spain possession in Santa Cruz de la Cañada. Thy sacrifices of the Holy mass and the offering of your earnest prayers for the domain of the hethenism has been heard. Go forth & build Sanctuary to Jesus at Junction of the Rivers Chimayo and Quemado Pueblo. Where you will fiend an Image to be placid in said sanctuary for ever. Go forth in the name of the name of Apostolic & Roman Church. & geather alms & offerings from all Provinces with in reach of 44 days travel. And whoso ever gives one tenth of what he poses. Shall receive 12 years of indulgence and shall be blessed with 12 years of abundant crop of what ever he shall plant. He shall conquor over his Enimies. Even in war they shall prevail. Whosoever refues to aid you shall fail even to earn his daily bread—and thou shall not administer the holy sacraments to one who refuses to aid in building the holy sanctuary. Even until it is finished & dedicated to our Lord Jesus of Esquipula. Further the dememtions the sanctuary shall be 20. yards long & 12 yards wide. Walls one yard & half thick, made of adobes, and seven yards high, there to be 12 nitches in the walls 6 in each wall. You are to place 12 status one in each nitch. & Jesus of Esquipula in the alter. You are to declare to the entire country that; a visit to this sanctuary will heal eny person of eny disease what ever. Under the alter there will bee the holy Earth to be used by eny one as an antidote for eny disease, sickness, wounds, bites of eny Pioson or venenus caused by ratte snakes or mad dogs. This thou shalt pridict for ten years. Every Pilgrim must bring two candles, & an offering of Gold, Silver, live animals cows, sheep, goats, horses, mules, dunkies, (no hogs) corn, wheat, beans, onions fruits dry & green, you must make record of all who visits & the country. The visits must be made on their knees 100 yds & bare footed in the sanctuary they must remove their hats 300 yds from the Chapel. two bells must be moulded of Gold silver & cooper no other metal. two Golden candle sticks & 7. silver candle sticks. One high Cross made of silver. Two high lanterns of tin with long handles. All ornaments must be brought from France. This do & exort. & may no one put you asunder." Gabrial.[42]

In this section of the document, Padre Martínez allegedly writes that Peña receives a revelation from the angel Gabriel, who outlines the construction and the cultic practice to be carried out at the Santuario in a fashion that can only be described as biblical. The dimensions of the building, the ritual instruments, the positioning of the statues, and the instructions for pilgrims put the Santuario on the same rhetorical and religious level as the great Temple in Jerusalem or the heavenly city laid out in the Bible's apocalyptic texts. To be sure, the intent of this revelation is to declare the Santuario one of the holiest places in Christendom.

There is no historical proof whatsoever that this document was written by Padre Martínez, and its details and tone would suggest that it was not written by him. Martínez almost certainly knew of Bernardo Abeyta and would have included mention of him in any document he wrote about the Santuario's origin. So what should we make of this astonishing version of the story? This question can best be answered by looking at what the story achieves. It initially appears to privilege, like some of the other origin stories, the role of Catholic clergy. But it takes this emphasis in an unforeseen direction by providing not only Father Peña but also the dimensions, ritual practices, and healing dirt at the shrine with the ironclad imprimatur of divine revelation and angelic visitation. The document was written, then, possibly to validate the role of clergy at the Santuario but more likely to defend the aesthetics and particulars of the miraculous dirt and the popular pilgrimage that were mostly under the control of Hispano lay devotees. As such, the document represents a tactical approach to maintain lay access and usage of the Santuario even while buttressing that access and usage with a revelation bestowed on a possibly fictitious priest, and further validated by tying the whole story to Padre Martínez. Of course, the latter cleric had come to be known by 1900 (the supposed translation date for the document) as a defender of the Hispanos and their popular piety over and against the bureaucratic centralization of Archbishops Lamy and Salpointe and the American Catholic hierarchy. The document ultimately suggests that God wants the Santuario to look and function as a site of miracles and pilgrimage; and "may no one put you asunder."

Nonmiraculous Origins

I have argued here that origin stories and legends tend to tell us about the storytellers and their competing interests in the Santuario. Included among these tales of origin are those that refuse to find anything legendary or miraculous about the founding of the shrine. The earliest of these comes from L. Bradford Prince, the president of the New Mexico Historical Society and governor of the New Mexico territory from 1889 to 1893. In a history of New Mexico's churches, he wrote, "How and when the healing virtues of the sacred earth of this favored spot were first manifested, not even tradition tells us." Prince goes on to discuss Bernardo Abeyta, but the light appearing in the ground or any other miraculous occurrence is conspicuously absent. In Prince's account, Abeyta builds the Santuario as a sign of his gratitude for his relative prosperity, and the site happened to coincide with a place that had long been known for its medicinal soil.[43] A more recent history takes up the issue of the Esquipulas crucifix. The author, Don Usner, is a historian, photographer, and native son of Chimayó. He finds that the legends that swirl around the crucifix likely obscure a more rational origin:

> The common thread in all the tales of Bernardo's epiphany—the discovery of a buried statue or cross—may be easily explained: the buried object could be an artifact from Hispanic settlement of the valley before the Pueblo Revolt of 1680. Indeed, the site of Potrero matches closely with descriptions in Luis Granillo's journal for the location of the Juan Ruiz farm. Few if any people living in Potrero would have known that people occupied the area before, and as a consequence certainly would have been surprised to find an icon of the Christian faith buried in the soil.[44]

Thus, for Usner, the credulity that soaks the origin legends can be explained with the clarity of historical hindsight. The discontinuity of Spanish settlement and a Catholic predisposition to accept the miraculous easily provide an explanation for the oddity of finding Christ in the dirt.

Surprisingly, at least some of the official rhetoric of the Catholic Church in relation to the purported miracles at the Santuario is consistent with the rational, nonmiraculous accounts proffered by Prince and Usner. The Catholic Church's relationship to miraculous apparitions and other kinds of miracle stories embraced by laypeople is notoriously complex. By the late nineteenth and early twentieth centuries, authorities in the Catholic Church were working out a relationship with modernity that simultaneously promoted certain apparitions (especially Marian) and the centralization of devotional practice. Official support for apparitions occurred when and where the Church felt that it could encourage popular religious participation while also ensuring support for the Church's own sociopolitical positions. These included greater administrative oversight of popular devotions and a tentative repositioning of the Church as a relevant actor in a time of declining church-state cooperation throughout the Catholic world.[45] In such a context, the Church often finds itself walking a fine line between supporting the faithful devotion of Catholics and disavowing the more "miraculous" aspects of popular lay devotions. This is especially the case when those devotions threaten to exceed the boundaries set by Church interpretation. Hence, official Catholic explanations at the Santuario modestly state, "It is probable that the crucifix found in Chimayo by don Bernardo Abeyta came from the South with an expedition."[46] Rather than being an irony that the Church would in this way underplay the miraculous nature of one of the Santuario's principal holy objects, this statement illumines the Church's intricate employment of various kinds of authority, dogmatic and historical.

Extra-ecclesiastical interpreters have noted that the apparition stories concerning the Esquipulas crucifix at Chimayó follow patterns that anthropologists have identified in relation to other Christian pilgrimage sites. This line of analysis introduces yet another potential connection between Chimayó and preexisting pilgrimages even beyond the more immediately apparent links with indigenous and Spanish traditions. The historian Elizabeth Kay identifies two related tropes that appear to overlay neatly with Chimayó's legends of the Esquipulas crucifix discovery. One is the oft-repeated folklore surrounding buried treasure in the Iberian Peninsula and throughout Spanish America. These stories flourished in the context of wealth-seeking conquistadors in search of fabled golden cities, for whom buried or hidden treasures presented significant appeal. And in more remote regions of New Spain such as New Mexico, with the frequent threat of conflict with Indians, it was not unusual for settlers to conceal whatever objects of value they were able to acquire or maintain far from the colonial metropolis. As we have seen, some of the apparition stories about the Chimayó crucifix do indeed conjecture that prior settlers had buried the statue in the ground only for it to be later discovered by Abeyta.

The second trope is the European "shepherd's cycle," which produced many miraculous or especially blessed images throughout medieval Europe.[47] In their canonical work about Christian pilgrimage, the anthropologists Victor and Edith Turner describe the "shepherd's cycle" in such a way that makes it difficult to dispute that Chimayó's apparition legends follow a similar narrative pattern in most if not all details. These tales, which emerged in various European contexts from the ninth to the thirteenth centuries, feature a shepherd who finds an image of the Virgin Mary in a hole in the ground. Often the shepherd is led to the location of the sacred object by a shining light or by the miraculous guidance of a saint or other heavenly being. The Turners draw on the work of a nineteenth-century Spanish historian who wrote in 1879 a description of the shepherd's cycle in his country that bears an uncanny resemblance to the Abeyta legends. Most notably, these features include "attempts to carry the image to a more comfortable and accessible place, return by the image two or three times to the site of the vision, resolution to build a church in the designated place, and frequent veneration of the image there by people of the town."[48] With the exception that Abeyta found an image of Christ instead of the Blessed Virgin, the story matches almost perfectly.

Of course, I do not point this out to devalue or "explain away" the origin legends that surround the Esquipulas crucifix at Chimayó, but rather to indicate to what extent the Santuario participates in—and even exemplifies—a long-standing European Catholic apparition and pilgrimage tradition. Moreover, as we have seen, several origin accounts for the Santuario emphasize Pueblo and indigenous Guatemalan inputs to both the crucifix and the presence of healing dirt. Not only are these indigenous connections quite historically likely, given the evidence presented here and elsewhere, there are also ample sociopolitical reasons for Pueblos and other American Indians in northern New Mexico to insist that their own religious and mythological understandings and practices have had concrete and enduring effects on the devotional lives of northern New Mexicans both in the past and today. That some of the most common Chimayó origin stories are quite congruent with European shepherd's cycle narratives does not mean that other unique combinations have not occurred in the region. These combinations indicate the simultaneous continuation of European traditions *and* the refashioning of indigenous ideas and behavior at the periphery of New Spanish and Catholic control. Nevertheless, at least one scholar has mistakenly tried to insist that northern New Mexico's Hispano Catholicism differed radically from prior European expressions of the faith, even going so far as to say that Hispanos in the Río Arriba area lacked the apparitions common to their Catholic counterparts farther south in Mexico and in Spain.[49] As we have seen, this contention is certainly not substantiated by the stories concerning the Santuario's origin: the apparition legends at Chimayó both echo early European apparition stories and demonstrate new combinations unique to the region.

* * *

One of the primary purposes of origin stories is to explain the state of things for the group to whom the story belongs. An example from the intersection of religion and U.S. politics demonstrates this point: evangelical Christians in the contemporary United States have commonly emphasized the Christian piety—dubious as it may have been—of the founding fathers to sustain their contention that the United States is a Christian nation. Conversely, contemporary proponents of a high wall between church and state are more likely to recount early American history with an emphasis on religious pluralism and tolerance, likewise to justify and achieve their current understanding of the nation. In the same way, stories about the origin of the Santuario, the crucifix, and the *pocito* tend to reflect the needs and desires of the person or group doing the telling. An emphasis on the Tewa origins of the site affirms the resiliency of Pueblo knowledge and worldviews. However, this version of the story also promotes the idea that a Christian holy place has undergone significant religious combination with the religion and culture of the surrounding Pueblos. Depending on the narrator, this latter phenomenon can be judged either as a sign of creative religious refashioning to meet popular needs or as a dire decline in Christian purity. Stories that emphasize the waves of Catholic evangelism around the Viceroyalty of New Spain may focus on the particulars of the Guatemalan Lord of Esquipulas. These accounts, often attractive to anthropologists and students of Spanish art and devotional practice, demonstrate the flows of symbols as well as political and religious influence around Spanish America. They also highlight the early development of Catholic venerations near the metropolis that spread only later to the peripheral areas such as northern New Mexico. Apparition stories promote the sacralization of the Santuario and its contents and location. As we have seen, some of these stories favor lay control of the place, while others accentuate the importance of clerical leadership and oversight. Finally, some analyses of origin stories suggest nonmiraculous rationalizations to demystify the apparition stories, or they attempt to situate the apparition tales in widely observed religious genres such as the shepherd's cycle.

In all these diverse cases, which often overlap even as people's needs for the Santuario overlap, various constituencies compete for a stake in the Santuario, that is, religious ownership. Perhaps the clearest exposition of this process can be found among official Catholic sources that interpret the Santuario's origin with a nod toward Indian influences but ultimately with an evident desire to administer and interpret the pilgrimage at the Santuario as an expression of Christian faithfulness. Lay Hispano involvement in the origin of the Santuario likewise points to the ongoing need for the Nuevomexicano community to maintain relatively autonomous control of their devotions and pilgrimage to Chimayó. More difficult to discern but no less exacting in terms of religious ownership are anthropological or other academic analyses that thrive on notions of causality, power, and cultural maintenance and change. One might argue that the latter case does not aspire to *religious* ownership per se. But archaeologists, historians, and anthropologists nonetheless make truth claims and follow their own processes of observation, participation, and (lest we forget) desire.

3

New Mexican Catholicism in Transition

Construction of the Santuario de Chimayó was completed in 1816 in Spanish territory, but it did not remain Spanish for long. In 1821 Mexico gained its independence from Spain, and in a moment, Chimayó went from being a distant outpost of a European empire to being a distant outpost of a new nation. However, with the conclusion of the Mexican-American War in 1848, New Mexico—along with most of northern Mexico—was annexed by the United States. Once again, in fewer than forty years, Chimayó and its Santuario entered a new nation and a new political and ecclesiastical era. As a place of Catholic worship, the chapel dedicated to the Señor de Esquipulas, renowned for its *pocito* full of miraculous dirt, moved not only from nation to nation but from one Catholic jurisdiction to the next, as first the Mexican Catholic Church and then the Catholic See of the United States took control of New Mexico's churches. Although it would seem that the Santuario was a house built upon shifting sands, the vast changes that shook nineteenth-century New Mexico reveal that the Santuario rested on a firm foundation.

Distance from metropolitan and national capitals makes northern New Mexico a hinterland, a periphery, only from the point of view of those at the imagined centers of nations and empires. And it is from that perspective that the Santuario and its environment must seem a place battered by geopolitical change beyond any kind of local control. But another way to examine the multiple transitions of the nineteenth century is from the perspectives of local actors, whether these be Nuevomexicanos with generations in La Cañada or more newly arrived characters from France and the United States. These voices and viewpoints, which sometimes do acknowledge their distance from national centers, nevertheless maintain a continuous conversation with local customs and institutions. When we consider these local negotiations with the momentous changes of the era, we can put the Santuario and the world of

Hispano popular Catholicism that it represents at the center rather than at the periphery of our analysis. From this vantage point at the center, we can observe and explore the rise and fall of different states and the changing priorities of Catholic authorities. From this point of view, we can appreciate the changes that did occur while also remaining attentive to the ways that actors both big and small worked to maintain stability as well as social and religious cohesion.

Of course, surviving historical documents do not always give clear, unimpeded insight into local histories and the day-to-day actions and experiences of most people. Indeed, during the years of the Mexican period and the transition to the United States, there is little to nothing about pilgrims' dealings with the Santuario in the historical record. However, there is a great deal of information about some of the principal actors of the era, and not an insignificant amount of information concerning Chimayó itself as an important site of rebellion, contestation, and continuity. By examining these stories and especially the pivotal figures of Padre Antonio José Martínez and Bishop Jean Baptiste Lamy, and to a lesser extent, Bernardo Abeyta, we can construct a narrative of the past that stays attentive to the ongoing healing and devotion of everyday people at the Santuario in the middle of the nineteenth century.

The New Mexican Catholic Church at Mexican Independence

The Franciscans had left their mark on New Mexican Catholicism through centuries of missions to the Indians and maintenance of Hispanic devotion, but by the opening years of the nineteenth century, the power of the order had begun to wane. As early as 1602, Oñate had petitioned the Spanish crown, under the auspices of the Patronato Real, to create a new diocese to oversee the missions and churches in his newly settled province. However, lack of political will as well as economic realities that would not permit the maintenance of a bishop and the construction of a cathedral meant that New Mexicans would remain under the care of the friars. Indeed, through most of the colonial period, the same Patronato Real that granted to the Spanish crown the right to name bishops also gave extraordinary, bishop-like powers to regular clergy in distant mission fields like most of New Mexico. In practice, this meant that the Franciscans could operate their churches within their own system of oversight and administration with little interference from Catholic dioceses further south in New Spain. Eventually, however, the Bourbon reforms of the late eighteenth century compelled the secularization of many former missions, and despite their protests, many Franciscans soon found themselves working with a small but growing number of diocesan priests. In New Mexico, official declarations of secularization well preceded actual removal of friars and installation of parish priests, but the trend was definite and irreversible.[1]

When Mexico gained independence in 1821, the Mexican Catholic hierarchy and priests were hardly united concerning the status of the new nation. Even with three centuries of Spanish presence in Mexico, the reliance of colonial government on friendly ecclesiastical authorities meant that nearly all the bishops, upper-level secular clergy, and the higher echelons of the ordered clergy were peninsula-born Spaniards. These men's loyalty to the Spanish crown was complete, and as the historian John Lynch points out, the Mexican push for independence was "a war of religion; [Catholic elites] totally identified the cause of religion with royalism, and warned that revolution in Mexico would cause the same destruction to the Church as the revolution in France." An archbishop informed the revolutionary forces that they would go "infallibly to hell."[2] Of course, not all clergy felt this way; several of the most important proponents of independence—for example, Fathers Hidalgo and Morelos—were themselves priests. These men, normally creoles or mestizos, were unhappy with the Bourbons and their desire to strengthen state control of the Church. Likewise, the pro-independence priests tended to be well-read and aware of the liberal philosophies of the European Enlightenment. Not many went as far as Hidalgo in revolutionary fervor, but Mexican-born priests were far more likely than their Spanish bishops to support independence, many becoming vocal nationalists.[3]

The preponderance of Spanish *peninsulares* at the highest levels of the Catholic hierarchy created something of a crisis in leadership for the new Mexican Church. Most Spanish clergy, including both diocesan and ordered priests, were either expelled or chose to leave Mexico in the years following independence. So great was this exodus, and so concentrated was Spanish power in the hierarchy, that by 1829 there was not a single bishop left in Mexico. By one estimate, the number of priests in

Mexico was halved between 1810 and 1830. Given the anticlerical bent of some of the revolutionary fervor, the Vatican remained unsupportive of much of Latin America's various independence movements. The popes who served during the 1820s and 1830s often associated independence from Spain and the rejection of royalism with a loss of ecclesiastical authority, and the Holy See was slow to reappoint bishops in Mexico. In fact, no new bishops assumed their posts until 1831, when Pope Gregory XVI finally began to name new bishops for the ten-year-old nation. The Diocese of Durango, which oversaw the territory of New Mexico, received its new bishop in February of that year, José Antonio Laureano de Zubiría, a strong supporter of the nation of Mexico.[4]

For the most part, the Mexican period in New Mexico witnessed a general decline in the number of clergy. In this context of reduction in total numbers, a realignment occurred: the long-mandated secularization of the missions and parish churches finally gained ground. However, this change did not happen overnight. In 1821 many of the Spanish Franciscans who remained in New Mexico were expelled along with so many of their countrymen around the new nation, and the Diocese of Durango tried at this time to replace them with diocesan priests. Some seculars were posted to New Mexican parishes, but the majority of these men remained for a very short time before returning south. A look at the number of priests in various years of the Mexican period illustrates both the decline in overall numbers and the slow shift from Franciscan to diocesan leadership. At independence in 1821, New Mexico had twenty-four priests, twenty of whom were Franciscans and four were seculars. By December 1826, priests had declined to twenty, with twelve friars and eight diocesans. In 1838 the number of priests hit an all-time low of eleven for the entire territory, of whom only three were remaining and aged Franciscans. While Santa Cruz de la Cañada did experience diocesan leadership briefly around the time of independence, the priest posted to the parish did not stay long, and Santa Cruz and its surrounding villages were some of the last places to be served by Franciscans. Not until 1834, when the last friar died, did Santa Cruz finally receive a permanent priest from the Diocese of Durango.[5]

The writing had been on the wall for some time for the Franciscans, even prior to Mexican independence, and the efforts of the Durango diocese to develop native priests in New Mexico did begin to bear fruit in the early years of the Mexican Republic. In fact, during the years around independence, an influential group of young New Mexicans traveled south to Durango to attend seminary and receive ordination as priests. Most notably, this group included both Antonio José Martínez, one of New Mexico's most important nineteenth-century leaders, and Juan Felipe Ortiz, the scion of an important New Mexico family who would serve as the vicar and representative in Santa Fe of the bishop in Durango.[6] Unlike the Franciscans who came before them, these new priests and leaders combined two important characteristics: their diocesan connections to the Mexican See and their local New Mexican heritage. This new development in Catholic leadership meant that the Church in post-independence New Mexico imagined itself less and less as an active mission field and more as a regular, if remote, regional body of the Mexican Catholic Church. However, since the new priests were mainly local men with generational ties to the unique Catholicism of colonial New Mexico, they also continued to support—or at least turn a blind eye to—some of the features of local Catholic practice such as the Penitente Brotherhood, the folk art and devotion of the *santeros*, and the growing complex of pilgrimage and healing that was developing around the Santuario de Chimayó.

Padre Martínez's centrality to this era of New Mexico's history can hardly be overstated, and he has an outsize influence on some of the major events of the Mexican period, including several episodes that had an effect on the Santuario. While his story will not be retold in its entirety here, especially since it has been so well related elsewhere, the parts of Martínez's life that intersect significantly with Chimayó and the Santuario are valuable for this account.[7] One immensely important initiative was the seminary that Martínez opened and ran in Taos starting in 1833 with the express approval and encouragement of Bishop Zubiría in Durango. As many as thirty men were trained for the priesthood at Martínez's seminary, which meant that he was responsible for the education and pastoral formation of a generation of New Mexico's priests in this period. This group included one of the first diocesan—that is, non-Franciscan—priests to serve the historic parish of Santa Cruz de la Cañada, the parish that covered Chimayó. This priest, Father Juan de Jesús Trujillo, was ordained in 1836, only a year before the Chimayó Rebellion, a topic covered in more detail below.[8]

The placement of local New Mexicans in parish leadership was not the only distinctive feature for the Catholic Church during the Mexican period; the other truly novel feature of the time was a hands-on bishop who made regular visits to this part of his diocese. Bishop Zubiría of Durango visited New Mexico on three separate occasions, in 1833, 1845, and 1850. Remarkably, before 1833, the last time that New Mexico had been graced with an episcopal visitation was over seventy years before, in 1760, when Bishop Pedro Tamarón y Romeral had toured this northernmost section of his diocese. At that time, every one of the more than twenty clergymen in New Mexico was a Franciscan, and the Penitentes almost certainly had not yet come into being. When Zubiría first came to New Mexico, the major changes in clergy makeup discussed above were already well under way. There were only fifteen priests, but of those a mere four were elderly Franciscans; the remaining eleven were made up of the new wave of diocesan priests, many with local origins.[9] Despite Zubiría's greater oversight and control over these diocesan priests—or perhaps because of it—he was not timid in sharing his displeasure over the state of the churches in New Mexico. He was alarmed by the apathy and moral decrepitude of many of the priests, and his observations of the Penitente Brotherhood, their penitential practices, and their growing control of local religious and social life scandalized him deeply. Before returning to his seat in Durango, Zubiría wrote and issued a lengthy pastoral letter full of admonishments and precise directives. The priests were to reorder their personal and professional lives. He also lashed out at the Penitentes, not only for their flamboyance but for their entrenched positions of religious power in New Mexico over and against a sparse and sometimes apathetic clergy.[10]

Bernardo Abeyta and the Santuario in the Mexican Period

After Bernardo Abeyta finished construction of his Santuario in 1816, there is surprisingly little in the historical record about the place. However, it would be a mistake to assume this means that nothing was happening at the Santuario or in the lives of the New Mexicans who were beginning to rely on its religious images and its miraculous dirt for healing, communal religious observance, and focus of pilgrimage. During the same period, the monumental change from Spanish rule to

Mexican independence occurred alongside the rapid decline and expulsion of the Franciscans and the tepid rise of diocesan clergy to take their place. These tectonic shifts in New Mexico's political and religious institutions, which lay entirely outside the control of the vast majority of New Mexico's population, coincided with the rise of the Santuario as a site of relatively unsupervised Catholic devotion and community-based social organization. In this sense, the flourishing of the Santuario can be understood as a popular reaction to the rapidly changing leadership and institutions in Mexico and the Catholic Church.

Bernardo Abeyta never dominates episodes captured in the historical record from the construction of the Santuario until his death in 1856, but his name appears enough and in sufficiently important places that we can be sure that he remained an important community and religious leader in the Río Arriba region. The most salient fact about Abeyta, discussed below, is his longtime position as an *hermano mayor* of the Penitente Brotherhood in La Cañada. Before we turn to that essential portion of his activities, it is worth lingering briefly on Abeyta's role as a devout Catholic respectful of the Church hierarchy as well as a church outfitter. First, recall that Abeyta, according to the legends of the discovery of the Esquipulas crucifix, tried to place the holy item on the altar in his local parish church in Santa Cruz. When, with the prompting of the crucifix itself, he decided to build a chapel near his home in El Potrero in Chimayó, he did so with the full support not only of the local priest, Fray Álvarez, but with the documented approval of the diocese in Durango. Moreover, during the Mexican period Abeyta and the local parish made the effort to renew the diocesan permission for the Santuario on at least five different occasions, in 1826, 1829, 1833, 1845, and 1849.[11] This indicates that it was important to Abeyta that the Santuario be able to host Masses, even if these happened only infrequently due to sparse and overextended priests. Finally, either through donations or out of his personal finances, Abeyta managed to furnish the Santuario with artwork and various liturgical items and vestments. Of course, the main crucifix on the altar, the Señor de Esquipulas, claimed a miraculous provenance, but the dozens of other *santos* and *bultos* had to be commissioned and purchased from the artists. Diocesan records show that at least three official inventories were made of the Santuario between 1818 and 1826; these documents mention the Esquipulas crucifix as well as a *bulto* of Nuestra Señora de los Dolores, a smaller version of the Esquipulas statue, thirty-eight other sacred images, and seven glass windows. Various other items such as chasubles and candles also figure in these inventories. All of this is to say that Abeyta's commitment to his Santuario, its functionality, and its beauty was important not only to local devotees and pilgrims but also to official Catholic representatives to the chapel.[12]

There is little doubt, given this evidence, that Abeyta intended his Santuario to be a chapel where both local devotions and authorized Catholic Masses could take place; this does not mean, however, that Abeyta did not have other functions in mind for the Santuario. As a farmer and trader who likely had travelled widely in New Spain (given his knowledge of the Lord of Esquipulas), Abeyta would also be well aware of the commercial possibilities at popular sites of pilgrimage. The historian Ramón Gutiérrez suggests that Abeyta built his chapel not as the result of a legendary miraculous apparition of the crucifix in the ground but rather as a canny business decision to create a pilgrimage destination atop a preexisting and known site of Pueblo healing. Since the place was already regarded as special and restorative, it was a ripe opportunity waiting to be exploited and soon attracted many visitors. Gutiérrez writes, "The pilgrims needed hospice and needed to be fed, and for these functions cottage industries emerged. As people moved to and fro, Chimayo's woolen and agricultural products began to circulate widely throughout northern New Spain." In this analysis, Chimayó's famous weaving industry may have the Santuario to thank. Gutiérrez continues, "Prosperity for Chimayo's residents shortly followed."[13]

Chimayó, along with Abiquiu, was one of the principal centers of Penitente activity in northern New Mexico at this time, and it is likely that Abeyta, in addition to its commercial impact, also had the brothers of the order in mind when he constructed the Santuario. There is no reason to think that the Santuario functioned as one of the Brotherhood's *moradas*, that is, as a stand-alone, semi-private space for both secret and public Penitente rituals. But given Abeyta's important position among the Chimayó Penitentes, we can safely suppose that the brothers of his order were frequently part of the celebrations, pilgrimages, and devotions related to the Santuario. In fact, we may conjecture that Abeyta's leadership of the Penitentes was a significant aspect of his religious leadership and innovation in the region. He was the author of at least one influential constitution for the order, one that was revised and reprinted into the twentieth century. The historian Michael Carroll suggests that there are several possible links between Abeyta's position within the Penitentes and his devotion to the Lord of Esquipulas. One of the most prominent legends of the crucifix puts Abeyta with a group of his Penitente brethren at the time of its discovery; both Esquipulas devotion and the Penitentes are highly focused on Christ's passion; and there is some suggestion that the full name of the Penitente order as the Brothers of Padre Jesús Nazareno is also a name that was used for the Santuario's Christ by Bernardo Abeyta's son, Tomás de Jesús Nazareno de Esquipulas Abeyta, who was apparently the namesake of both the Esquipulas Christ and the Penitente order. Of course, none of these linkages is precise or verifiable, but when historians endeavor to uncover popular histories, the lack of archived documents does not erase the importance of strong circumstantial evidence. If nothing else, it can be affirmed that Bernardo Abeyta had a multifaceted and powerful impact on the religious life of northern New Mexicans throughout the Mexican period and beyond.[14]

The Santuario's effect on northern New Mexico, given Abeyta's influence, was multiple: it was a sanctioned Catholic worship space, a boon for Chimayó's economy, and a likely gathering place for the Penitentes. But also, of course, it was from the beginning a place of healing. The various origin stories of the Santuario almost all revolve around the power of both the figure of the crucified Christ and the power of the earth in which he was found to bring succor to the suffering. In 1813, when Fray Álvarez of Santa Cruz wrote to the diocese in Durango to endorse Abeyta's request to build the Santuario, he does not explicitly mention the *pocito* or the healing dirt. But he is quite clear that the local people had considered the site as one of healing for some time. As mentioned in the previous chapter, Álvarez wrote, "I declare that the miraculous Image of the Lord of Esquipulas has been venerated for three years in the Shrine that is attached to [Bernardo Abeyta's] home. . . . This place is frequented by many people, and they come as pilgrims from twenty and even more leagues distance to offer up their devotions to the Sovereign Lord and to experience relief or healing of their suffering."[15] In the priest's account of the pilgrimage and the healing associated with it, he focuses on the figure and power of God through Christ, which has the virtue of both being true for the earliest visitors to Abeyta's shrine and an affirmation of theological orthodoxy concerning miraculous healing. But again, just because there is no specific mention of the holy dirt in the extant Catholic documents about the Santuario and its predecessor house-shrine in Abeyta's dwelling, does not mean that there was no tradition of using the dirt of the place for relief of suffering. If we take seriously the Tewa myths that the mud of the locale was known for its healing properties, and if we attend to the ethnically mixed population of eighteenth-century Chimayó that was known—like Abiquiu—for witchcraft and the arts of *curanderos*, and we notice the explicit mention of healing related to the pilgrimage in Fray Álvarez's letter, we can begin to suggest with some certitude that the healing earth near Tsi Mayoh hill may have been as or more attractive than Abeyta's Lord of Esquipulas crucifix.[16] To be sure, by the end of the nineteenth century, pilgrims had been going to the Santuario for years specifically to experience the healing power of the earth in the *pocito*, a fact examined in more detail below. However, before we turn to that subject, other events in Chimayó and in the rest of New Mexico take center stage.

The Chimayó Rebellion

In the years immediately following independence, both the Mexican government and the Mexican Catholic Church sought to redefine their roles in New Mexico. Playing a part in both of these spheres, Padre Martínez of Taos was elected in 1830 to serve in the deputation that had been called together to form the territorial legislature for New Mexico as part of Mexico. In these chaotic and transitional times, Martínez and the other leaders in the deputation rightly worried that threats from both Indians and advancing Anglo Americans from the expanding United States would soon lead to a serious crisis all along the northern territory of Mexico. In an 1831 exposition of his feelings on the territorial deputation, Martínez complained that the deputation lacked "legislative, executive, and judicial powers; it is useless to the territory and harmful to its citizens." A short-lived Santa Fe periodical from the same time period called *El Crepúsculo de la Libertad* shared Martínez's concerns for New Mexico and feared that the "deplorable abandonment" by the distant federal center of Mexico would soon lead to the "dismember-ment [of New Mexico] from Mexican territory." The paper further predicted that a U.S. takeover was a distinct possibility and more than hinted that such a change in government would be welcome to many New Mexicans.[17]

This must have been a difficult concession for Martínez and his dioc-esan contemporaries, whose patriotism for Mexico had propelled them through the transformation of New Mexico from a staunchly Francis-can mission field to a respectable outpost of the Diocese of Durango. The strengthened diocesan oversight of the New Mexican Catholic Church had the benefit of remaining relatively stable from pre- to post-independence eras in part because the polity of the Catholic Church was a reliable constant even in a region with too few priests. And where the official representatives of the Catholic Church did not reach, New Mexicans had the long folk traditions of their faith and dependable lay leadership to provide social cohesion.

The Mexican national government could boast of no such stability, and floundered to find a way to govern effectively. The territorial deputation struggled along for a decade, a time during which New Mexicans largely continued economic and political patterns that had held sway during the final years of Spanish rule. These patterns reflected the autonomy of a territory long accustomed to being ignored or forgotten on the periph-ery of empire. When the Mexican government appointed a governor in 1835 to establish and enforce the centralization of authority in the nation, many New Mexicans were wary. The governor, Albino Pérez, a native of Veracruz far to the south, was charged with the difficult tasks of estab-lishing firmer ties with Mexico, defending the frontier in northern New Mexico from both Indians and Anglo American incursions, and—most of all—raising sufficient revenues to help fund the infant Mexican state. In his first months in office, Governor Pérez imposed several kinds of taxation and trade restrictions to try to increase his budgetary resources to administer New Mexico, and he liberally fined or otherwise punished those who could or would not abide the directives of the new regime. Not surprisingly, the new taxes and state control of sources of revenue were not popular with the majority of the people.[18]

A handwritten manuscript from 1837, likely by Albino Chacón, a city official in Santa Fe under Pérez, provides a firsthand account of the growing opposition to Pérez's regime not only among the overtaxed poor but also among the small numbers of economically advantaged families of the territory. The document notes that New Mexico, by the time of the governor's arrival, had become increasingly dangerous due to the fact that the Republic of Mexico had done so little in its first years to ward off Indian attacks. When Pérez moved to control the frontier against these attacks, he quickly found himself embroiled in "lawsuits and grudges" and the "puerile intrigues" of the small ruling class that predated Mexican independence. When the Navajos made successful advances against the Mexican forces, even threatening the area around Santa Fe, the

> most impartial persons considered in fact that the administration and coming of Señor Pérez to New Mexico had actually increased all the evils, both by the rapid consumption of the scarce resources of the country in the salaries of his retinue, and in the quarreling and intrigue that he tolerated in his administration, without producing any good whatever that his qualifications and good intentions had promised.

To salvage things, Pérez appointed local son Ramón Abreu as prefect of the district around Santa Fe, but Abreu proved to be nearly as unpopular as the governor when he too began to levy taxes to supply the troops. As taxes like these continued to rise even amidst some military losses, Pérez's administration teetered.[19]

The event that sparked Pérez's downfall occurred in Chimayó. The judge in Santa Cruz de la Cañada, Juan José Esquivel, tried a case involving many of his own relatives. When he acquitted them, the prefect Abreu got involved, found Esquivel's ruling to be partial, and ordered that it be overturned. When Esquivel refused to comply, Abreu had him jailed. In the charged atmosphere that already existed in the region against the Pérez administration, and in an area of New Mexico that had long enjoyed strong local leadership, Esquivel's imprisonment was the stroke that led to open insurrection. A group surrounded the jail, freed Esquivel, and regrouped in the nearby mountains. From this stronghold, on August 3, 1837, the rebels formed a revolutionary government from their seat in the newly declared Cantón de La Cañada. At this time, they issued a "Plan of Rebels," a document significant especially for its rich evocation of religious language alongside more mundane concerns:

Long live God and nation and the faith of Jesus Christ. The most principal points that we defend are the following:

1st. To be with God and nation and the faith of Jesus Christ.
2nd. To defend our homeland to the last drop of Blood as to achieve the intended victory.
3rd. To not allow the plan of the Department.
4th. To not allow any taxation.
5th. To not allow the bad order of those who try to impose it.

God and nation, Santa Cruz de la Cañada, August 3, 1837, Encampment[20]

The rebel junta, now joined with a large force of disgruntled northern New Mexicans from Chimayó to Taos, descended toward Santa Fe. Governor Pérez could only raise 150 men to counter the rebels, a number that proved insufficient. He was captured in his retreat, and the rebels of the Cantón executed him on August 9. The two thousand men of the rebellion entered Santa Fe and proceeded to elect a man named José Gonzales as their new governor.[21]

Of course, the issue of taxation and poor government was clearly important to the rebels, but the language about God, nation, and the Christian faith that bookmarks the rebels' plan was more than mere rhetorical flourish. By the time of the 1837 rebellion, Chimayó—largely under the influence of Bernardo Abeyta—had become a place of local religious power and devotion due to the Santuario and one of the most important centers of Penitente activity as well. The Santuario and the Penitente Brotherhood emerged both as continuations of Spanish Catholic piety *and* as lay innovations born of the unique Pueblo, *genízaro*, and poor Spanish populations of northern villages. The new rebel governor, José Gonzales, was himself a *genízaro* familiar with the customs of various Pueblos as well as Spanish village life.[22] That he was chosen to lead the rebel government reflects many northern New Mexicans' often poorly articulated but nonetheless powerful desire to maintain the social and religious structures and leadership that made sense to them. Greater Catholic as well as federal political centralization was, thus, anathema to them. The Cantón's rebel plan, although vague in scope, imagines a northern New Mexican homeland under God and the Christian faith as they knew it. Their revolutionary activities, to a great extent, were imbued with their religiosity. Penitente leadership in the revolt is not certain, but during their occupation of Santa Fe, the rebels went first of all to the parish church to express their thanks. Padre Martínez of Taos celebrated Mass in the Santuario during the short time in which the rebels were in control of the region. The historian Fray Angélico Chávez speculates that the Mass was likely said for the Penitente Brotherhood in Chimayó, Martínez's "pet extra-parochial congregation." If this is so, there is strong reason to believe that Penitentes were influential members of the rebellion.[23]

The assassination of Governor Pérez and the establishment of *genízaro*-led home rule, however, was not what many political and Church leaders desired, despite their shared contempt for Governor Pérez's unpopular military and tax policies. Soon after Gonzales was elected governor of the independent Cantón, the former governor and statesman Manuel Armijo took the helm of a counterrevolutionary force. Those following Armijo, in addition to wanting to see order restored under Mexican rule, berated the Río Arriba rebels as uncouth savages, explicitly suggesting that the racial mixture in Chimayó and other northern villages had resulted in wild men unfit to govern. Albino Chacón, no great supporter of the murdered Governor Pérez, was one of the government officials who supported Armijo against the rebels because of their unsavory characteristics; he called them "treacherous deceivers, . . . men of the braided hair . . . who have abandoned the looms to rebel against the country." The looms, of course, refer to the already successful weaving industry in Chimayó, and the "braided hair" was a thinly veiled reference to the cultural and ethnic mixing with the Pueblo and *genízaro* populations throughout the northern half of New Mexico.[24] Even for fellow New Mexicans, then, the villagers of northern New Mexico had become a people unto themselves, with suspect ethnic and economic markers and intolerable modes of cultural and religious expression.

Thus the religious, ethnic, and social structure that imbued Chimayó and the Río Arriba region motivated the rebels in a diffuse but powerful way that was ultimately unacceptable, and perhaps even incomprehensible, to the elites farther south in the territory. A long-remembered exchange between the rebel leader Gonzales and Armijo illustrates this disconnect. Gonzales, echoing the basic objectives of his rebellion, declared to Armijo, "We do not need your government, we do not care about its armies, which we have whipped, and we do not need [its] laws. This country can be governed, and be governed well, under the laws of God, and the execution of His law is all that is necessary." If Gonzales does not exactly recommend a theocracy, he at least imagines a regime that relies on local religious social structures and leadership. Armijo's retort demonstrates that the two men did not understand their ostensibly shared religion in the same way: "You cannot rule under the laws of God. His law says: 'Thou shalt not kill,' and you have committed murder. It says: 'Thou shalt not steal,' and you have appropriated unto yourselves that which belongs to others." Rather than a list of statutes confined to the realm of personal ethical decisions, Gonzales and his fellow rebels imagined the law of God as the warp and weft of their entire social and cosmic order. In this law of God, the alliances and admixtures among Spanish villagers, *genízaros*, and Pueblos, united by Franciscan and earthy piety, healed by intercessions and holy dirt, were not peripheral aberrations but fundamental and sufficient.[25]

Armijo's forces put down the Chimayó Rebellion shortly after it began with little bloodshed. Only five leaders of the revolt, including José Gonzales, were executed, and the Pueblos who had collaborated with the rebels were left in relative peace. Some historians have suggested that the 1837 Rebellion, although not ultimately successful, demonstrates how independent the northern villages and Pueblos had become in the final years of Spanish rule and during the chaotic first decades of the Mexican period. The historian and anthropologist James F. Brooks points out that, although "Pueblo warriors from Santo Domingo were directly responsible for [Mexican Governor] Pérez's assassination," the Pueblos still counted for one-sixth of the entire population of New Mexico. Keeping the Pueblos and their Hispano allies in the northern villages peaceful was economically and politically necessary during a period in which trade as well as skirmishes with eastern Plains Indians roiled the northern frontier. Mexico's ongoing plans to impose greater central authority both in the department of New Mexico and in the nation as a whole continued to be largely untenable in the independent north, with the Chimayó Rebellion being the most conspicuous example of the northerners' autonomy and internally cohesive sense of community. If Armijo could claim victory and the restoration of order, he could do so only with the tacit understanding that little had actually changed in terms of Mexican political and economic control of La Cañada, Taos, and the rest of the Río Arriba.[26]

Padre Martínez had a small role to play in the rebellion, though it is difficult to discern whether his involvement is representative of the Catholic Church in general or of the priest's own shrewd dealings with his various constituencies. Due to the padre's political strength in Taos, at least some of the elites in Santa Fe assumed that he had something to do with the uprising itself. Martínez later defended himself against these accusations; his version of events must be read carefully since his remarks are meant to exonerate himself, but they nonetheless provide another viewpoint on Catholic involvement with the rebels. Martínez's report likewise opens yet another window onto the population center that surrounded the Santuario de Chimayó. Martínez, shortly after the uprising got under way, went to Chimayó upon the invitation of a member of the Esquivel family to say Mass for the rebels. It is likely that the Esquivel who issued the call for the priest was the anti-Pérez Chimayó judge who had sparked the rebellion in the first place, and it is notable that Esquivel was the current *hermano mayor* of the local chapter of the Penitente Brotherhood. Esquivel's position in the order, the use of the Santuario, the fact that the Santuario's owner, Bernardo Abeyta, was also a Penitente leader at this time, and the known strength of the Penitentes throughout the Río Arriba all suggest that the Brotherhood's membership and adherence to the rebellion were related. This supposition about the order's involvement in the Chimayó Rebellion does not exactly implicate Father Martínez, but the padre continued—even in the course of his self-defense—to crow about his position as the officially named supervisor of the "Penitential Third Order of St. Francis."[27]

After he met with the rebellious Penitentes at the Santuario, Martínez continued on to Santa Fe to work on the negotiations to move the territory of New Mexico toward official departmental status within the nation of Mexico. By the time he got back to his home in September, his Taoseño parishioners had largely joined the rebellion and grown suspicious of their priest and his involvement with the Mexican government. According to Martínez, his erstwhile parishioners threatened him with imprisonment, treated him shabbily, and made him sign an oath of allegiance to the rebellion. At this point, Martínez headed south once again to Santa Fe, ostensibly to escape the growing danger in which he found himself. We must keep in mind that what we know of the priest's activities is based on his own reporting, but it is at this time that Martínez claims he began issuing calls for his rebellious parishioners to end their uprising. After only a short stay in Santa Fe, at that point held by Gonzales, the proclaimed rebel governor of the Cantón de la Cañada, Martínez returned north to Taos. While Martínez was en route, Armijo arrived with his forces from the south and restored Mexican rule. Always aware of the way the wind was blowing, Martínez made a hasty report to Armijo to swear his ongoing allegiance to the latter.[28]

A couple of letters that Martínez wrote to Bishop Zubiría in Durango during and after the Chimayó Rebellion suggest that Martínez's Mass in the Santuario early in September 1837 may have been a turning point in the relationship between the priest and the independent-minded Penitentes of the northern region. As early as September 25, not even two months after the beginning of the uprising, Martínez wrote to Zubiría that "an unusual but unexpected event has occurred due to the lawless character of the population of the town of Santa Cruz de la Cañada, *the filth of New Mexico.*" Given this vitriol and the date of the letter well before the end of the rebellion, one wonders if Martínez's stay in the Chimayó area and his involvement with the rebels in both La Cañada and back in his own Taos had soured his formerly valued relationships with lay leaders in the Penitente order. After the rebellion was over and Martínez had returned to the good graces of Armijo and other political elites of the Mexican regime in Santa Fe, the priest wrote a second missive to Zubiría in which he once again takes pains to malign the people of the Santa Cruz area. In this letter, he recounts his journey to Santa Fe after escaping his disgruntled people back in Taos. "On the 19th [of October] as I was traveling through La Cruz de la Cañada another gathering was being formed by the inhabitants of the same [place], the rectory of San Juan, mission of Picurís, and the Indian Pueblos. . . . On the very day that I passed through La Cañada the rebels ran after me, but they were unable to catch up to me!" In the same letter, after recounting his role as chaplain to Armijo's battling soldiers, Martínez remarks to his bishop that northern New Mexico was deeply troubled and that the rebels, although vanquished, remained intent on spreading "pagan-ism, pillage, and death." In a matter of months, the powerful priest goes from providing Mass and perhaps guidance to Penitentes in La Cañada to publicly suspecting both Pueblos and other citizens of northern New Mexico of godlessness and irredeemable violence. The final years of the Mexican period thus feature an environment around the Santuario that had become more and more isolated and independent from the official representatives of the Church.[29]

The U.S. Takeover

The anger and discontent that northern New Mexicans harbored against the artless taxation schemes of the Mexican government did not dissipate after the suppression of the Chimayó Rebellion. Likewise, widespread but often clandestine disregard for Bishop Zubiría's 1833 condemnation of the Penitente order and New Mexico's popular religious aesthetic continued apace in the years just prior to the American takeover. Thus, when in 1846 Colonel Stephen Watts Kearny led American forces into Santa Fe and took control of New Mexico without bloodshed, the calm was illusory. To be sure, not all New Mexicans were troubled by the prospect of becoming part of the United States; Padre Martínez in Taos was both an early predictor of the U.S. takeover and an influential sup-porter. In 1845 Martínez wrote to Zubiría, "I will venture to predict that sooner or later this Department will become a portion of our neighbor Republic of America. There every religion is tolerated according to its constitution. . . . As I have said, this time is quickly approaching, and our government is not taking steps to overcome this intrusion." Martínez, a man who knew his audience, warned Zubiría that this would mean the introduction of Protestantism into New Mexico. But when Kearny soon fulfilled Martínez's predictions, the priest quickly accepted an invita-tion to meet with Kearny and swear allegiance to the new government. Besides positioning himself favorably with the new regime, Martínez likely felt that U.S. administration of the territory could hardly be less negligent or tone-deaf than had been the government of Mexico. His assessment was not shared by the Pueblos and many Nuevomexicanos in the northern towns and villages whose open rebellion had so recently been put down.[30]

Kearny appointed an Anglo businessman from Taos, Charles Bent, to serve as provisional governor of the new American holding of New Mexico. However, in a series of events remarkably similar to those of the 1837 revolt in Chimayó, a coalition of non-elite Nuevomexicanos and Pueblo Indians from Taos and other villages all around the north rose up in rebellion, took control of Taos, and assassinated Governor Bent. Soon, two thousand fighters amassed in Santa Cruz de la Cañada to march on Santa Fe. As in 1837, this rebellion was not able to withstand organized military resistance. By early 1847, American forces had largely restored order and punished the leaders of the rebellion. Even though peace and a treaty with Mexico would not come until later in 1848, New Mexico from 1847 onward would be part of the United States.[31]

In the broadest terms, it can be said that 1847, then, is also the date when the Santuario de Chimayó "entered" the United States. Just over thirty years old, the shrine was still owned at this time by the now elderly Bernardo Abeyta. But since at least 1837, Chimayó, like the rest of La Cañada, had been known principally for its cantankerous and autonomy-seeking spirit. Over the course of the Mexican period, Chimayó's connections with New Mexico's secular government as well as with religious oversight in the Catholic Church were significantly weakened even as internally cohesive standards of political and religious community grew in importance. On the political side of things, the Chimayó Rebellion had begun when local kinship patterns—which had been honored by local justice Esquivel—were overturned and challenged by the centralized Mexican authorities in Santa Fe. The resulting revolutionary government, although short-lived, represented a tension between local autonomy and state control that persisted through the Taos revolt and well into the American territorial period. On the Catholic front, Chimayosos and other northern New Mexicans, who had come to rely for much local religious leadership on the Penitentes, were forcefully rebuffed in 1833 by Bishop Zubiría, who condemned the Brotherhood and called for its dissolution. The local priest in Santa Cruz during this period, Padre Trujillo, also represented a rift with tradition. Even though he had been one of Martínez's seminarians and thus someone with local roots, he diligently obeyed Zubiría's dictate against the Penitentes.[32] Padre Martínez himself, perhaps the best ally in Catholic officialdom that northern New Mexicans could claim, eventually turned on the people of La Cañada, branding them "the filth" of New Mexico. His hasty switch of loyalties to the Americans at the time of the Taos uprising completed and compounded the isolation of the kind of Catholicism still practiced by many northerners in and around the Santuario. In brief, even though the Santuario, its holy dirt, its miraculous crucifix, and its pilgrims in 1847 were annexed into the United States, their connections to both political and religious authorities in Mexico had already become tenuous and beleaguered.

Colonel Kearny was acutely aware that New Mexico, like the rest of the Mexican territory he and the American army were entering, was Catholic. No doubt, Kearny could not have understood the fractious nature of New Mexican Catholicism in this period, but he did endeavor to salve the situation with blanket assurances for Catholics. In addition to his claim that fully a third of his army was made up of Catholics, Kearny declared,

> New Mexicans: We have come amongst you to take possession of New Mexico, which we do in the name of the government of the United States. . . . We come as friends, to better your condition and make you part of the republic of the United States. . . . In taking possession of New Mexico, we do not mean to take from you your religion. Religion and government have no connection in our country. There, all religions are equal. . . . The Catholic and the Protestant are esteemed alike. Every man has a right to serve God according to his heart.[33]

While statements like these seemed to have assuaged the concerns of Catholic leaders like Padre Martínez, it is unlikely that the religion of the Penitentes, the Santuario, converted Pueblos, and Nuevomexicano villages was what Kearny had in mind when he made rhetorical space for Catholicism in U.S.-controlled New Mexico. The increased religious autonomy of many New Mexicans would continue to wax in the early territorial period.

New Mexican Catholicism and Local Foreign Leadership

The impact of the arrival of Jean Baptiste Lamy to New Mexico (1851) and the eventual establishment of the Diocese (1853) and then the

Archdiocese (1875) of Santa Fe has been amply covered and so does not need to be rehearsed again in full here.[34] Relevant, however, for the present story are the ways Franco-American oversight of the Catholic Church in territorial New Mexico, for the most part, accentuated the isolation and autonomous religious practice of Hispanos in Chimayó and other northern villages. Already before Lamy got to New Mexico, his predecessor, Bishop Zubiría in Durango, had made repeated calls for the elimination of the Penitentes and the removal of folk art from the churches.[35] Zubiría found these visual and ritual traditions to be plebeian and déclassé; Lamy agreed but also was more precisely worried about the lack of discipline in his ecclesiastical province. To remedy the situation, Lamy and his lieutenant, Father Joseph Machebeuf, focused on discipline and construction projects. The discipline was achieved in part by removing stubborn native New Mexican clergy from their posts but also by flooding the new diocese with French-born priests and religious. The building projects included the great cathedral in Santa Fe as well as dozens of other churches around the territory.[36]

Most historians argue that Lamy's leadership represented a distinct break with the Catholic supervision of the colonial and Mexican national periods, and while that is true in many cases, Lamy's disdain for the popular practices and aesthetic basis of northern Hispano village Catholicism was continuous with that of the Spanish and Mexican bishops and official custodians who had occasionally made their way to New Mexico prior to the U.S. takeover. Lamy's impulse, in contrast to his predecessors, was to administrate and control rather than condemn and eliminate. To this end, in 1856 he issued a document ponderously titled "Rules That Must Be Observed by the Brothers of the Catholic Confraternity of Penitentes." These rules, not surprisingly, attempted to reorder Penitente organization such that Lamy himself as bishop would have greater control and access to information. The *hermano mayor* of local chapters was to provide membership lists to the local parish priests, and the Penitente brothers were to swear obedience to the bishop. While Lamy explicitly stated that he found nothing heretical about the current constitution of the Penitentes, his imposition of additional rules and scrutiny of membership rolls demonstrate his desire to recapture the order and reformulate it as a more typical lay confraternity under parish supervision.[37]

Lamy's main efforts, however, to establish greater control over Catholic life in New Mexico did not have to do with the Penitentes but rather with a restructuring of the fee system for sacraments that had long been in place throughout the territory. In 1852 he issued a "Christmas Pastoral," a letter to be communicated to all the faithful under his care. In former times, the Franciscans and the parish priests all the way up to the bishop had been supported by significant fees for celebration of the sacraments, especially for the rites of passage of baptism, marriage, and Christian burial. In many cases, the poverty of the people meant that Catholics were unable to participate fully in the sacramental life of the Church, one of the factors that had led to the development of folk traditions and the robust lay leadership of the Penitentes. Lamy rightly recognized that these fees were problematic, but the solutions he articulated in his Christmas letter were not well-received by many clergy and laypeople alike. He drastically lowered and regulated the fees-for-sacraments and replaced that lost income with an insistence on faithful tithing—that is, a percentage of all income had to be given to the Church. To enforce this new policy, Lamy wrote, "if, despising this law of the Church, you decide not to subject yourselves to ecclesiastical authority, we will be forced, although with much sadness and regret, to deny you the sacraments and to consider that you no longer belong to the Catholic Church."[38] These new tithing requirements led to internecine fighting between Lamy and several of the native clergy, most famously Martínez in Taos, and the overall effect on the people was immediate and ominous. As the Jesuit historian Thomas J. Steele writes, referring to Lamy's new insistence on tithing, "New Mexicans might have heard echoes of the Mexican government's centralization in the mid-1830s which led to Governor Albino Pérez's assassination." Lamy did not face any threats on his life, but New Mexican Catholics' predilection for autonomy was severely tested by his reforms.[39]

The other way Lamy worked to increase the diocese's control over New Mexico's Catholics was through dozens of appointments of foreign priests—mostly Frenchmen like himself—to the territory's far-flung parishes. By the end of his tenure as bishop and archbishop in 1885, Lamy had imported 114 French priests, almost three-quarters of all the priests under his jurisdiction.[40] Additionally, he brought in an order of nuns from Loretto, Kentucky, to run schools. That he felt compelled to appoint so many outside priests and religious educators to his diocese indicates Lamy's ultimate inability to connect with or trust local Catholic leadership. On some level, he recognized that this lack of trust was a significant stumbling block for him and his successors. In 1881, near the end of his career, Lamy wrote the following to the Vatican:

> Finally, our Mexican population has quite a sad future. Very few of them will be able to follow modern progress. One cannot compare them to the Americans on the grounds of intellectual liveliness, know-how, and industry. . . . If the bishop who will follow me has not lived among the Mexicans for a long time, and if he did not show a great interest in them, they will become quite discouraged. Seeing themselves on the one hand under American discipline and, on the other, imagining that the Americans prefer foreigners to them, their faith, which is still lively enough, would grow gradually weaker, and the consequences would be dreadful.[41]

Tellingly, the problems Lamy predicts for his successor were precisely the problems that had plagued his own efforts to centralize authority in the diocese and diminish local autonomy in the churches and chapels of the territory.

Of course, what Lamy meant by the faith of the "Mexicans" growing "gradually weaker" was that they would be less and less likely to attend Mass, pay tithes to the Catholic Church, and rely on parish priests to help them mark major events in their lives. However, as we have seen, northern New Mexicans had long before Lamy's arrival developed relatively autonomous religious and social structures to meet the people's various needs. The resilience of the Penitentes is a key example of the self-contained religious culture that sustained Nuevomexicano village life. And so it is that Lamy was rebuffed in his efforts to control and channel the Penitentes in much the same way that Bishop Zubiría had found his own dictates concerning the order summarily ignored throughout his decades of oversight of the region. In 1879, many years after he issued his "Rules That Must Be Observed by the Brothers of the Catholic Confraternity of Penitentes," Lamy found himself condemning the Penitentes for their disobedience to his authority.[42] As discussed below, Lamy's desire to take ownership of the Santuario de Chimayó met with similar failure.

The archbishop who followed Lamy, Jean Baptiste Salpointe, had even greater troubles with the Penitentes and the religious autonomy of Río

Arriba. His experience as a priest under Lamy had already introduced Salpointe to what the latter considered the "criminal extravagances" of the Penitentes. Not only was Salpointe scandalized by the penitential rites of the order, he also found it incomprehensible that these same bloody ceremonies were attended "by numerous good old women devoutly saying their beads." The tableau of laymen mortifying their own flesh, marching, and intoning their penitential chants was bad enough without the approval and open devotion of old women, the pillars of so many Catholic congregations. Salpointe, like Lamy, issued his own rules for Penitentes, but the new archbishop was more explicit in his scorn. In 1888 he declared,

> With regard to the Society called Los Penitentes we firmly believe, that it fully deserves all blame. Consequently, it must not be fostered. This society, though perhaps legitimate and religious in its beginning, has so greatly degenerated many years ago that it has no longer fixed rules but is governed in everything according to the pleasure of the director of every locality, and in many cases is nothing else but a political society. . . .
>
> . . . [M]ass must not be celebrated in the chapels [*moradas*], where the Penitentes observe their rites and abuses. Moreover, we command that the following rule be observed by our Priests toward the Penitentes who celebrate the wake over the dead bodies, with scourging, not excluding eating and drinking and despised our ordinances and penalties, published to that effect in 1886. They are to be deprived of the Sacrament until they amend.[43]

In the wake of these comments, several Penitente groups did, in fact, attempt to find some reconciliation with Salpointe, but he remained frustrated—even perplexed—with community support for the Penitentes. His bald assertions about Penitente decadence and heterodoxy demonstrate once again that Franco-American control of New Mexican Catholicism in the late nineteenth century remained vexed.

The Quiet and Private Operation of the Santuario in the Territorial Period

Given Archbishop Lamy's agenda to gain greater levels of control over both the churches and devotional life of the Catholics in his diocese, it would not be surprising to discover that he had made a bid to take command of the Santuario. Like the Penitente order, the Santuario operated largely under lay leadership, it exhibited at least some traces of pre-Hispanic traditions (albeit Catholicized), and it lay in the contentious and autonomous La Cañada area. While there is little indication that a massive Good Friday pilgrimage had developed during the territorial period, there is ample evidence that pilgrims came to the Santuario throughout the year from all over the Río Arriba area (and possibly farther away) to seek healing from the holy dirt in the *pocito*. Certainly, this would have drawn Lamy's attention. This popular folk practice, however, is mentioned nowhere in extant documents related to the archbishop. This, of course, does not mean that Lamy knew nothing of the Santuario and its unique customs; it is more likely that the majority of visitors to the Santuario made their journeys, offered their prayers, and gathered the dirt in relatively innocuous ways, and so did not merit official comment from Lamy, as did more contentious issues like the Penitentes and rebellious northern priests like Padre Martínez.

Despite the lack of official mention of the Santuario in Lamy's papers, there is anecdotal evidence that Lamy desired Bernardo Abeyta's popular chapel for the archdiocese. The source is L. Bradford Prince, an Anglo American transplant to New Mexico who had served as the governor of the territory in the 1890s. By the time he related the story of Lamy's interest in the Santuario, he had become the president of the Historical Society of New Mexico, a fact that does not necessarily vet his comments as historically reliable but does provide at least some level of authority. Prince relates that after Bernardo Abeyta's death, his Santuario had passed on to his daughter, Carmen Chavez. Chavez had maintained the place and continued to welcome pilgrims and health seekers. Prince, with the rhetorical flourish of his day, tells the story of how the archdiocese, through a young priest, tried to stake a claim to the Santuario:

> Troublous times arose in [Carmen Chavez's] days to try her soul. The old Mexican priesthood, amiable and easy going, had been the friends of her father and of her youth; and encouraged the faith of the people which had such wonderful results in almost miraculous cures. The early French priests were similarly friendly. . . . But at length came a young man fresh from the seminary, full of the importance of his office and of

the power which it possessed, and insisted that the Santuario property should be given absolutely to the Church authorities. In vain the amiable owner explained that it was her patrimony, coming down from her father and that her support was obtained from the voluntary offerings of those who benefited by its healing power. But nothing less than an absolute conveyance of the property would suffice. Her refusal brought threats and finally a practical excommunication, the youthful autocrat refusing to baptize, marry, or bury any of the family until his demands were complied with. Still the good woman maintained her independence, and at last the priest was removed to another field and harmonious relations were again restored.[44]

This account is rich for a number of reasons. First, it suggests that both Mexican and French clergy had been supportive of the Santuario not only as a Catholic chapel but as a pilgrimage site and place of successful healing. Second, by Chavez's own admission, the Santuario was her personal property and means of economic livelihood. Third, the upstart young priest did not offer to purchase the Santuario, but demanded it be conveyed to the Church with no remuneration. And, at least in this version of events, it seems that the young father himself was the enterprising force behind the demand—no mention is made of the diocesan chain of command. Moreover, Prince recalls especially the priest's youthful arrogance and impetuousness as part of the overall negative interaction.

One of Prince's contemporaries, Benjamin Read, a historian and lawyer with a Hispano heritage on his mother's side, was commissioned by the archdiocese to answer Prince's allegations concerning the attempted confiscation of the Santuario. Read dismissed the credibility of Prince's account: "Mr. Prince having failed to give dates and names and also to cite his authorities; the said statements are therefore, allowed to remain in the realm of fiction." But Read felt compelled to convey the archdiocese's response to Prince's portrait of the "youthful autocrat," and acknowledged that he, Read, had obtained reliable information from the Church authorities. Read identifies the young priest as J. B. Francolon, the parish priest at Santa Cruz from 1881 to 1892, dates at the very end of Lamy's tenure and the beginning of Salpointe's turn as archbishop. The difference in Prince's and Read's two accounts is one of tone rather than factual detail:

It is true that Father Francolon, acting under the instructions of his superior, Archbishop Lamy, called on Dona [sic] Carmen and asked for a conveyance of the Santuario chapel to the Catholic church, explaining to her that he had been directed by his superior to request from her the conveyance; that if it was not done no further religious services were to be held in the chapel, neither would it be recognized as a church unless it was placed under the control of the ecclesiastical authorities. To Father Francolon's proposition the senora [sic] refused to accede. Then it was that Archbishop Lamy ordered Catholic religious services to be discontinued, and the matter ended then and there.

Read denies that this was an "excommunication" of Chavez, but he does note that after this episode, Father Francolon found his ministry in the area so hampered that he relocated to Colorado Springs.[45]

I was not able to uncover documentation of this episode in the life of the Santuario in the archives of the archdiocese. However, the many congruent details in the two accounts as well as the fact that Read was commissioned by the Catholic Church to set the matter straight suggest that the basic contours and characters of the story are correct. Since Lamy stepped down in 1885, the years in which the request for conveyance must have occurred are between 1881 (the beginning of Francolon's placement in Santa Cruz) and 1885. It is unclear why Lamy waited until this late stage of his ministry to try to obtain the Santuario for the archdiocese, but that he would do so is consistent with his overarching goals of centralizing Catholic life under the purview of the archdiocese. Unfortunately, at this distance, we likely cannot know whether Lamy had specific interest in the Santuario other than as a church outpost of the parish in Santa Cruz. The story, confirmed by both Prince and Read, is that the churchmen seemed concerned solely with the use of the Santuario for Catholic worship services.

Despite this, Prince's story features the miraculous dirt and the power of the Santuario to bring healing to pilgrims, while Read's version downplays this aspect of the site. At the time of Prince's and Read's dispute, in 1915 and 1916, the archdiocese was under yet another Frenchman, Jean Baptiste Pitaval. Backed by Pitaval, Read declared, "I am authorized to say that the Catholic Church representatives in this archdiocese, either archbishop or priests, notwithstanding their consideration for the good faith of the people, have never paid the least attention to the so-called miracles, supposed to have been wrought at the Santuario de Chimayo."[46] This statement cannot be taken at face value, as it ignores the historical record of clergy support for the construction of the Santuario as a site of pilgrimage and healing. Rather, it opens a window onto the position of the Church in the first decades of the twentieth century, namely, that the Santuario was a potentially viable place to hold Masses but that the dirt and miracles were nothing more than "good faith of the people," perhaps to be tolerated but certainly not promoted. In terms of religious ownership, however, the legal holding of the property was only one part of the story that leaves us with several questions: What about the livelihood that the Chavez family was earning from the Santuario? Why were Francolon's actions so unpopular with the people of La Cañada? What was the Santuario for the people who visited it regularly in the territorial period? How did it "belong" to them even as it was owned by the Chavez family and claimed by the Catholic Church?

The other part of the story—the part that seeks to address these and other questions—has to do with the popular use and appreciation of the Santuario not just as a church building but as a powerful place where access to divine healing was uniquely available. Unlike the highly documented trails left by institutionally conspicuous people like Archbishop Lamy and Padre Antonio José Martínez, relatively little remains to point us toward the daily experiences of ordinary visitors to the Santuario. In the incipient English-language press in Santa Fe, an article about the Santuario came out in 1885 that provides some indication of how visitors to the Santuario ritually accessed the miraculous power of the place:

> Perhaps it is not generally known that there is a spot of consecrated ground within a day's drive of Santa Fe, where there is not a day in the year but that some distressed one visits the place, has the "Novena" read, applies the consecrated dust to his or her body on the five points representing the five wounds our Savior received at the time he was crucified, and goes away firmly believing that they will get well. The writer was told by the devout layman that has officiated in this chapel for thirty years that not a case that has visited the holy place, in good faith, but has recovered.[47]

The opening statement that "it is not generally known" most likely refers not to the majority-Hispanic population of northern New Mexico but to the English-speaking audience of businesspeople and transplants in Santa Fe. The journalist interviews a long-term caretaker of the Santuario, possibly a member of the Abeyta/Chavez family, who explains the use of the "consecrated dust" in terms that relate explicitly to Christ's passion. Such a short description by an outsider cannot tell us much about the Santuario's daily rhythms, but the focus here on the wounds of Christ resonates both with the central image in the Santuario—the crucifix of the Lord of Esquipulas—and with the ritual emphases of the Penitentes, who in this period were flourishing throughout the Río Arriba area.

María Martínez, the famous potter from San Ildefonso Pueblo, visited the Santuario twice in 1890 when she was then ten years old. The memories of her two visits were not recorded until fifty years later, when Martínez retold her life story to the anthropologist Alice Marriott, and therefore are likely colored by the passage of time and later interactions with the Santuario. Nevertheless, Martínez's memories represent some of the best evidence available about ordinary usage of the Santuario in the territorial period and, more specifically, how the Santuario functioned for Catholic Pueblo people. The memories indicate that the native people from many of the surrounding Pueblos enjoyed kin and friendship relationships with many of the "Spanish" in Chimayó and other nearby villages. Likewise, Martínez and her family, although residents of San Ildefonso Pueblo, clearly knew with great precision how to access the healing power of the dirt in the Santuario.

Martínez fell seriously ill with a persistent fever early in 1890. Coming in and out of consciousness, she discovers that her mother has made a promise in return for her daughter's recovery. María first asks if the promise was to dance, presumably a Pueblo dance related to Pueblo deities. But no, the girl is told that the promise is to make a pilgrimage to the "Sanctuario of the Santo Niño" in Chimayó. María's mother explains, "He's the one that takes care of children and is good to them. I promised you would go there and make thanks to him yourself, as soon as you are able." In contrast to the 1885 journalist's account of devotion at the Santuario, which was primarily focused on the suffering figure of Christ on the cross, Martínez and her family seek help from the Holy Child, the Santo Niño de Atocha. Devotion to the Santo Niño at the Santuario is discussed in much greater detail in chapter 4, but we can note here that by the close of the nineteenth century, the original devotion to the Esquipulas Crucifix at the shrine had been displaced in large measure by a growing affection and connection to the miraculous Holy Child.[48]

Little María eventually regained some strength after her long bouts of fever, for which she and her family gave thanks to the Santo Niño. To show further gratitude, they prayed the rosary repeatedly and walked the sixteen miles from San Ildefonso Pueblo to Chimayó with her father, who fasted for the duration of the pilgrimage. Her mother and an uncle traveled by wagon to meet them at the church, where a "Spanish" old man emerged to attend to their needs and admit them into the Santuario. After leading them by the main altar of the church, which in María's memory held a statue of the Santo Niño, the man led them to the small chamber where the *pocito* is located. The evocative scene is worth quoting at length not only for a description of the Santuario in this time period but also for the ritual and sensory aspects of María's interaction with the holy dirt:

There was darkness behind the door [to the *pocito*]—darkness and a sense of depth. Mother drew María towards it. The child smelled an earthen dampness, like the darkness of the storeroom at home, and it surprised her. Most churches smelled like dry dust, not wet.

"There are steps going down," said Mother. "You must go down them. When you get to the bottom, take off all your clothes. Don't be afraid, because nobody can see you. Then take this holy medal and scrape off the earth on the sides of the hole. Rub the earth all over your body. That's what will make you well."

"Will you go with me?" María asked.

"Just you can go. This is your pilgrimage. After you have rubbed yourself with the sacred earth and dressed again, take the medal and dig out enough earth to fill your water bottle. That much you can take home with you, to drink there to make you well. While you are doing this, you should say your 'Our Father.' Don't think about any thing but your prayers and the Santo Niño."

When the little girl emerged from the earth, her mother supplied her with offerings to leave on the altar: purple cloth, a rosary, hides, and a little money. Her mother took the bottle of dirt from her and told her how she would mix it in water for the next four days and give it to María to drink to complete her healing.[49]

In María's childhood memories, the *pocito* is not the small hole in a side chapel of the Santuario, as almost every other account renders it. Instead it is a deep pit, scored by dozens of others who had scraped its holy sides to gather its earth. Of course, it is possible that the hole was bigger in that era and has been made smaller over time as part of renovations to the site. It is also possible that a small child's memory has reconstructed the place as dark and big and solitary. In either case, the room with the dirt then, as now, is a kind of inner sanctum where María, under her mother's tutelage, physically experiences the healing power of the place and of the Holy Child.

The old Hispano attendant serves in this context as a kind of official Catholic spokesperson and even argues with the child's mother about the importance and origin of the dirt itself. María's mother explains,

> "This is good earth. The Indians knew about it and how to use it a long time ago. Then the padres came and learned about its power, and the Santo Niño came and told them what to do, so they built the church here. Everybody knows the earth is good. It makes everyone well who drinks it, for the rest of his life."
>
> The old Spanish man had come out of the church and stood listening. He shook his head at Mother. "The Santo Niño makes the people well," he said. "He could do it on a mud-pile. He doesn't need any special Indian earth. . . . Well, the padres say that faith without works is dead."

This remarkable exchange reveals tensions between Indian and Hispano as well as lay and priestly understandings of the Santuario's miraculous earth. In María's mother's telling, the dirt (and Indian knowledge of it) predates both the Catholic priests and the Santo Niño, even though the latter is embraced as a worthy guide to the good earth. For the sacristan, who speaks for the padres, the dirt is merely incidental to the Santo Niño's holy power and essence. There is also evident friction concerning the status of the earth as "Indian," a source of pride for the Martínez family while a point worthy of contradiction for the "Spanish" caretaker. When later in the same year, 1890, María and her family make the Good Friday pilgrimage to Chimayó, some of these same tensions of owner-ship over the Santuario, the Santo Niño, and Catholic identity play out again when little María witnesses Penitente processions and finds them vastly different from her experiences of the joyous dances of her Pueblo people. Nevertheless, the Martínez family is in Chimayó not only to render devotion at the Santuario but also to spend time with friends and family members, both Indian and Nuevomexicano, who live in the vicinity. In sum, the Santuario in this period served as a focal point for both Hispano and Pueblo Catholics. These often overlapping groups practiced devotions both similar (prayers to the Santo Niño and use of the holy dirt) and different (solemn processions, priestly instruction, and Indian origin stories).[50]

* * *

On one level, the nineteenth century witnessed tremendous turmoil and radical change for New Mexico. The political disarray that fol-lowed Mexican independence meant that many New Mexicans found themselves unhappy with clumsy and heavy-handed Mexican taxation schemes. They also felt simultaneously unprotected by Mexican mili-tary forces on the northern and eastern frontiers of the territory and harshly conscripted into military misadventures. The resulting rebel-lious spirit coalesced in the willful region of La Cañada, exploding into open revolt in 1837 in the village of Chimayó itself. Even though put down by Mexican forces, the rebels' propensity for autonomy—which had been nurtured through the centuries of benign neglect under Spain and the Franciscans—meant that both Hispano farmers and their Pueblo neighbors were hardly eager to transform their community and religious structures to accommodate new political regimes. When the United States invaded and took over the region in 1846 and 1847, yet another round of rebellions and renegotiations took place. In contrast to the transition to Mexico, this major change also included the first substantial restructuring of the Catholic Church in the area in 250 years when Jean Baptiste Lamy took control of a new diocese created not in Mexico but in the expanding United States. Once again, the religious and folk traditions of northern New Mexicans, including both the Penitente

Brotherhood and the pilgrimage to Chimayó, persisted even when Lamy and Franco-American Church officials tried to curtail them.

On another level, the rhythms of northern New Mexican communities remained mostly constant. Long accustomed to the self-determination of relative isolation and supported by efficacious traditions of penance and pilgrimage, the people of the Río Arriba practiced their Catholicism in the orbit of the Catholic Church, but with their own narratives, identity, and structures of mutual support. Although the well-documented history of New Mexico's political and ecclesiastical regime changes in the nineteenth century certainly affected non-elites throughout the territory, experiences of healing, miracles, and the power of Christ continued to undergird the faith and health of thousands of people in the mountains and valleys from Santa Fe to Taos, from Chimayó to Abiquiu. If there was a substantial change in the religious life of the Santuario in the nineteenth century, it had little to do with the nation in charge or even the bishop. Instead, the person of Christ as healer at the Santuario changed at some unspoken moment from the crucified and suffering Lord on the cross to the winsome and puckish Santo Niño, the holy Christ Child. As we saw in the story of the young María Martínez, the Niño became the key divine personage at the Santuario, the custodian and partner of the miraculous dirt.

4

The Santo Niño de Atocha

In the late 1960s, the cowboy folklorist and novelist John L. Sinclair wrote an essay about the Santuario in which, like those who came before him, he described the legends of the Lord of Esquipulas and its apparition in the dirt to Bernardo Abeyta. But Sinclair brings the discussion forward to the later years of the nineteenth century when, for reasons unexplained, "there was a dwindling of interest in the Christ of Esquipulas—and today there is a complete ignorance of him among most of the pilgrims—because the 'miracle' of the *Santo Niño de Atocha*, or the Lost Child, had sprung into popularity." An incredible transformation in the focus of devotion had occurred at the Santuario. Pilgrims had once come to venerate the miraculous crucifix with the arboreal cross that hung on the principal *retablo* and to scoop up the healing dirt from the *pocito* from which he emerged. But by the closing decades of the nineteenth century, a small statue of a Christ Child dressed for travel in the side chapel of the Santuario had thoroughly eclipsed the suffering Lord on the cross. By the time Sinclair wrote his essay, the Santo Niño had even begun to replace Esquipulas in the origin myths of the Santuario; instead of the crucifix coming out of the dirt, the statue of the Holy Child was the miraculous found object, the church was built for him, and the holy dirt gained its power from his association. Sinclair continued, "All credit for healing now goes to the Infant Deity."[1]

Veneration of and intercession to the Santo Niño continue to reign as the prime devotions at the Santuario today. Who is the Santo Niño de Atocha, and how did he come to have such a prominent position in the Chimayó pilgrimage? The Santo Niño, in theological terms, may be just as much Jesus Christ as the crucified Lord on the cross of Esquipulas, but these two images of Jesus are, in many ways, radically different. The nonbiblical pilgrim Christ Child, however, has managed to capture and keep the fervent devotion of the vast majority of the pilgrims to the Santuario. In this chapter, I recount the origin of the Santo Niño de Atocha and tell how he made his way to the banks of the Santa Cruz River in Chimayó in the middle of the nineteenth century. Additionally, I examine his consolidation of power over the dirt and the miraculous cures at the Santuario as well as at the adjacent Medina Chapel, now known as the Santo Niño Chapel. The approachable and miraculous Child ultimately represents one of the main ways the day-to-day religious faithful have been able to make indelible impacts on the direction and focus of the Santuario. In this sense, the Santo Niño has made it possible for the Santuario's users to establish some modicum of ownership over the shrine. If they have moved away from the suffering Christ of the Esquipulas crucifix toward a wonder-working boy Jesus, and even retold the history of the Santuario with the Niño at the center, they have done so because the Holy Child has been more responsive to their needs. Or to put it another way, he belongs to them.

The Origins of the Santo Niño de Atocha

The Holy Child, perhaps not surprisingly, originates with his Holy Mother, the Virgin of Atocha. Our Lady of Atocha was one of three baby-toting statues of Mary in a shrine and monastery in Atocha, a stop on the royal road on the way out of Madrid. Founded sometime in the distant past, perhaps even in the first millennium of the Common Era, the place was obtained in the sixteenth century by the Dominican order, who began to sideline the other two virgins in favor of Our Lady of Atocha. Before that time, all three images were known for miraculous powers to grant favors, including healing, to devotees. While it is unknown exactly why the Dominicans decided to focus devotions on the Lady of Atocha, this stage in her history led to a definite surge in popularity not only locally but also among travelers and pilgrims who would come to the shrine especially to see the miraculous Virgin. Around the turn of the seventeenth century, Atocha became associated with the Spanish court, and from that rarefied vantage point, she became part of Spain's imperial administration of the Americas. It is worth noting that the Christ Child that the Lady of Atocha carried on her arm was not generally considered the source of the favors and miracles; instead, the Virgin herself was the font of power. The protection of mothers before, during, and after childbirth was a common intercession that she may have inherited from another of the trio of virgins in the original shrine, Our Lady of Pregnancies. In any case, the original image of Atocha was not the Santo Niño but his powerful mother, who cared for local peasants, pilgrim supplicants, and the Spanish nobility.[2]

As early as the late sixteenth century, veneration of Our Lady of Atocha had accompanied the Spanish conquest into Peru, but the most important establishment of her veneration in relation to the Santo Niño occurred significantly later in Zacatecas, Mexico, in a little mining town called Plateros.[3] Despite the prevalence of Franciscan missions and Catholic leadership throughout northern Mexico, which at this time still included New Mexico, Dominicans had long held sway at the Plateros church, and they were the ones who brought the Virgin of Atocha to the region sometime in the late seventeenth or early eighteenth century. The historian Juan Javier Pescador suggests that the arrival of the Virgin was tied to the area's rising economic fortunes as a hub of mining; the Spanish elites went where fortunes were to be made, and the Virgin of Atocha accompanied them. In this sense, she was hardly a popular image. Moreover, the principal devotion of the village of Plateros in the colonial period, supported by the nearby city of Fresnillo, was to the Señor de Plateros, a crucifix beloved for its own miraculous power and its role in various processions throughout the region. Indeed, the Lady of Atocha had fallen on such hard times in Plateros by the end of the eighteenth century that the priests in Fresnillo had taken to removing the Christ Child from the statue and dressing him separately for celebrations of Candlemas, the Catholic feast that celebrates the baby Jesus's presentation in the temple.[4]

Once unmoored from his mother, the baby began to take on a life, and a life story, of his own. By the first decades of the nineteenth century, concurrent with Mexican independence from Spain, the statue of the child Jesus began to be inventoried separately from any of the Madonnas in the Plateros church, and by 1838, the Santo Niño de Atocha had made a definitive move from a side chapel to be ensconced on the main altar of the church.[5] The Niño's image at first took after the original statue of the Virgin of Atocha (and her detachable child) in Plateros. Given the region's importance in silver mining, it is not surprising that his clothes were plated in silver; in addition to that finery, he held a globe and a rosary in his hand, and often sported a traveler's cape. Soon, as the image of the child was reproduced in *retablos* and in stand-alone statuary reproductions, his aspect also came to include other symbols of the pilgrim: the wide-brimmed hat, the walking staff, and the scallop shell. As stories of his exploits began to develop, and intercessions were made to him specifically for his miraculous intervention, other symbols also accrued to his image. These included a basket for carrying food and drink, and sometimes, broken shackles upon his little legs.

Historians of the iconography of the Santo Niño de Atocha have suggested that this conglomeration of symbolic items has resulted from the conflation of the Niño de Atocha with the Santo Niño Cautivo, or "Captive Holy Child." This statue of the child Jesus was created in Spain and exported to Mexico in the seventeenth century, but on the way, it was captured and held for ransom by Moors in Algeria. After this was paid, the image finished its trek to Mexico City, where it still resides. Broken shackles were affixed to it at one point to commemorate its liberation from its captivity.[6] Perhaps related to the Moorish captivity of the Santo Niño Cautivo, another popular story concerning the Moors has also come to be associated with the Holy Child of Atocha. The legend is set back in Atocha in Spain before the Christian Reconquista. The Moors had imprisoned Spanish Christians in great numbers and were keeping the prisoners incommunicado except for visits from small children. The families of the prisoners prayed constantly for divine succor for their captive loved ones.

> One day a child dressed like the pilgrims of that time came into the prisons carrying in one hand a basket and in the other a staff with a gourd full of water at its tip. To the astonishment of the Moors, the gourd and the basket of bread still were not empty after all of the captives had been served and each one, as he received his portion, received also a blessing. According to the legend, Christ had returned in answer to the prayer of the women of Atocha. As a child He came to serve those without spiritual or earthly help.[7]

Ironically, the stand-alone image of the Santo Niño of Atocha developed in Mexico rather than Spain, but the story of his miraculous abilities was projected back into a legendary situation of hardship and opposition.

The ambulatory nature of the Child contributed to his miraculousness, since he could move about freely to help those in need. Moreover, his association with prisoners made him attractive in his Zacatecas context to those in compromised economic situations or feelings of being trapped by circumstances or sickness. This extended his appeal to the many miners in the region but also those who were victims of violence, unchecked illness, or oppressive relationships. In 1848 a man named Calixto Aguirre wrote and widely published a novena to the Santo Niño de Atocha, which both documented the growth of the Niño's cult and contributed to its spread. As part of the nine-day prayer sequence, various miracles attributed to the Holy Child were memorialized in prose and in etchings that depicted him as a young boy in pilgrim's dress, roaming about the Mexican countryside helping the dispossessed. In the various miracles in the novena, the Santo Niño brings food to an imprisoned woman and advocates in the courts for her release, heals the victims of violence, protects miners from danger, and cures various internal ailments.[8]

Juan Javier Pescador convincingly argues that the rise of the Santo Niño in this period is closely mapped to the rise of the liberal Mexican state and the accompanying decline in clerical authority. Not only did the little pilgrim help the working and agricultural classes against the vagaries related to the precarious nature of their lives, he also responded to their physical and legal needs directly, without the intercession of priests or Church-sponsored liturgies. Pescador explains that "the narratives [in the novena] did not portray religious authorities in indispensable roles, and in no case do they appear as the initiators or facilitators of the miraculous interventions." He adds that priests and members of the Catholic hierarchy remained "outsiders in the relationship between the faithful and the Santo Niño de Atocha."[9] It was precisely this autonomy of the Santo Niño, in combination with his grassroots miraculous power, that made him such a popular focus of devotion for the independent-minded Hispanos of the northern Río Grande, who, in this same period, were seeking ways of maintaining their religious traditions in the face of major changes in Catholic oversight of the new U.S. territory of New Mexico.

The Santo Niño in Chimayó and the Commodities of Devotion

After the publication of Calixto Aguirre's novena in 1848, the popularity of the Santo Niño began to spread widely throughout Mexico and Central America, though there is evidence that he was venerated in New Mexico even before this date. A *bulto* of the Christ Child, not Atocha, was listed in the 1818 inventory of the Santuario de Chimayó, but the Santo Niño was also on the scene in the art of a prolific artist of the period known only as the "Santo Niño *santero*," named thus for his favorite subject. The Santo Niño de Atocha's cult had most certainly been introduced to northern New Mexico by 1857, when a girl in Santa Cruz was christened Manuela de Atocha.[10] An additional datum that suggests that devotion to the miraculous Child was especially strong in the Santa Cruz de la Cañada area is that by 1864 there was record of a small village near Santa Cruz that had taken for its own name El Santo Niño.[11]

Of course, the devotion to the Santo Niño must have been growing in the region prior to these clear signs of it in the historical record. This means that Bernardo Abeyta, in his later years as owner and steward of the Santuario and its central sacred objects—namely, the Señor de Esquipulas and the holy dirt—was very likely quite aware of the meteoric rise of the Santo Niño in the devotional lives of his neighbors, and perhaps in his own intercessions as well. As a businessman, he must have also been aware of the trends and shifts related to this new cult. E. Boyd, the premier curator and art historian in twentieth-century New Mexico, carried out a close comparison of inventories of the goods present in the Santuario in its first decades. By examining the changes between the 1818 and the 1826 inventories, reported to the Diocese of Durango, Boyd could conclude that, as of the later date, sales were taking place from within the Santuario: "Wax, candles, wine, rings for arras [tapestries], embroideries and even little dust cloths might be construed as property of the chapel, but such quantities of blankets, yardage of cloth and carpeting, pairs of hose, and miscellaneous reliquaries and ex-votos point only to a stock in trade." Given the unusually high number of *santos* and *bultos*, Boyd speculates that these items may also have been available for purchase. Adding to this semi-commercial portrait of the Santuario are two additional facts. First, a man named Juan Vigil was employed by Abeyta to be his storekeeper and salesperson. And second, the atypical layout of the Santuario includes the two rooms adjacent to the entrance before the nave of the church itself; these rooms are best explained as storerooms for Abeyta's inventory of goods for sale.[12]

The fact that the Santuario—like nearly all places of pilgrimage—served then, as it does now, as a place of both religious and commercial functions is not surprising. The introduction of the Santo Niño and his intense and immediate popularity help us understand the forces at play in Chimayó that tied together the semi-autonomous Catholicism of the people and the ritual and commercial arrangements they had in place to accommodate their economic needs. The two main historiographical approaches to explaining the incorporation of the Santo Niño into the essential character of the Santuario both deal, in different ways, with the ideas of religious competition and collaboration. In what follows, I look at these two approaches to understanding the Santo Niño at the Santuario with a focus on how the devotion to the little and miraculous Christ Child was claimed and centered in various privately owned but publicly used religious spaces.

The first and most common historiographical strategy to explain the Santo Niño's rise in popularity at the Santuario can be called the "religious competition" approach. In this explanatory framework, devotion to Catholic images like Esquipulas, the Santo Niño de Atocha, or other images popular in New Mexico such as San Francisco, San Juan Nepomuceno, or Our Lady of Guadalupe is tied to the commercial as well as the transactional nature of the people's relationships to their saints. Saints and images of Jesus receive intercessions because they are powerful granters of favor. The sick are healed, the weak are strengthened, and the imprisoned are given justice in response to the prayers, promises, and other devotions of the faithful. In this devotional context, the weaker party—the intercessor—is yet able to exert influence, and even make demands, on the stronger party—the saint. There are countless stories from Latin America and other parts of the Catholic world in which images or statues of saints are disciplined in order to encourage them to produce the desired results. An example from New Mexico is a story about the Santo Niño. It is told that, in 1862, a group of Navajo abducted a Hispano child from the village of Placitas, just north of Albuquerque. The distraught mother took her image of the Santo Niño de Atocha from his honored place on a shelf in the house and stuffed him away into a box. Not many days afterward, the woman heard the sound of bells coming from inside the box. Opening it to find the source of the ringing, she retrieved the Niño and put him back on his shelf. Moments later, her kidnapped son walked across the field in front of the house and through the front door. This story is typical not only because it features

two of the Santo Niño's specialties, the care of children and the liberation of prisoners, but also for the way the mother was able to compel the
Holy Child's intervention by hiding his image away.[13]

But these kinds of exchanges between saint and devotee are only one
aspect of the religious competition argument. Another aspect deals with
how religious authorities, institutions, and private individuals can, and
often do, use intercessory devotions for commercial or other kinds of
gain. In these cases, access to the source of divine power is traded for
money, influence, or other items of value. These contexts of exchange
depend on religious ownership or control of access to divine power. In
other words, the ownership of an image, a sacred place, or access to a series of ritual actions provides the opportunity for economic exchanges,
whether these be in the form of charging for services (as in the Catholic
Church's collection of tithes or other fees for administration of the Mass)
or as a way of attracting "customers" to one's place of business (as in the
case of Abeyta's Santuario, which offered free access to the holy dirt and
sacred images but offered goods for sale nearby). Of course, if someone
is able to offer religious access more effectively or more inexpensively,
religious competition arises as devotees seek to get the best value.[14]

This contention is at the heart of the "religious competition" approach
to the rise of the Santo Niño in Chimayó. In brief, this argument claims
that a contemporary of Bernardo Abeyta named Severiano Medina went
to Fresnillo in Zacatecas and purchased a statue of the Santo Niño. He
returned to Chimayó with the ascendant image and built a chapel just
yards away from Abeyta's Santuario sometime in the 1850s in order to
take economic advantage of some of the pilgrim traffic. Devotion to the
Santo Niño had already been growing all around the region, and word
had spread that the Child Jesus was active all over the Santa Cruz valley at night, miraculously meeting the needs of his devotees, so much
so that the little sandals on his feet were often worn bare. Although not
the originator of this version of events, Stephan de Borhegyi's influential
account of the history of the Santuario repeats this etiology for Medina's
Santo Niño Chapel, and Borhegyi also reiterates how the Santo Niño
found his way into the Santuario: "In a desperate attempt to rescue the
dwindling revenue the owners of the Santuario, the Chaves [sic] family,
obtained another Santo Niño figure and announced that in the Santuario, not only the Santo Niño but San José, San Rafael, and Santiago also

Figure 4.1. The Medina Chapel, often known as the Santo Niño Chapel, 1925–1945? T. Harmon Parkhurst, courtesy of Palace of the Governors Photo Archives (NMHM/ DCA), 008934.

traveled through the country at night and needed new shoes." By placing their new Santo Niño *bulto* in the room adjacent to the *pocito* of holy earth, the Chavez family furthered "the confusion that already existed. The Santo Niño now reigns supreme in both churches."[15]

That the Medina Chapel was originally built specifically to house a devotion to the Santo Niño de Atocha is not certain; in fact, the first mention of the place in association with the Christ Child is not until 1936.[16] And it was not until 1948, almost a hundred years after the Medina Chapel was built, that the Anglo American folklorist and writer Elizabeth DeHuff somehow came by the story of religious competition between the Medina and Chavez families over the devotion to the Santo Niño. Her version of events, though poorly documented, soon came to dominate historical accounts concerning the presence of the devotion in the Santuario. As mentioned, Borhegyi uncritically accepted DeHuff's story and even accentuated the fear of monetary loss as the main motivator for the emplacement of the Santo Niño in the Santuario. The historian Ramón Gutiérrez likewise accepts the competition argument between the two families, but he is less sardonic about the Medina family's original motivations for their chapel. Instead of attributing the new chapel to a bald grab for profit, Gutiérrez recounts legendary causes for the chapel akin in tone to Abeyta's miraculous encounters with the Lord of Esquipulas. One story holds that Medina was cured of rheumatism by praying to the Santo Niño and so built the chapel in gratitude. Another focuses on the proliferation of the Niño's nighttime miracles around La Cañada. Yet another echoes the story from Placitas: a man and his daughter were in the vicinity of the Santuario when they heard a bell ringing from under the ground. When the man dug up the bell, he also found a statue of the Santo Niño, and the chapel was built to house the miraculous image.[17]

Two questions are raised. First, did Severiano Medina build his chapel specifically for the veneration of the Santo Niño de Atocha? And second, did he build the chapel in order to compete with Abeyta's Santuario? The "religious competition" argument answers both questions affirmatively and necessarily links the two questions together. But as we move into an examination of the second major historiographical approach to the Santo Niño in Chimayó, it is worth noting that if Medina did *not* desire to compete with the Santuario for pilgrims' business, then there is less reason to believe that his chapel was originally built to be a site of popular and public veneration. It *may* have been built as a result of Medina's deep and personal devotion to the Santo Niño, but it just as likely could be the result of a variety of religious and community motivations.

In short, the second explanation as to why the Santo Niño gained ascendancy in Chimayó argues that the Medina Chapel was merely a Penitente *morada* located near the Santuario that had little or nothing to do with Holy Child of Atocha. (*Morada* is the name for the church-like structures built by Penitente orders in which to carry out their meetings and some of their ritual activities.) In this line of reasoning, the Santuario was the place where the Niño was first introduced in Chimayó, and his cult grew there and only later came to occupy a place of importance in the Medina Chapel. The main proponent of this argument is the historian Juan Javier Pescador, whose close research reveals that no mention of the Santo Niño in relation to the Medina Chapel is made in the historical record until after the sale of the Santuario to the Archdiocese of Santa Fe in 1929 (see chapter 5). Rather, there are multiple suggestions that Medina's chapel was used not as a public church or secondary pilgrimage site but merely as a gathering place for the local order of Penitente Brothers.

To make his case, Pescador first notes that María Martínez, during her 1890 visits to Chimayó as a child, did not visit the Medina Chapel but instead encountered the Santo Niño in the Santuario. Likewise, her father identifies a nearby church-like structure as a Penitente *morada*.[18] More convincing is Pescador's second piece of evidence: none of the principal journalistic or historical sources about Chimayó from the early decades of the twentieth century identify Medina's chapel with the Atocha veneration. In fact, one of these sources from 1916, in obvious reference to Medina's building, writes that near the Santuario "is the campanile of another church with an interesting God's acre, ascribed to the Penitentes or Flagellantes. It is one of the few real campaniles in the Southwest, a tower all by itself and separate from the main auditorium."[19] His final piece of evidence is a 1935 dissertation on the Penitentes by Dorothy Woodward. Woodward clearly and repeatedly identifies the Medina Chapel as a Penitente *morada*.[20] In sum, there is no documentary record before 1936 of the Medina Chapel being a major site of cultic competition for the Santuario. Moreover, while there is no reason to believe that the Santo Niño was unimportant to Severiano Medina, there is no historical evidence that he promoted a public veneration of the Niño in the building that multiple sources claim was a *morada* rather than a shrine.

If Pescador's revisionist answer to the "religious competition" arguments is true, then the Santo Niño's rise to become the central figure of devotion in the Santuario de Chimayó must be accounted for in some other way. In other words, if the Abeyta and Chavez families did not install their own Santo Niño to compete with the Medinas, then why and when did the Holy Child come to enjoy his current importance in the Santuario? The most likely answer is that the Santo Niño's tremendous growth in regional importance throughout Mexico and New Mexico in the late nineteenth century made him a desirable figure, and his presence in the Santuario is a natural extension of the people's devotional needs and foci. The Santo Niño's care for children, his nightly forays to help the needy, and his special care for the disenfranchised made him a powerful ally to the Hispano and Native American populations in the Río Arriba area during a time of intense political and economic transitions.

From Crucified Lord to Miraculous Child: Changing Sources of Christian Power at the Santuario

The shift in devotional focus at the Santuario de Chimayó from the legendary crucifix of the Lord of Esquipulas to the miracle-working figure of the Holy Child of Atocha shows that popular Catholic religious commitments can and do change in response both to shifting needs and to novel characters and narratives that arise. As we have seen, this process of change at the Santuario was not a clean break between Esquipulas and Atocha; rather, the stories of the former concerning emergence from the ground overlapped onto the latter even as did the miraculous power of the healing dirt. In this sense, there is continuity of sorts between the two images, and the continuity has to do not with the fact that they are both images of Jesus at different points in his life but with the miraculous power that he channels and represents in response to the people's needs. Historically, it is impossible to reconstruct exactly why New Mexicans moved their allegiance from the Santuario's legendary crucifix to the Santo Niño during the second half of the nineteenth century, and the historical records from that time do not provide the kind of ethnographic interviewing that would offer us insight into people's motivations and decisions. Instead, as we have observed, the available material focuses on the commerce of pilgrimage shrines as well as on accounts of the Niño's growing fame as a miracle worker. While precise answers explaining the change in devotion at the Santuario may elude us, it is yet possible to examine contextual factors and shifts that can help us account for the Niño's sudden rise in popularity and his ongoing dominance.

First, we must wonder how a common image like the crucified Christ, so central to the Gospel accounts of Jesus's life and his theological significance in Christianity, could be supplanted by an image of Jesus as a boy, a representation that is not important in the canon of Christian scriptures or in Catholic Christology. One possible answer to this conundrum is to recall the origin of the Santo Niño de Atocha as a statuary attachment to Our Lady of Atocha, a Spanish version of the Virgin Mary, who later found herself exported throughout the Spanish Empire. If the Santo Niño is understood in relationship to Mary, as a typical component in thousands of depictions of the Madonna with Child, then, by extension, we can associate the Holy Child with Catholic Marian devotions. To be sure, Marianism has long been a central feature of Spanish Catholicism and of the Spanish evangelization of the so-called New World.[21] The absolute ubiquity in Mexico of the Virgin of Guadalupe and the strong devotions to Our Lady of San Juan de Los Lagos and Our Lady of Zapopán tend to overpower devotions to particular images of Jesus. However, there is evidence that images of the crucified Christ and the passion and suffering of Jesus had greater purchase earlier in the history of New Spain and Mexico. For instance, the anthropologist Jennifer Scheper Hughes has found that, in gross terms, there have been more devotions to the crucified Christ in Mexico than to his mother.[22] In New Mexico, the history of the Penitente Brotherhood is highly Christocentric, with a pronounced and well-known commitment to the suffering of the Christian Passion. The Penitentes' central figure of devotion has always been Nuestro Padre Jesús Nazareno, an often life-sized image or *bulto* of the suffering Christ, his body pierced and whipped and a crown of thorns upon his head. In his study of the Brotherhood, the historian Michael Carroll finds that historical Penitente devotion mentioned Mary only as a device to accentuate the suffering of Jesus.[23]

Despite the Christocentric proclivity of popular devotions in early nineteenth-century New Mexico, there is reason to believe that the Marianism so popular throughout Latin America had begun to make significant inroads by the mid- and late nineteenth century. To be sure, the French clerics who entered New Mexico after U.S. annexation were deeply committed to Mary and to the Marian devotion of the rosary.[24] Of course, the Santo Niño is not Mary, but if we consider the Holy Child to be a Christ figure with a direct connection to the mothering care and nurture of the Virgin, he may have achieved popularity in northern New Mexico because of his ability to "bridge the gap" between the suffering adult Jesus and the family-oriented holy Mother of God. Although there is no historical evidence of this, Carroll reasonably speculates that Bernardo Abeyta's commitment to the Christ-figure of Esquipulas may have been maintained largely through Abeyta's personal devotional life rather than by popular acclamation. After his death in 1856, the growing cult to Atocha was able to quickly enter the Santuario, buoyed by New Mexicans who found a boy Jesus to be more suitable to their needs than the Guatemalan crucifix.[25]

To be sure, the particular specialties of the Holy Child—perhaps more than his conceptual connections to his Virgin Mother—also explain his quick rise to prominence in the Santuario. As a protector of the weak, of the oppressed or imprisoned, and especially of children, the Niño could provide the kinds of immediate succor that people requested in their intercessions. Several of the Child's fantastical interventions in the lives of children have already been mentioned as well as the various miracles that form the basis of the 1848 novena. These stories allow little doubt that devotees have long appreciated the Santo Niño's capacity to meet them in their places of trial and need and to accompany them tenderly with his basket of food and gourd of water. His status as a boy is itself significant, argues the historian Alexander Frankfurter, who connects the Santo Niño de Atocha with numerous other Christ Child devotions from around the Catholic world. Frankfurter suggests that a child, as opposed to more challenging images of Christ, is "compelling and un-threatening," and resonates with the experiences of those who may be caught between "both strength and weakness."[26] The Child contributes to a devotional setting where childlike gentleness and lack of guile be-come qualities that translate to powerful protection for the small and the weak. Hence, the much-attested symbol of Atocha devotion has long been and continues to be a pair of children's shoes. These shoes, which the faithful leave by the dozens in the Santuario, are not only replace-ments for the ones that the Niño wears out in his nightly rounds but also talismans of protection for devotees' own children.

Yet another possible reason for the Santo Niño's popularity at the San-tuario has to do not with his boyhood but with his status as a pilgrim. The art historian Yvonne Lange has studied many images of the Atocha Child in *retablos* and devotional paintings on tin (*láminas*), and observes that they come in two variations: with and without leg irons. In all cases, however, the little boy wears the clothing and carries the paraphernalia associated with Spanish pilgrimage. He is generally seated and wears a long robe, a traveling cape, and a wide-brimmed hat to protect his face and head from the elements. The cape is often adorned with the cockle-shell, a symbol of baptism and the vows of faithfulness that motivate the pilgrim; he likewise carries other items associated with pilgrimage such as a staff, a water gourd, and, occasionally, a basket filled with bread, symbolic of the Eucharist. When the image of the Santo Niño includes

Figure 4.2. Statue of the Santo Niño de Atocha, located
in the sacristy of the Santuario. Author's photo.

shackles, this likely signals a blending of the Atocha Niño with the Niño
Cautivo, a less popular image of the Christ Child in Mexico City. In Atocha's legend, the shackles refer not to the other Holy Child but rather
to the Niño's narrative connection to the imprisoned.[27] Some have suggested that the image of the Santo Niño in the Santuario is actually a
Holy Child of Prague that has been refitted and dressed as Atocha.[28] This
would likewise suggest that the pilgrim aspects of the Child rather than
a precise provenance of the statue or image are what allow the Niño to
resonate with his devotees. Pescador confirms this, suggesting that the
pilgrim identity of the Niño reflects the needs of the people in the Mexican milieu in which he arose. Instead of emphasizing colonial authority,
as did the original Babe connected to the imperial Lady of Atocha, the

emergent and stand-alone pilgrim boy nodded to the "wandering and motion" that marked the lives of Mexican farmers, miners, and townspeople. A pilgrim boy was much more able to carry out the desired miracles of liberation and assistance than a stationary baby.[29]

Finally, the miraculousness and accessibility of the Santo Niño are likely what most contributed to his sudden popularity at the Santuario. In this regard, he can be understood less as a boy version of Jesus Christ, the central figure of Christianity, and more as a young member of the assortment of saints—both officially canonized and folk—that dot Latin America and are extremely popular in the Mexico-U.S. border region.[30] There is no doubt that the Santo Niño originated as the Christ Child, a boy version of Jesus. However, the faithful pilgrims who go to the Santuario to fulfill promises to the Niño and to seek his intercession treat him so identically to how other saints are treated that it is easy to dissociate him from Jesus, the Son of God.[31] In this sense, the Santo Niño, as a miracle worker and granter of petitions, is a more obvious partner to work alongside the holy dirt of the *pocito* than the suffering and magisterial Christ upon the Esquipulas crucifix. This point, however, should not be taken too far, since advocations of Jesus Christ are commonly venerated like saints throughout Latin America. Examples include the Cristo de Chalma and the Cristo de Totolapan in Mexico and the Lord of Malta in Bolivia, not to mention the Lord of Esquipulas in Guatemala.[32] At issue is devotees' access to divine power; in many cases, but not all, that power is more directly available through a saint, or through a Christ acting like a saint. And so the accessible and relatable Santo Niño gains ascendancy over the Esquipulas crucifix, not because the latter is not powerful but because the Child is more approachable, and perhaps even more prone to make deals.

In his study of a borderlands folk saint, the historian Paul Vanderwood explains the appeal of the saint over direct contact with the Triune Godhead of Christianity. He writes that many Catholics

> prefer the services of a go-between—someone close to God but somewhat less awesome, less exalted and so more apt to respond to a human being's trivial needs, and therefore more approachable. Under the circumstances, it makes sense to have an intercessor, an advocate, who is acquainted with the heavenly terrain. So the needy turn to saints . . . whom they find more

Figure 4.3. Visitors to the Santuario often leave pairs of children's shoes for the Santo Niño. Author's photo.

like family, and they expect these saints to carry their concerns to the Almighty. In exchange they promise to extol the saint with prayer and devotion. The premise is that saints need humans as much as people need saints.[33]

The contractual nature of the saint/devotee relationship puts at least some agency in the hands of the petitioner. And the unique aspects of saints often give them specific attractiveness; for instance, as we have seen, the Santo Niño is especially associated with children, the imprisoned, and the sick. The reciprocal relationship that Catholics have with saints, while not equal, represents a better opportunity for a positive outcome, especially if the devotee can make a pilgrimage or offer some other tangible devotion to the saint. Ultimately, what animates devotion to saints, or those who act like saints such as the Santo Niño de Atocha, is their reliability and effectiveness.[34]

The Santo Niño's responsiveness to intercessors' appeals puts those same intercessors in a position of power over their religion. They can become the administrators of their own healing, or the healing of their loved ones, simply by approaching the Niño. For instance, one mother tells her son's story:

> We have what we call the Santo Niño de Atocha there. . . . You get some of that dirt from that little cave that he has there. And, you know, you can take it, and—and you rub it. And let me tell you—I had my son that was very sick. He had, like, a cancer, in the leg. And I had been praying all the time. He was just a little kid. He was maybe not more than ten years old. And I took him to Chimayó. And I put some of that dirt on that leg. My son belongs to the Eighty-second Paratroopers now.[35]

No elaborate theologies, sacred orders, or exegetical skills are needed for the devotee of the Santo Niño; the miracle comes from the Holy Child and the dirt. The semiotician Larry Russell has identified "self-reliance" as one of the major symbolic themes of the Chimayó pilgrimage, and he likewise shows that the Santo Niño is an obvious expression of that self-reliance: "the popularity of the irrepressible Santo Niño reflect[s] the struggle of Hispano village life to survive as a focus of cultural life." Healing, viewed in this context, is obtained because the Holy Child and his devotees insist on it even as these same devotees tenaciously remain central to the everyday life of the Santuario.[36]

The Popular Persistence of the Santo Niño de Atocha at the Santuario

The current administrators of the Santuario, the Sons of the Holy Family and the Archdiocese of Santa Fe, have gone to significant lengths to diminish and refocus popular devotion away from the Santo Niño. The priests of the Sons of the Holy Family have been in charge of the Santuario as a property of the Catholic Church since the 1950s, and their administration of the shrine is covered in more detail in chapter 7. It is appropriate to point out here, however, how the priests have reformulated the narrative, and even the space, of the Santuario to try to reinterpret the Santo Niño's role at the site. The archdiocese bought the Medina Chapel from the Medina family in 1992, after the Church had already owned the adjacent Santuario for over sixty years. By the time of the purchase, the Medina Chapel was well known regionally for its image of the Santo Niño and as a place of auxiliary devotion to the image of the Santo Niño in the Santuario. This situation continued for several years until the current parish pastor in Chimayó, Father Julio González, remodeled the Medina Chapel and renamed it the Children's Chapel, or the Chapel of the Holy Child of Atocha. Since then, publications of the Sons of the Holy Family explain that the Santuario de Chimayó complex consists of two chapels, the Chapel of the Christ of Esquipulas and the rechristened Holy Child Chapel. González and the other priests have endeavored to reconnect the dirt in the Chapel of the Christ of Esquipulas (which everyone continues to call the Santuario) with the Esquipulas crucifix on the main altar screen. The Children's Chapel, still popularly called the Medina Chapel, is home to several elaborate and colorful images of the Santo Niño, on the main *retablo* in that chapel as well as in a dedicated side chapel with a newly carved statue and hundreds of pairs of children's shoes.

A booklet for sale at the Santuario, published by the priests who oversee the two chapels, makes the current official interpretation of the Santo Niño explicit. The text begins with Christological concerns: "The crucified Christ and the Holy Child are the same person." What differs is the focus of devotion. Devotion to the image of the Esquipulas crucifix "points to the suffering and passion of Jesus for the forgiveness of sins, while the devotion to the Holy Child points to the childhood of Jesus." The Medina Chapel, after its redesign, is now replete with bright and often cartoonish depictions of saints and the Holy Family. This aesthetic differentiation with the darker and more somber Santuario is intentional and attempts to connect devotion to the Santo Niño to an idealized childhood and nuclear family: "the Chapel of the Holy Child is devoted to [Jesus's] childhood, the love for life and its colors, to innocence and purity. The Chapel of the Holy Child is a song that praises God for the gift of life and the joyful years of the childhood of Jesus."[37] Other of the priests' publications as well as placards in the visitors' center reconnect the dirt of the *pocito* specifically with the miraculous apparition of the Esquipulas crucifix to Bernardo Abeyta.[38] A tourist or visitor unfamiliar with the Santo Niño who comes today to the Santuario could, based on his or her interaction with display materials, conclude that the Santo Niño has nothing to do with the holy dirt or the purported miracles at the church; this is despite the fact that the vast majority of pilgrims for more than a century have decisively linked the healing and the *pocito* with the Santo Niño de Atocha. Notwithstanding the Catholic Church's public interpretation concerning the Holy Child, an older statue of the Santo Niño remains ensconced with a kneeler in the sacristy of the Santuario. The presence of this object belies the efforts of the priests to move popular devotion in the Santuario building back to the Esquipulas crucifix. The considerable number of hours that I have spent observing devotees and their movements through the space of the Santuario reveal that, after the *pocito* itself, the Santo Niño statue in the sacristy, encased such as it is in a box of dingy white plywood, is the object of the greatest public devotion. People kneel before the statue, often with tears in their eyes, and offer their prayers of intercession and supplication for themselves and their loved ones. It is not uncommon to see a mother encourage her children to kneel and say a prayer, gently showing them how to cross themselves and to brush their fingers on the statue. In contrast, the remodeled Medina Chapel, for all its vibrancy and new artwork, is often empty or occupied solely by tourists moving around its interior in the way people mill about an art museum.

* * *

By the end of the nineteenth century and continuing to the present, the Santo Niño de Atocha, understood as the boy Christ or as an autonomous and powerful folk saint, has been the central figure of devotion at the Santuario de Chimayó. The history of his presence and influence at the church appears to be rooted, at least in part, in the commerce and proprietary relationships that surround religious shrines and pilgrimage sites. Whether the Santo Niño in Chimayó emerged first in Abeyta's Santuario or in the Medina Chapel has led historians to speculate on the role of religious and economic competition in this devotion. Likewise, Atocha's persistent popularity has led us to reflect on how a pilgrim boy, the son of Mary and a personality who seems open to exchanges and promises, has outshone the much more orthodox, but perhaps less accessible, image of the crucified Lord of Esquipulas. The Holy Child belongs to his devotees in a way that means he is approachable and constant, and maybe even a little pliable. He is loved because he is close, and he makes things happen. This kind of popular ownership of religious power, although related to the physical space, tradition, and Catholic nature of the Santuario, transcends and challenges legal or material claims of ownership as well as doctrinal authority. These kinds of ownership and authority inevitably overlay each other, sometimes in cooperation, sometimes in contestation, but just as often with seemingly no interaction whatsoever. In the following chapter, we move to a discussion of the ownership of the Santuario not only as real estate but as an idea of beauty in the eyes of diverse beholders. In this story of physical sale and Anglo fascination with the aesthetics of the Santuario, the Santo Niño and his utter salience for Hispanic devotion in northern Mexico and the Southwestern United States figure not at all.

5

Selling the Santuario

By the time New Mexico became the forty-seventh state in 1912, the Santuario was nearing its centennial. The transition from territorial status to statehood at first had little effect on Chimayó, and the church remained a locally and regionally important place of pilgrimage for Hispanics within the expanding nation. However, changes were on the horizon as more and more people from the eastern part of the country made their way west, some of them settling permanently in the Río Arriba region. Among some of the new visitors and settlers from the east, a trope emerged that cast New Mexico as a place where ancient Pueblo civilization came together with Spanish gentility to create a gracious home for adventurous Anglos. For some, this created an environment in which elite New Mexicans, especially those with an artistic bent, began to think of the Santuario as a place of timeless innocence, a folk relic of a more spiritually wise people.[1]

Early twentieth-century descriptions of the simple devotion of the people in Chimayó serve as a microcosm of widespread Anglo attitudes concerning the Hispano population and Hispano aesthetic in northern New Mexico. For instance, former territorial governor Bradford Prince, president of both the Historical Society of New Mexico and the Society for the Preservation of Spanish Antiquities, intoned in 1915,

> The people [of Chimayó] are contented to live almost entirely on the products of their own valley. Money is little needed where requirements for happiness are so few; and the community illustrates the philosophy of content, which proclaims that happiness is not attained by the multiplication of possessions, but by the satisfaction of a few real wants of man, and the absence of desire for anything that is unattained.[2]

This romanticized vision of Nuevomexicano village life was deeply attractive for eastern transplants even while it ignored the significant political, demographic, and economic changes that were occurring in the new state.

Northern New Mexican villages like Taos, Abiquiu, and Chimayó— due to a growing tourist industry—began in this period to be valued for their picturesque qualities. Tourists in automobiles learned about destination points from travel brochures produced by new businesses catering to these visitors. A 1929 Santa Fe Transportation Bulletin recommended a stop at Chimayó to observe the Santuario; the information provided demonstrates that the shrine was not merely of architectural interest but also exposed the tourist to the exotic cultural practices of a credulous and perhaps magical people and their healing dirt:

> The usual method employed to obtain the benefit desired was to take a small amount of the earth and make of it a sort of tea, or drink. Those who came from a distance usually took back with them a small quantity of the earth as a safe-guard against possible illness in the future. If an invalid were too ill to be brought to the "Sanctuario" [sic], earth was taken to him. However one may account for these strange results, it cannot be doubted that there are possibly hundreds who attribute their health and healing to the miraculous power of the "Sanctuario."[3]

The brochure does not advertise healing for the Anglo tourist but rather the opportunity to gaze upon a people who were being healed by the holy dirt, a manufactured experience of imagined simplicity and immediate faith. And since the Santuario remained in the hands of the Abeyta and Chávez family, visitors in the earliest decades of the century could visit the private church without the imposition of official Catholic interpretations of the healing miracles.

Indeed, the relationship of the people of Chimayó with the Santuario in the early twentieth century remained, in key ways, outside the control of the Catholic Church, meaning that the rituals and healing miracles that persisted in the chapel remained distinctly connected to Hispano village life. To be sure, priests could be called upon for baptisms, marriages, and deaths, but they had to travel from Santa Cruz. The majority of the time, the Santuario, the Oratorio on the Plaza del Cerro, and other local chapels in the village served as gathering places for the faithful for prayer and festival celebrations.

Due to this ongoing dearth of official Catholic oversight, Chimayó in the first decades of the twentieth century continued to be a place where the Penitentes carried out both their fervent rites and their pastoral mission to local families in grief or need. The Santuario itself was likely a site of Penitente ritual, given Bernardo Abeyta's personal leadership role in the Brotherhood, as was the Medina Chapel (see chapter 4), and the nearby Plaza del Cerro likewise witnessed much Penitente activity. Holy Week featured various Penitente rites and processions through Chimayó and the surrounding communities. Residents who were children in the early years of the century later remembered impressions of late-night chanting and praying, bleeding torsos from penitential self-flagellation, and particular ritual reenactments. These included Good Friday observances of the Stations of the Cross, community singing of hymns, and solemn meat-free meals.[4]

Despite the religious vitality of Chimayó, national and international forces well beyond the bounds of northern New Mexico were inevitably affecting the rhythms of life. The arrival of the railroad in Española in 1880 had already ushered in a new era of outside access to the region's natural resources. Nuevomexicanos in the rural economies of the villages were attracted to wage-earning jobs in these new extractive industries as well as on the railroad itself.[5] As men and women left the villages, often seasonally, for outside labor, the patterns of land usage and mutual support changed. The historian Suzanne Forrest suggests that these economic transformations resulted in at least two important cultural changes. First, the semi-communal use of land for agriculture was disrupted when an individual's productivity and earnings began to outweigh prior mutual goals centered on livestock and crops. If, for example, a young man was away working on the railroads or in lumber during planting season, his reliance on his wages was matched by his lack of involvement in village agricultural production. Second, the transfer to a money-based system left villagers more open than ever before to the fluctuations of national capitalist markets.[6] While this meant economic success for some, most Hispanos remained tied to menial and low-paying jobs even as the mutual support of village life became less and less reliable. The Santuario, yet in private hands, likewise found itself tied to these inevitable changes.

On the eve of the Great Depression, the Chávez family's stewardship of the Santuario suggests that the family, like many others in the region, had fallen into dire circumstances. The Santuario with its sculpture and artwork had always been valuable to pilgrims and devotees as a place of prayer, healing, celebration, and contemplation. But in the changing economic environment, the Chávezes found themselves in what must have been the excruciating position of selling items associated with the church. A front-page story in the *Santa Fe New Mexican* from February 9, 1929, reports that the family had already sold three *bultos* to the Spanish and Indian Trading Company and that other dealers and art collectors in Santa Fe had been offered the Santuario's carved wooden doors. Others were reporting that the entire church was for sale. Unconcerned with the plight of the family, the newspaper pleads, "Is the 'Lourdes of America', the world-famed chapel of Sanctuario of Chimayo, painted by a score of artists, declared by many the most beautiful thing in New Mexico, to be dismantled, its sacred relics peddled to curio dealers, and the ancient Place of Miracles to be used for some commercial purpose?"[7]

The short answer was no. But this was a turning point for the Santuario.

Anglo Preservationists and the Spanish Colonial Arts Society

Mary Austin, the author of over thirty-five books and numerous plays and essays, had settled in Santa Fe in 1924 after a peripatetic and eruditely adventurous life. She found Santa Fe, and New Mexico in general, a fit place to be her "land of journey's ending." In this, she was certainly not alone among the literati of the era. Several other artists, writers, and culture mavens settled in a colony of sorts on the famed El Camino del Monte Sol in Santa Fe, a narrow and winding street lined with quaint adobe cottages. The artist Frank Applegate was her nearby neighbor and frequent collaborator. Others in the general area included Alice Corbin Henderson, Gustave Baumann, and John Gaw Meem; farther afield, Georgia O'Keeffe, Mabel Dodge Luhan, and occasionally D. H. Lawrence were also part of her circle. Along with Luhan's house in Taos, Austin's home on El Camino, La Casa Querida, served as a frequent salon and guest quarters for members of this new Anglo cultural elite.[8]

Austin loved New Mexico for all of the normal reasons: its incredible topography, its climate, and its seeming otherness within the United

States. But she also loved it for what she referred to often as the "Indian blood" of the people, both in the Pueblos and in the admixture she discerned in the Hispano villager. The people of New Mexico themselves, or at least as they appeared in Austin's mind, became for her a project of curation and restoration that would guide her in her new home. She declared, "What I felt in New Mexico was the possibility of the reinstatement of the hand-craft culture and of the folk drama."[9] Her first impulse was to collect and save—she feared that the simplicity, guilelessness, and familial morality of New Mexico's villagers were under threat, and she worried that these same villagers did not have either the tools or the inclination to preserve their own historical way of life. Her new friend Frank Applegate, of like mind, had long been collecting *santos*, hand-crafted furniture, and punched tin.

On the one hand, Applegate had dreamed of organizing some kind of revival of Hispano village crafts to stimulate the desperate economic situations of many in the state. On the other hand, Applegate wanted to preserve a particular aesthetic that appealed to him and his artist friends who, like him, had hoped to find in New Mexico an antidote to their disenchantment with modernity. This latter impulse potentially conflicted with the former objective of economic development for the villages. The historian Charles Montgomery notes, "'Reviving' Spanish colonial craftsmanship in the 1920s meant discouraging innovation and subduing techniques that did not suit preferred notions of authenticity." These notions, adds Montgomery, were "premised on a highly selective and stylized story of efflorescence and decline."[10] Austin, who concurred wholeheartedly with Applegate's vision, soon joined him, gathering Hispano folk literature, drama, and songs. Together, they became some of the most active exponents of the preservation of an idealized vision of New Mexico's Spanish and Indian past.

Before Austin's arrival in New Mexico, an earlier group had organized itself in 1913 into the Society for the Preservation of Spanish Antiquities in New Mexico, but it was under Austin's and Applegate's leadership that this group was transformed and eventually settled on the name of the Spanish Colonial Arts Society. The 1929 certificate of incorporation for the society defines its work not only in terms of preservation but also in terms of revival and supervision. The mission of the members was "to acquire, preserve, and protect places, property, both real and personal, things and articles relating to or exemplifying or representing Spanish Colonial art, and to provide for the custody thereof; to restore places, things, buildings and property, both real and personal relating to or exemplifying Spanish Colonial art."[11] In response to what it considered to be the destruction of traditional New Mexico village life and culture, the society focused itself on acquisition and custodianship. Its members believed that it was only through the society's proper oversight and vision that the handiwork, folk life, and aesthetic integrity of New Mexico's Hispano past would be rebuilt, maintained, and, ideally, sealed in time, like an ancient creature caught in amber. Austin understood the society, thus, to be ultimately responsible for what she described as the "rebuilding of that shattered culture."[12]

Another key figure in the revival of the so-called Spanish colonial arts was the architect John Gaw Meem. Meem was one of the foremost exponents of the "Spanish Pueblo style," marked by adobe construction, flat roofs, exposed beams, and other features reminiscent of both Pueblo and Spanish mission buildings. Following in the footsteps of other architects who had pioneered this style around the Southwest and California in the first decades of the twentieth century, Meem left an indelible mark on New Mexico's cities.[13] However, one of his initial interests and inspirations was New Mexico's various village churches, including the Santuario de Chimayó. Early in the 1920s he served as the supervising architect for a group dedicated to these places called the Committee for the Preservation and Restoration of New Mexico Mission Churches.[14] No doubt, Meem's expertise and aesthetic vision made him an ideal candidate to join with Austin and Applegate in the Spanish Colonial Arts Society.

After the official incorporation of the group in October 1929, the society's first action was to purchase a *retablo* from the Llano Quemado chapel south of Taos, but the plight of the Santuario soon piqued members' interest. The artist Gustave Baumann had also sent word that the Santuario's unique *bulto* of Santiago astride his horse had already been sold and that other pieces were on the block. His intelligence on the situation was passed along to E. Dana Johnson, the editor of the *Santa Fe New Mexican*, at which point the paper published news of the impending sale of the chapel's artworks and architectural features.[15]

It is not surprising that Johnson would make this front-page news; while he himself was not a member of the Spanish Colonial Arts Soci-

Figure 5.1. *Bulto* of Santiago on his horse, once sold but now restored to the Santuario. Author's photo.

ety, like many in his social circle, he was committed to maintaining the aesthetic and cultural distinctiveness of his adopted state. In his obituary, society member Alice Corbin Henderson wrote, "[Johnson] supported every cause and movement that tended to keep New Mexico, and Santa Fé its ancient capital, a symbol of the races that made it— to preserve its essential character and integrity."[16] The unsigned story (likely by Johnson himself) that detailed the Santuario's plight lists several cultural preservation organizations that had already voiced interest in raising funds for the Santuario's purchase, including Meem's church preservation group, the New Mexico Historical Society, and, of course, the Spanish Colonial Arts Society. Conspicuously absent from the list is the Archdiocese of Santa Fe; in fact, the article cites Santa Fe's Father Bernard, who confirms that "there was nothing in the rumor that it was desired to build a Catholic Chapel on the site. He said it had not been used for Catholic services for many years."[17]

When the story broke, Mary Austin was lecturing at Yale, a vantage point that allowed her to move quickly to raise the six thousand dollars necessary to purchase the Santuario outright from the beleaguered

Chávez family. The great majority of historical sources about the sale describe the donor as anonymous, although Austin did identify the person as Catholic and is elsewhere said to be a "Yale alumnus."[18] The poet and New Mexico transplant Winfield Townley Scott at one time claimed that the donor was Olivia Murray Cutting, the mother of New Mexico senator Bronson Cutting.[19] The latter was a trustee on the board of the Spanish Colonial Arts Society, which suggests he may have facilitated a gift from his mother, but the donor's identity is likely unknowable.

The 1929 Sale

The actual handover of funds to the Chávez family came together as a piece of newsworthy theater. At some point in the weeks prior to the Santuario's sale, the archbishop of Santa Fe, Albert T. Daeger, had been made the chair of the Spanish Colonial Arts Society, and so it was from his hand that the money officially was exchanged during a staged ceremony of transfer. Other society members present at the ceremony included Meem, Austin, Applegate, Alice Corbin Henderson, and Gustave Baumann. The newspaper editor Johnson and several others were also present as witnesses. The deed of the property, importantly, did not go to the Spanish Colonial Arts Society but was turned over immediately to the Archdiocese of Santa Fe; indeed, the image that remains from the sale features Meem handing the deed to Archbishop Daeger while a man who may be José Chávez stands in the background. The article that covered the story of the sale in the *Santa Fe New Mexican* reports that a "delegation from Chimayo headed by Jose Chavez" was on hand, but no other mention is made of the locals, and only Meem is quoted: "One more beautiful and historic thing associated with Santa Fe has been preserved." Meem went on to say that church services would be restored to the building as soon as possible.[20] His comments suggest that Meem and others from the society had achieved their goals. First, the picturesque history and aspect of the Santuario as viewed by Santa Fe Anglos had been maintained intact, and second, the scope of Santa Fe's artistic and touristic circle had unquestionably been expanded the thirty miles to the north to encompass the shrine as a sort of extension or outpost of the aesthetic ideals of Canyon Road and El Camino del Monte Sol. Even the reinstatement of Catholic Masses in the Santuario,

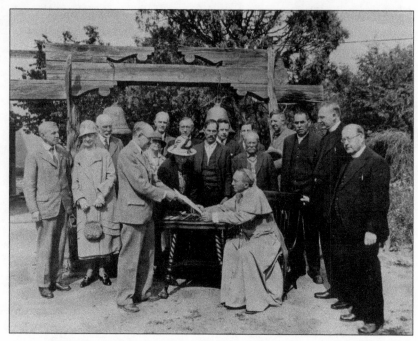

Figure 5.2. John Gaw Meem presents the deed to the Santuario to Archbishop Daeger, 1929. The woman in the white hat near Meem is Mary Austin. The two men to her left are members of the Chávez family. Beatrice Chauvenet Pictorial Collection, Center for Southwest Research, University of New Mexico.

for the Santa Fe observers, was less about restoring the pious function of the place and more about retaining the folk drama of village rituals.

It is remarkable to what extent Austin's and Applegate's romantic preservationist objectives were met in Chimayó. It is worth quoting at length from a letter that Applegate sent to Austin dated February 20, 1929, fully eight months before the sale was finalized:

> Just at present, the Sanctuario seems to be safe. The people of Chimayo have gotten together and will not allow the old man who claims he owns it to sell. Also, they came down to Santa Fe together and took back the Bultos, including Santiago, and the large chest back to the Sanctuario today. . . .
>
> Of course it is unsafe as long as it is in Native hands. They are likely at any time to go on a restoring fa [illegible] and ruin it, as they almost did when the[y] put on wooden towers and tin roof a few years ago. . . .

> Of course it should be one of the churches of the natives. It will always
> be. . . . as long as they control it. I suppose it should be under the control
> of the Archbishop with a guarantee that it should never be altered and
> whenever it is repaired not to make changes.[21]

Of course, the most telling moment in the letter is Applegate's confidence that the Chimayó "natives" will be unable to care adequately for the Santuario. He is quite explicit in his fears: the people of Chimayó will adulterate the place by making updates and changes to the building that might detract from the "Spanish colonial" aesthetic valued by Applegate and his cohort.

The calculation to place the chapel under the archdiocese's control indicates that the nascent Spanish Colonial Arts Society, of which Archbishop Daeger was a prominent member, considered the Catholic Church to be a safer custodian of the place than the people of Chimayó. Nonetheless, one can yet sense Applegate's reluctance to turn full control over to the Church. Both the newspaper and Mary Austin's private communications reveal that some sort of agreement had been forged with the archdiocese that no changes would be made to the structure of the building without the express approval and oversight of the Spanish Colonial Arts Society, mostly likely under the supervision of Meem.[22]

It is not altogether clear what role Archbishop Daeger played in these events other than the fact that the Spanish Colonial Arts Society gave him the six thousand dollars that was used to buy the Santuario from the Chávez family.[23] In fact, Austin's own feelings about the role of the archdiocese in New Mexico are complicated and sometimes critical. An episode from her home illustrates this point. The famous novelist Willa Cather wrote a good deal of *Death Comes for the Archbishop* while living in Austin's house. Austin was not pleased with the book.

> When it was finished, I was very much distressed to find that she had
> given her allegiance to the French blood of the Archbishop; she had sym-
> pathized with his desire to build a French cathedral in a Spanish town.
> It was a calamity to the local culture. We have never gotten over it. It
> dropped the local mystery plays almost out of use, and many other far-
> derived Spanish customs. It was in the rebuilding of that shattered culture
> that the Society for the Revival of the Spanish Arts was concerned.[24]

Austin thus links the Archdiocese of Santa Fe and its French roots under Archbishop Lamy with the very genesis of the Spanish Colonial Arts Society. That an agreement could then be reached with Daeger suggests that this archbishop, given his leadership in the society, must have shared at least some of the preservationist goals if not the entire vision of Hispano village life that Applegate and Austin so valued.

If this agreement between the Spanish Colonial Arts Society did indeed exist, it may have been only in verbal form, as no known written trace of it persists to the present day. To be sure, absolutely no mention of the society's oversight and control of renovations is made in the legal documents of the Santuario's sale.[25] Some significant changes to the exterior of the Santuario had already been made, presumably by the Chávez family, in the early 1920s prior to the sale. The flat earthen roof over the nave of the chapel was covered with a metal gable, a common solution to roof leaks in older adobe architecture. At the same time as this renovation, the flat-roofed bell towers on the façade were also topped with metal gables, and the openings for the bells were framed in wood. After the purchase, a metal roof was likewise added to the adjoining sacristy and the room containing the *pocito*.[26]

As recently as 2004, a series of emails were exchanged between administrators of the Spanish Colonial Arts Society, which now exists as an important museum and research center in Santa Fe, debating whether a renovation that the archdiocese was carrying out on an altar screen in the Santuario could be regulated, or at least monitored, by the society for fear that the renovation was doing damage to the integrity of the site. David Rasch, a Santa Fe–based official in New Mexico's Historic Preservation Division, found some indication in the historical record that the Church needed to seek the society's permission to do any alterations, but when he consulted the county deed, no mention was made of this restriction. Indeed, the archdiocese did not seek the Spanish Colonial Arts Society's input in the case of that renovation, nor in any other in recent memory.[27]

A question that must go partially unanswered is how the Chávez family and other Nuevomexicano devotees of the Santuario felt about its sale, since little or no record remains to document their responses. It is not difficult to imagine that they were unhappy with the economic circumstances that forced the sale or with the rhetoric of Austin, Ap-

Figure 5.3. Santuario before renovation, ca. 1917. T. Harmon Parkhurst, courtesy of Museum of New Mexico (NMHM/DCA), 014375.

Figure 5.4. Santuario, ca. 1935, after the renovations to the roof and bell towers. T. Harmon Parkhurst, courtesy of Palace of the Governors Photo Archives (NMHM/DCA), 008932.

plegate, and others who so vocally claimed to be saving the Hispano culture. In fact, at least in some cases, memory of the Santuario's sale among locals in Chimayó has obliterated the involvement of Austin, her colleagues, and their claims of ownership. In a 2004 feature story in the *Santa Fe New Mexican* about the history of the Santuario, the reporter interviewed Abeyta's great-great-grandson Raymond Chávez, then fifty-seven years old, about his and his family's memory of the transaction between Austin, Applegate, and the archdiocese. When Chávez was informed of the 1929 sale, he responded, "I don't believe it," and added that he had never heard the story before. In fact, according to his own grandfather, Francisco Chávez, the family traded the Santuario for cattle. "Six-thousand dollars was a lot of money back then, and if the Chávezes would have kept that money, that would have made them better off than I knew them to be." In other words, scions of the family do indeed remember the transfer of the Santuario to be based on economic necessity, but the role of the Anglo literati in Santa Fe in the affair has not become part of Chávez family lore.[28]

Whose Santuario? Whose New Mexico?

The sale of the Santuario to the Catholic Church in 1929 marks a turning point not only for the Santuario but also for the changing fortunes of northern New Mexican Hispano villages. As the economic livelihood of places like Chimayó shifted from semi-communal agricultural ventures to wage labor mostly outside the bounds of the village, other changes also took hold in the way religious life was regulated.

These changes had everything to do with the slow but inexorable incorporation of New Mexico into the social imagination and sense of nationhood of the United States. For Anglo aficionados and appreciators like Mary Austin and her artsy confreres, New Mexico represented a spiritual tie to the indigenous and Hispano past of the Southwest and a source of artistic inspiration in the starkness of its landscapes. But it also represented an aesthetic project writ large. Preservationist organizations like the Spanish Colonial Arts Society and John Gaw Meem's village church preservation league worked like an enormous piece of installation art in which whites smitten with their own romantic renderings of New Mexico could build and maintain picturesque tableaus throughout the state. In many ways, the purchase of the Santuario allowed these new residents to freeze an image of New Mexico religious life. The miraculous dirt was exactly the kind of detail that made the Santuario such an appetizing piece of vernacular architecture, not to mention the priceless *retablos* lining the walls and the fine folk drama of penitential pilgrimages.

Much of this process remained insistently racial: The Hispano was best appreciated by the outside artist when he was understood as the more-or-less pure descendant of either the spiritual and mystical Indian or the dramatic and chivalrous Spaniard. When outsider aesthetes recognized racial mixing among the Nuevomexicanos, it was often in an almost biologically determined explanation of Hispanos' discrete artistic and ethnic heritages. For instance, in her autobiography (on the page directly before her retelling of the purchase of the Santuario), Mary Austin writes,

> The colonists who first came here [New Mexico] originally came direct from Spain; they had not much tarrying in Mexico. They brought with them what they remembered, and as soon as they began to create, they made things in the likeness of the things of old Spain, modified by what they found here among the Indians. . . . They accepted the Indian house, but added a fireplace; they brought chests, but added tables and chairs in the Spanish pattern. They made *santos* and *bultos* in the pattern of the holy images of sixteenth-century Spain. They mixed with the Indians, the peon class, and brought into their blood an Indian strain, Indian capacity for making things, for design and color. . . . It takes more than a hundred years to destroy patterns in the blood.[29]

Clearly, it was important to Austin that the Hispano villager represented overlap if not melding of the Spanish and the Native American. Her engagement with Nuevomexicanos as mostly Spanish with some Indian thrown in, of course, was not unique but was rather part of the overall aesthetic branding that was taking place at this time all around the Southwest and California. As the historian Suzanne Forrest points out, "while Indians had appealed to American romantics from the beginning, there was a problem with Mexicans who had been almost universally despised as dirty, backward, ignorant, and lazy. To romanticize

Mexican culture, it had to be 'cleaned up' and relabeled as Spanish."[30] The growing tourism industry likewise learned from the successful commodification of Indians and began to market Nuevomexicanos as "Spanish Americans" with explicit mention that they were the remnants of the Conquistadors.[31] It is thus significant that Austin's and Applegate's preservationist group was called the *Spanish* Colonial Arts Society.

By the time of the Santuario's purchase in 1929, Anglo leaders in Santa Fe had already begun to formulate explicit language about New Mexico's ostensibly tricultural heritage, but for the most part, the Indians and the Nuevomexicanos were the parties responsible for providing quaint and earthy color to the story, while the presence of the Anglos in New Mexico went uncommented. Austin's romanticization of the Spanish and Indian "blood" of authentic New Mexico plays into this rhetoric even as she uncritically exercises her own role as an economically powerful custodian of the picturesque folk. The ritual studies scholar Ronald Grimes, in his research on the pageantry associated with the annual Santa Fe Fiesta, shares an important example of this rhetoric from a 1967 script of the fiesta's main drama. At the end of a rehearsal of New Mexican history, the narrator intoned, "Our tri-cultural co-existence—in neighborly peace and harmony—is the fruit of Don Diego's [de Vargas] peaceful *reconquista*."[32] The U.S. takeover after the Mexican-American War is obliterated from the story in such a way that professed celebration of Nuevomexicano and Indian history becomes a component of colonialism. The purchase of the Santuario, in the same fashion, is presented (by Austin, Applegate, and their cohort) as the salvation of a timeless Spanish treasure that the "natives" cannot possibly handle, despite the ongoing ritual use of the church by Nuevomexicanos from all over the region. The needs of these worshipers figured relatively little in the calculus of preservation.[33]

Indeed, at first blush it might seem strange that the Spanish Colonial Arts Society would turn ownership of the Santuario over to the archdiocese, especially under the influence of Mary Austin, who had proven herself critical of the American Catholic Church in New Mexico. But this decision should be understood as one more calculated move in the aesthetic project of Hispano village preservation. In short, the villagers were to be appreciated for their simplicity, their mystical and dramatic spirituality, and the air of Spanish romance and chivalry that surrounded them, but they were ultimately not to be trusted with maintaining themselves in patterns that the Santa Fe artists found acceptable. At the time of sale, it seems that Archbishop Daeger, as a member of the Spanish Colonial Arts Society himself, was a trustworthy partner in this endeavor, although one wonders if he was more interested in ecclesiastical control of the chapel than in promoting the community rituals, pageantry, and miraculous healing that perhaps appealed more to his other colleagues in the society. To be sure, if the Anglo tastemakers of Santa Fe wished to remain in control in perpetuity of the Santuario, then they certainly made a mistake by entrusting ownership to the archdiocese.

But what of the people of Chimayó and other faithful Nuevomexicano pilgrims to the Santuario? Even though they had clearly failed as far as Austin was concerned in terms of being able to administer their own religious space, what was to become of their interaction with the Santuario, its images, and its dirt? For the thirty years after the chapel left control of the Chávez family, not much changed for the local people in terms of use and access to the church. The Santuario, now owned by the Catholic Church, seems to have remained a mission of the Santa Cruz de la Cañada parish, though records of this relationship in the Official Catholic Directory are spotty through the first decades of the twentieth century; after 1931 the Santuario no longer appears as an official mission of Santa Cruz, but this is likely an absence in the documentary record rather than a reflection of actual life.[34] As they had done for more than a century, the people of Chimayó relied on visiting clergy to celebrate Mass and receive the sacraments. Their other religious needs remained met by household devotions and the ongoing ministrations of the Penitente order.

The archdiocese's inability to act quickly to restore the crumbling Santuario and to initiate regular Masses in the church indicates an important disconnect between the original preservationist aspirations of the Spanish Colonial Arts Society and the administrative realities of a poor and widespread New Mexican Catholic Church. To be sure, pilgrimage and miraculous healing continued to take place at the Santuario after its sale. But this had little to do with the efforts of the Anglo artists and elites from Santa Fe who so desired to stage Chimayó as an ongoing piece of primitive theater. Nor can the ongoing centrality of the Santuario as a place of Hispano devotion be attributed to Archbishop

Daeger or his immediate successors, who were also not able to either stifle these devotions or change the daily rhythms of the Santuario for the next three decades of the twentieth century. But despite the continuing local control of the chapel, its dirt, and its role in annual festivals and pilgrimages, the English-language press in Santa Fe found several opportunities in the following years to recast the sale of the Santuario as its saving grace. A feature story in a tourism-focused magazine went so far as to claim that the Nuevomexicano Catholics of the region had longed for its sale: "the villagers of Chimayo saw their fondest wish granted when Archbishop Albert T. Daeger accepted the little chapel on behalf of the Catholic Church."[35] As dissonant as this statement is with the reality of long family ownership of the Santuario, it nonetheless gives a fair picture of the success the Spanish Colonial Arts Society achieved in terms of forming Anglo understanding of what Nuevomexicanos wanted and needed for the maintenance of their own religious practices. In this understanding, of course the villagers wanted the Church to own their Santuario to validate as well as to oversee their faith. This played directly to midcentury tourists who looked to the Hispano villages to have their assumptions confirmed about the simple piety and Catholic allegiance of the ancient people of the land.

6

The Pilgrims and Pilgrimage

A white woman in her fifties is sitting outside the Santuario with a small cooler, the kind construction workers sometimes use to pack their lunch. The cooler, I see, is full of dirt from the *pocito*. We start to talk, and I learn that she has driven down from Colorado Springs expressly to get the dirt, which she regards as highly miraculous. Her adult son is dying from cancer: "he has twenty-three tumors in his brain." Her family had never heard of the Santuario, but her son's best friend is from Albuquerque. The friend took the son to the Santuario and rubbed the dirt all over his head. "He's lived two months longer than they expected." So today the mother is here, filling a cooler. The dirt inside will be for the son, but she also plans to use it for pains in her own legs, and her husband is recovering from a stroke. Their journey to the Santuario, if not a classic pilgrimage, has nonetheless been a purposeful movement to receive a miracle, to step out in faith, to hope for God's renewed care. She says to me, "When you went in there, did you get a sort of condensed feeling? Like something was hovering over you?" I offer, "They say it's a holy place." "Yes," she says, as she runs her sandy hands over the calves of her legs.

People come to the Santuario. Mostly, they come to see, to learn, to pray, to snap photographs, and to gather dirt. In 2014 the Santuario's administrator estimated that the place received 500,000 visitors a year; 30,000 of these come en masse during the Christian Holy Week, and 20,000 of these come on Good Friday alone.[1] Good Friday, of course, is the day Christians commemorate the crucifixion of Jesus. His suffering on the cross atoned for human sin, and preceded his resurrection from the tomb on Easter, when Christians celebrate the victory of God over sin, the triumph of life over death. The Good Friday walking pilgrimage at the Santuario de Chimayó is one of the largest pilgrimages in the United States, but the Santuario receives pilgrims as well as tourists throughout the year who come walking, driving, and biking. Drawing on archival research, newspaper reports, and other scholarly sources, as well as my own fieldwork from my various visits to the place, this chapter explores the Santuario as a place of pilgrimage and as an increasingly popular tourist destination. What do pilgrims and tourists find so fascinating? Why do they keep coming? What do they do when they are there, and how does the holy dirt "work" for such a diverse group of visitors? For everything it is and has been for Nuevomexicanos, and for its status as an official church of the Archdiocese of Santa Fe, the Santuario is now also a place of immense attraction for all kinds of people. The folklorist Enrique Lamadrid reports, "The journey to Chimayó itself is more diverse every year. Thousands of immigrant Mexicans have found their way to the Santuario in recent years." He adds, "Groups of Protestants regularly join in the journey, along with devotional Azteca dancers and enthusiasts of New Age spirituality, bikers and lowriders."[2] The woman from Colorado Springs with her cooler of holy dirt was one of thousands, and like them, she made a claim on the Santuario and became, in a small way, part of its story.

To this point, this book has presented a historical narrative of the Santuario and its people based on archival records, newspaper reports, and other pieces of historical evidence. Going forward, the book turns to the Santuario's recent past and contemporary circumstances. Some of the same source materials used to knit together the church's history remain important here. Interviews, participant observations, and other sorts of personal interactions supplement those sources and also provide concrete insights and testimonies about the importance of the Santuario in people's lives today.

The Good Friday Pilgrimage, 2015

We parked the car at the Nambé junction, just north of Pojoaque and not too far south of Española, as the sun was coming up. The shoulders of the roads around the junction were mobbed with cars and pickup trucks, people were spilling out of them, and both lanes of the road to Chimayó were packed with slow-moving vehicles. My companion, an old friend as well as a liturgics scholar, and I chatted quietly in the cool morning air as we started to walk with purpose along with the rest of the crowd toward Chimayó. Most people, like us, walked in pairs or in small groups; many of these looked like intergenerational family gatherings. In several cases, I saw middle-aged people and their children get out of vehicles while an older person stayed back, napping or drinking coffee behind the wheel of the parked cars on the roadside, presumably waiting to pick up their family members later in the day after they had arrived at the Santuario. In general, the early-morning mood was festive but subdued—little shouting, no loud music, but some laughter and plenty of conversation. A few pilgrims were carrying prayer books or rosaries, and their lips moved silently in prayer as they walked. My own mood was one of excitement and anticipation. So many of the stories I had read and heard about the Santuario centered on the experience of the Good Friday pilgrimage, and my chance to participate had finally arrived. I was grateful for the cool but sunny day and also anxious to talk to other participants, ask them questions, and learn about their understanding of the pilgrimage.

Our unscientific survey of the crowd suggested that over 90 percent of the pilgrims were Hispanic. In general, they wore comfortable clothing and light jackets, and some carried walking sticks reminiscent of the Santo Niño's pilgrim staff (though without the water gourd). The much smaller number of Anglo walkers and pilgrims tended to be decked out with backpacks, outdoorsy water bottles, and broad-brimmed hats, some even carrying fiberglass hiking poles. A few pilgrims rode bicycles, jogged, or walked dogs, and we even saw one teenage pilgrim cruise past us on his skateboard, with his long black t-shirt flapping in the breeze. We estimated the average age of the walkers to be around thirty-five, with an even distribution of men and women. In the forward movement of the walking crowd, many were there not only to get to the Santuario on Good Friday but also to spend a day together with family and loved ones. An older Hispanic woman who has made the pilgrimage every year for decades told me that she now considers it a "family reunion" where extended aunts, uncles, waves of cousins, and old friends meet every year to walk together and reconnect. Similarly, a retired university administrator was there with his adult daughters and one of his granddaughters, who had gathered from around the state. Although he mentioned that he did use the pilgrimage "to think about the Passion," he was obviously delighted to be with his family. His daughters likewise commented how pleasant they find the day spent together, engaged both

Figure 6.1. Pilgrims walking to Chimayó on Good Friday, 2015. Author's photo.

in religious pursuits and the maintenance of cross-generational family traditions.

As the sun rose higher in the sky, we walked with the crowd of pilgrims through the cottonwoods that line the road from the turnoff on the main highway to the Pueblo of Nambé. At the old adobe mission church in Nambé, the first large gathering of auxiliary people had gathered with lines of water stations, fruit, a first aid table, and several portable bathrooms. After the Pueblo, the road rises into the high desert and features some small but striking rock formations as well as the scrubby bushes and small trees that carpet the landscape. Longtime pilgrims, who could remember freezing cold or rainy Good Fridays, expressed gratitude for the day's clear, cool weather. Several church congregations, public health outfits, and even private families had set up water and snack stations along the way, and many shouted out their greetings and encouragement to us as we passed by. There were also some religious opportunists of sorts on the pilgrimage route. The first was a pair of robed Benedictine monks who had set up a tented area a little off the road to receive confessions from pilgrims. We also encountered two separate groups of evangelical Protestants eager to greet us with water and literature. Neither group had harsh words for the pilgrimage itself; instead, they were content to wish us well and leave us with tracts and booklets with a generic message of Jesus's salvation on the cross. Among our fellow pilgrims there were several church youth groups. At least one of these was carrying a large white cross on their pilgrimage, taking turns hefting its weight. We saw this group stopped at various times on the route to read scripture and pray together with adult leaders. A smattering of other pilgrims were, like the youth, carrying heavy crosses.

We arrived to the grounds of the Santuario shortly before noon. Based on the dozens of feature stories I had read about the pilgrimage and some of the comments I had already heard from former pilgrims who had complained of the "commercialization" of the pilgrimage, I expected an almost carnival-like atmosphere, lines of commercial booths, and so on. There certainly were more people selling things than on a more typical day at the Santuario, but, to my surprise, my imagined encounters with roving t-shirt and tchotchke sellers did not occur. In fact, as the Archdiocese of Santa Fe has expanded its real estate holdings around the Santuario, more and more of the nearby properties are owned by the Church. Signs prohibiting sales on church grounds without permission were well posted. To be sure, near the line to get into the Santuario itself, an artist displayed her portraits of saints, various food booths stretched down the street, and the shops that already dot the area around the Santuario were doing brisk business.

The place was packed. Below the Santuario in the devotional garden space on the banks of the Santa Cruz River, Archbishop Michael Sheehan took intercessory prayer requests from the large crowd. We listened attentively for a while to various intercessions for families, drug addicts, and immigrants before moving away to sit near the river to eat our lunch. The bank of the Santa Cruz was full of people picnicking like us, listening to the burble of the stream on the one side and the buzz of the crowd on the other. As we ate, we watched two men. One played a hand-held drum in a quick rhythm while the other, dressed head-to-toe in white, danced and gathered stones from the river. In his dance, he made as if to offer the stones toward the sky in the various cardinal directions. They avoided my admittedly feeble attempts to engage in conversation and find out what they were doing. After the dance, they gathered a pile of posters displaying an image of the Aztec solar calendar on them, perhaps to sell. The vast majority of the crowds, however, were making more customary use of the Santuario, waiting in line to pray inside and to gather dirt, or visiting with family and friends outside.

Around one o'clock, Father Julio, the Spaniard who serves as the current pastor of the Chimayó parish, oversaw a procession of images around the grounds of the Santuario. The procession, to some extent, symbolically communicated two intertwined narratives, one of Jesus's passion and the other of the Catholic evangelization of New Mexico. The four images of the procession and their bearers gathered in the road that crosses in front of the Santuario and the Santo Niño Chapel. Most of the bearers, who were all men, were preselected volunteers who had dressed for the occasion in the brown cowls of the Franciscans, the order most influential in bringing Catholicism to the reaches of northern New Mexico and to Chimayó itself. Other bearers were conscripted from the crowds and given hasty instruction in Spanish and then in English, after a few noted that they could not understand Spanish. A life-size, non-Guadalupan depiction of Mary was the first image in the procession, followed by her son, dressed in a red robe and wearing a crown of thorns. The third statue was a replica of the crucifix of the Lord of Esquipulas from inside the Santuario, and the final figure in the procession was a colossal bier upon which lay the dead body of Christ. At a signal from Father Julio, the Franciscan stand-ins hoisted the images to their shoulders and began a slow march of about half a block; behind them, below their banner, the local Chimayó chapter of the Penitente Brotherhood walked and intoned a melancholy hymn. Mary led the way for a very short distance when the procession paused, and she turned to face her suffering son while a woman plaintively sang the Via Dolorosa in both English and Spanish. After the song was complete, Jesus moved in front of Mary and led the rest of the way. During the short remainder of the march, the focus shifted to the crucified Lord and eventually to his corpse atop the bier. At this point, the procession paused once again so that another woman, this time dressed from head to toe in black, hair covered by a lacy black mantilla, sang a wailing lament with a decidedly Iberian flair. The procession ended somewhat lamely as the statues were parked in a gated patio below the Santuario itself, which could not be entered due to the long line of pilgrims stretching out of sight down the road, waiting their turn to go in.

Figure 6.2. Pilgrims wait to enter the Santuario on Good Friday, 2015. Author's photo.

The message of Franciscans marching Mary and Jesus to Chimayó was on display in the procession, and the replica of Esquipulas, promoted by the Church as the central devotional figure of the Santuario, also tried to refocus the crowds on the core biblical narrative of Good Friday, the crucifixion and death of Christ. But also on display for all to see was the relative lack of interest in the procession; much of the crowd stayed put either in line to enter the Santuario or in the various places of rest and gathering outside the church rather than moving themselves to better observe the drama of the procession. It is significant that the crowds, and their overarching desire to enter the room with the *pocito* and the holy dirt, had effectively blocked entrance to the Santuario for the processional images. It is not that Mary and Jesus and the salvific drama of Good Friday had no meaning for them, but the center of gravity was the interior room of the Santuario where the dirt awaited, close by the sacristy full of cast-off crutches, photos of loved ones, and the beneficent if dingy statue of the Santo Niño de Atocha.

When the procession wound down, my companion and I decided we would wait our turn to enter the Santuario. (Several pilgrims on the route and on other occasions told me that they long ago gave up going into the Santuario on Good Friday because the line was prohibitively long. "I know what it looks like in there, and I can come get dirt another day.") From the end of the line to the moment we exited the church took just under one hour and gave us the opportunity to rest and reflect after the morning's walk. While we waited to enter, we met three Nuevomexicanas who had walked from Pojoaque, several miles past the Nambé turnoff where we had begun our own walk. One of the women was a veteran from the war in Iraq and also had recently lost her father. She told me how she was there to pray for him and his memory as well as for her own healing from a series of surgeries resulting from battle injuries. I asked her what part of the Santuario she "gravitated" to, and she immediately responded "the room with the *pocito*."

Hours spent in observation of the Santuario suggest that many feel the same as this particular pilgrim. While some visitors and pilgrims do spend time in prayer in the nave of the church, with direct view of the Esquipulas crucifix, most walk reverently down the center aisle, where they may or may not acknowledge the image of the crucified Christ by genuflecting or crossing themselves, before moving through the low door to the sacristy. In the much smaller sacristy and the even smaller room that contains the *pocito*, people linger. They huddle with family around the well of dirt, sometimes applying it to achy body parts right there, and they spoon quantities of the earth in to plastic bags and other little receptacles. Then they move into the low-ceilinged sacristy to sit on the benches along the wall and pray as they wait their turn to kneel before the Santo Niño. Others slowly scan the thousands of photos that paper the old adobe walls, each one a story of suffering, longing, and hope. On the day of the Good Friday pilgrimage, this kind of detained reflection is allowed but logistically unlikely. The thousands who do elect to wait in line shuffle down the aisle so as to make a quick stop by the *pocito*. To accelerate the process, a volunteer is stationed at a card table in the sacristy on this day with hundreds of prepackaged baggies of holy dirt; despite this, many still gather their own earth from the *pocito* even as other volunteers frequently replenish the hole with five-gallon buckets of dirt from a large pile outside. Although I have not witnessed the act itself, the staff at the Santuario insists that all the dirt is blessed by a priest before it is introduced to the hole in the little room, akin to the blessing of holy water.

Exhausted by a long day of walking, waiting, talking, and watching, we left the Santuario around three o'clock in the afternoon. When we reached our car, we headed south toward Santa Fe to get something to eat. Pilgrims continued to pack both sides of the road to Nambé, although we also noticed a fair amount of vehicle traffic heading away from the Santuario. By the time we got out to the main highway between Santa Fe and Española, the number of pilgrims had thinned, but we still witnessed several dozen people walking, even as we approached the northern edges of the Santa Fe metropolitan area, more than twenty miles from the Santuario. The heat of the day had risen significantly, but we supposed that these pilgrims hoped to finish their walk in the cool evening and early night hours. By this time of day, we were happy to be driving to a place to sit, eat, and rest. Our Good Friday pilgrimage had come to its end.

Theories of Pilgrimage and the Santuario

Anthropologists and other scholars have tried to make sense of religious pilgrimages for many years. Without a doubt, the most influential theory to emerge from these efforts comes from the reflections of Victor and Edith Turner. The Turners, in their study of various Christian pilgrimages around the world, came to understand pilgrims as actors in a ritual process akin to a rite of passage—to wit, they refer to pilgrimage as a "liminoid phenomenon." By this, they mean that pilgrims enter an in-between, *liminal* place wherein various social functions are achieved. These include

> release from mundane structure; homogenization of status; simplicity of
> dress and behavior; communitas; ordeal; reflection on the meaning of basic religious and cultural values; ritualized enactment of correspondences
> between religious paradigms and shared human experiences; emergence
> of the integral person from multiple personae; movement from a mundane center to a sacred periphery which suddenly, transiently, becomes
> central for the individual, an *axis mundi* of his [sic] faith; movement itself, a symbol of communitas, which changes with time, as against stasis,
> which represents structure.[3]

To summarize the Turners' important insights, the pilgrim, along with other pilgrims, voluntarily enters into a time of movement that allows for religious reflection, a feeling of unity with fellow travelers and a renewed sense of belonging (communitas), and the experience of the peripheral as a type of re-centering and renewal that the pilgrim carries back to regular life after the pilgrimage.

The Turners' theoretical framework for understanding pilgrimage is often fruitful when applied to the pilgrimage to the Santuario. If we accept that pilgrims to Chimayó, especially those who make the journey on foot on or around Good Friday, do indeed enter a liminal space in their lives, we can observe that many of the oft-observed social functions in other Christian pilgrimages likewise occur on the way to Chimayó. Individuals and families leave the everyday environs of their homes to enter the ritualized space of the roadsides surrounding Chimayó, and on the road, all share in the exertion of walking miles through the desert. Pilgrims to the Santuario often report that they are renewed and that the pilgrimage gives them a chance to reflect on their Christian faith, on particular intercessions, and on gratitude to God for blessings already received. For instance, residents of the village of Chimayó report that they know of pilgrims—and now their descendants—who have been making the pilgrimage since World War II in response to a promise they had made to God in gratitude for the safe return of their loved ones.[4] In addition to these expressions of faith, pilgrims also tell of the communitas that results from the liminality of pilgrimage. One pilgrim, who had made a hundred-mile trek to Chimayó with a group from his church, stated, "Can you imagine how you feel when you've walked with a group, and you get close? You get very close to 'em. Cuz they're, they're like family. By the time you get there, and you're just one big family, and you don't want it to quit."[5]

The Turners' theoretical explanations of pilgrimage and its relationship to the processes of liminality and communitas are not their only helpful insights concerning the pilgrimage to Chimayó. In their work, the Turners also provide a typology of kinds of pilgrimage that can help us think about the various ways diverse groups of people make their way to the Santuario. In one case, they note that pilgrimages sometimes "bear quite evident traces of syncretism with older religious beliefs and symbols." As we have seen, the preexisting Pueblo use of healing mud near Tsi Mayoh hill provides a convincing suggestion of a syncretic-type pilgrimage site that attracts pilgrims who, consciously or not, make connections with pre-Hispanic traditions in northern New Mexico. Another type that applies readily to the context of the Santuario is the devotional Catholic pilgrimage that developed in the post-Tridentine period. This kind of pilgrimage emphasizes the "fervent personal piety" of participants and contains an inherent critique of secularization and technological advance. Pilgrims who go to Chimayó to express their Catholic piety and to remain connected to family and ethnic traditions over and against social anomie can be understood, say the Turners, as "modern" in their reliance on mass media and communication and transportation networks, yet they are simultaneously "antimodern" in tone because they continue to embrace apparitions and miracles.[6] For instance, in the Chimayó pilgrimage, the state's security forces are heavily deployed to maintain the safety and order of the pilgrims even as these same pilgrims gather holy dirt and pray for the Santo Niño's miraculous intervention in their lives.

The popularity of the dirt itself is another aspect of the pilgrimage to the Santuario that coheres well with the Turners' observations of many other Christian pilgrimage sites around the globe. Specifically, they note that as pilgrimages grow, they inevitably "fall increasingly under ecclesiastical sway" even while "ceremonial symbols multiply and are elaborated." The growth and importance of the Santuario absolutely led to ownership and subsequent higher levels of supervision by the archdiocese even as the popular uses of the Santuario continued to revolve around the holy dirt and the relatively autonomous Santo Niño. In contexts like this, tension generally develops between the enforced orthodoxy of ecclesiastical representatives and the more freewheeling creativity and dogged practicality of popular religious currents. If we focus our attention on the holy dirt in the *pocito* as the most remarkable feature of the Santuario compared to other New Mexican colonial-era churches, we can see, with the Turners, how the dirt functions in this tension between the Church's hierarchy and popular practice: "Any religious system which commits itself to the large-scale employment of nonverbal symbolic vehicles for conveying its message to the masses runs the risk that these vehicles will become endowed by believers with magical efficacy." The "risk," of course, accrues only to Church authorities who would want to interpret the symbols (like the dirt) in a way that limits the "masses" using said symbols for "magical" purposes. Despite the theological or doctrinal conflicts that might simmer between official ecclesiastical explanations of Chimayó's famous dirt and popular reliance on the dirt for healing and miracles, the pilgrimage itself continues to belong more to the thousands of pilgrims every year than to the archdiocese. To wit, the Turners find that "there is something inveterately populist, anarchical, even anticlerical, about pilgrimages in their very essence."[7]

Nonetheless, not all of the pilgrims who make their way to the Santuario do so in an anticlerical way. Many of the Good Friday pilgrims may also take part in much smaller Catholic Church–sponsored pilgrimages at other times of the year. The Archdiocese of Santa Fe organizes regular hundred-mile pilgrimages to the Santuario in support of vocations. (Broadly conceived, "vocations" can refer to a process of spiritual discernment leading to any profession, but in Catholicism, the word more often refers to people choosing to enter ordained ministry as priests or as religious.) The anthropologist Paula Elizabeth Holmes-Rodman took part in a hundred-mile women's pilgrimage for vocations; through her participant observation, she confirmed strong experiences of communitas and noted that, as the Turnerian view of pilgrimage maintains, this communitas reinforced fidelity to the official structures and doctrines of the Catholic Church. Holmes-Rodman writes that typical Catholic beliefs and practices

> were *not* contested but rather, confirmed, authenticated, and idealized through participating in the pilgrimage. For these women, pilgrimage was an occasion for "full-time" Catholicism, emphasizing suffering, prayer, and healing, meant to enhance, guide, and define in its idealness the everyday Catholic life of the other fifty-one weeks of the year.

However, even this highly normative experience of pilgrimage was not without its own small traces of popular direction. Holmes-Rodman observed that, despite the pilgrimage's stated purpose to promote Catholic vocations, not once was this purpose mentioned before, during, or after the pilgrimage by the women participants. They instead spoke often of their own motives for making the pilgrimage, which—reflecting the Santuario's position in the lives of the mostly Pueblo and Nuevomexicana participants—not surprisingly revolved mostly around healing, family concerns, and personal faith.[8] It is therefore possible to confirm basic Turnerian ideas of communitas being nurtured during the liminal space and time of the Chimayó pilgrimage; this communitas often renews participants' Catholic commitment and piety even while leaving the door open for popular redirections of, if not outright challenges to, ecclesiastical expectations and emphases.

The majority of anthropologists who have considered the pilgrimage to Chimayó have relied—with good reason, as we have seen—on the theories of Christian pilgrimage articulated by Victor and Edith Turner. As one scholar put it, "we follow Victor Turner" and recognize with him that celebrations, festivals, and pilgrimages "move from 'structure to antistructure and back again to transformed structure.'" These kinds of events "not only channel but reforge energies and can have a transformative function."[9] Walking to Chimayó, viewed through this interpretive viewpoint, becomes an exercise in leaving one's day-to-day life to join a radically equalized, energetic, and even joyful community of pilgrims (communitas), so that one can return to daily routines rejuvenated and with one's core narratives and self-understandings reinforced by the liminal experience of pilgrimage.

However, any academic theory has its limitations, and some have raised some serious critiques of Turnerian notions of pilgrimage. The principal problem has to do with the universalizing features of the Turners' notions of pilgrimage; critics point out that a structure-reinforcing yet anti-structural communitas is not necessarily the outcome of all pilgrimages. Two influential voices in pilgrimage studies, John Eade and Michael Sallnow, point out that

> pilgrimage is above all an arena for competing religious and secular discourses, for both the official co-optation and the non-official recovery of religious meanings, for conflict between orthodoxies, sects, and confessional groups, for drives towards consensus and communitas, *and* for counter-movements towards separateness and division.[10]

In other words, the Turnerian paradigm for understanding pilgrimage can be reductive and deterministic. It is not that communitas *never* occurs during pilgrimage, but that other features or results are also likely. For instance, as Eade and Sallnow mention, various constituencies involved in any given pilgrimage often compete for control of the discourses, meanings, and practices that make up multivalent pilgrimages. The massive nature of pilgrimages, in this interpretation, is not a likely cause of unity but rather the opposite. Sallnow explains, "The mere fact of a mass gathering at a sacred site is unlikely to indicate any unanimity of meaning or motive among the participants." In fact, such large gatherings are "more likely to reveal severely discrepant or discordant understandings of the cult, even among those nominally sharing the same faith."[11]

My observations of the pilgrimage to Chimayó, during Holy Week and at other times of the year, confirm what many other observers have noticed: there often does develop a special sense of camaraderie and purpose among those who travel to the Santuario, especially when they are taking part in a self-proclaimed pilgrimage. Moreover, as the Turners predict, a large and multifaceted Christian pilgrimage, like the one to Chimayó, results in contested uses of the ritual and its material accoutrements for "magical" purposes. Namely, the dirt from the *pocito* is popularly recognized for its healing powers while Church authorities insist that the dirt is no more than a sacrament-like symbol of God's loving care for the suffering. This contested apprehension of the pilgrimage site corroborates Eade and Sallnow's point that pilgrimages are often sites of competition, a multiplicity of discourses and interpretations, and even discord. They would perhaps point to the competing claims about the Santuario's miraculous dirt as proof that a Turnerian focus on communitas and the reinforcing of structure is inadequate. The anthropologist Simon Coleman, who has researched Christian pilgrimage sites in Great Britain, offers a constructive way out of this theoretical tension:

> The important point here is between viewing a cultural resource as an unchanging symbol of continuity and seeing it as the launching point for liturgical and interpretative creativity. . . . While one mode valorizes the exemplary and essentially replicable nature of sacralized history, the other interacts with traditions in a way that involves a more fluid, mutually transformative process.[12]

Coleman's important insight allows us to view the various uses and understandings of the holy dirt at Chimayó not as a breakdown of Turnerian analysis of pilgrimage, but rather as a contested yet ultimately fruitful place of tension and creativity among the many constituents who lay claim to the Santuario. The dirt can aid the priests in their proclamation of official Catholic doctrine concerning the divine cause of healing, sometimes mediated through material objects like water, oil, or—in Chimayó—earth. At the same time, the popular voices and actions of the pilgrims confirm over and over that the dirt itself holds power to heal. In practice, however, these two interpretations—which exist among others—are in conflict on paper more than in day-to-day life. The priests and shrine administrators rely on the holy dirt and its associated healing power to maintain the Santuario as a site of pilgrimage even as the pilgrims are generally quick to affirm that the dirt's power is ultimately a sign of God's blessing and care.

The Chimayó Pilgrimage over Time

Like all religious and cultural practices, the pilgrimage to the Santuario de Chimayó has undergone changes over the years. By tracing these changes, as well as the constants, we can gain insight into the ways pilgrims have maintained ownership over their own religious practices in this specific place. The presence and importance of the healing dirt in the *pocito* has remained consistent throughout the pilgrimage, serving as the Santuario's *raison d'être*. But other factors have evolved considerably, including the numbers of people who take part in the pilgrimage every year, its relationship to Holy Week, the rise of pilgrimages for special purposes, and the increasing role that tourism plays at the Santuario. From the beginning, the Santuario has thrived because of the pilgrims. Voting with their feet, the pilgrims have made and continue to make the Santuario their own.

There is not a great deal of archived evidence of the pilgrimage during the first century of the Santuario's existence, although there are enough well-documented mentions of pilgrims to the church that there is no reason to doubt that pilgrimage occurred. The earliest of these mentions appears in 1813, before construction of the Santuario was even complete.

As mentioned in chapter 2, the local priest in Santa Cruz de la Cañada, whose territory included Chimayó, wrote a letter to the bishop of Durango in support of Bernardo Abeyta's desire to construct a church. The priest, Fray Sebastián Álvarez, states, "This place is frequented by many people and in pilgrimage they come from even twenty and more leagues [approximately sixty miles] away to give their prayers [votos] to the Sovereign Redeemer, and to experience relief and healing of their ailments."[13] Fray Álvarez's statement indeed indicates that the pilgrimage predated the Santuario. Given the Tewas' uses of the local mud for healing and longtime identification of Tsi Mayoh hill as the site of an earth navel, the preexistence of a popular pilgrimage to gather the healing dirt is not surprising. Abeyta, as a result of miraculous apparition or canny business decision, ensconced an image of the Lord of Esquipulas on his property, which created the perfect combination of elements to lead to the construction of the Santuario.

It is likely that the establishment of Mexican independence in the 1820s and the subsequent relaxation of restrictions on trade led to greater travel to and from Chimayó. Before independence, the majority of legal trade occurred on the north-south axis of the Camino Real from Santa Fe to Mexico City. After the Spanish empire was defeated, east-west trade routes, which had already operated illegally, were normalized. The opening of the Santa Fe Trail and trade with the United States as well as the Old Spanish Trail and commerce with southern California allowed the goods and produce of northern New Mexico to access new markets.[14] According to one architectural historian, the resulting "boom years" in Chimayó were augmented by the pilgrimage traffic. People who came to the village to pray at the Santuario found a flourishing "trade center, where local people bartered their fruit and chiles for potatoes and wheat from the San Luis Valley in southern Colorado." The famous Chimayó weaving industry was likewise growing rapidly during this period.[15]

For the remainder of the nineteenth century, pilgrims continued to come to the Santuario from the villages and Pueblos surrounding La Cañada. Oral histories gathered from elderly residents of Chimayó in 1995 reveal family stories of the shrine that predate the 1929 sale to the Catholic Church. In these stories, the massive Good Friday pilgrimage has not yet been established; rather, the pattern of pilgrim visits to the Santuario is more scattershot and based on health-related needs. One such story involves the memories of Mama Libradita, the daughter-in-law of Carmen Chávez, herself the daughter of Bernardo Abeyta. Mama Libradita frequently told stories of her position as one of the family caretakers of the shrine. "They came in wagons and stayed overnight there, sleeping in their covered wagons. . . . More and more people started to come, and miracles were happening." Some of these visitors would pay Mama Libradita to say rosaries for them.[16] This account of health-seeking pilgrims coheres well with María Martínez's 1890 visit to the Santuario for healing from an intense fever, an episode described in detail in chapter 3.[17] Besides seeking miraculous healing in the *pocito*'s dirt or from the intercession of the Santo Niño, it was also during the nineteenth century that the tradition was forged of making an annual pilgrimage to the Santuario out of gratitude. In one instance, an older Chimayó resident named Benigna Chávez remembered that, many years ago, her family's prayerful petitions led to the miraculous recovery of her cousin Ramón, who had been lost in the sierras as a four-year-old boy. "Ramón's mother made a vow that she would visit the Santuario every year to give thanks for the miracle, and she made her son promise to do it after she died."[18] In sum, pilgrimage patterns that are still common at the Santuario—namely, occasional journeys, typically by car (formerly by wagon) to gather dirt or give thanks for healing—were well established among Nuevomexicanos early in the shrine's history and continued unabated through the Santuario's first centenary and beyond.

The Holy Week walking pilgrimage that Chimayó is famous for today appears to have gotten its start in the years following World War II.[19] Its impetus was a group of veterans of the infamous Bataan Death March; approximately 1,800 men from the New Mexico National Guard suffered in the battles and ordeals associated with Bataan, and when the survivors returned home, they made a walking pilgrimage from Santa Fe to Chimayó to seek healing of their bodies and memories.[20] On Sunday, April 28, 1946, more than five hundred pilgrims, including the survivors and their families, arrived at the Santuario and attended Mass; according to a newspaper report, "After the service with its sermon in Spanish had been completed, those in the patio surged into the chapel and the little side shrine was crowded with a patient stream of supplicants who gathered handfuls of soil from the dry well, which supposedly has curative powers."[21] Testimonials from participants reveal that they had made a vow to undertake the pilgrimage to Chimayó while they were yet in Japanese prison camps in the Philippines. The Santo Niño de Atocha's long association with care for prisoners augmented the layers of meaning for the pilgrim soldiers, as the art historian E. Boyd noted later in 1946: "In New Mexico, where so many men were at Bataan, He [the Santo Niño] had a special charge to perform." Although this first organized walking pilgrimage to Chimayó occurred in the weeks after Easter, it would soon move to its current position within Holy Week, with special emphasis on the Passion narrative of Good Friday.[22]

The annual Holy Week pilgrimage gradually grew, attracting more and more participants each year. Other visitors, including tourists, continued to come to the Santuario at other times of the year as well to seek health from the *pocito* and the Santo Niño. The 1929 purchase of the Santuario by the Spanish Colonial Arts Society had already demonstrated Anglo fascination with the Santuario and the perceived quaintness and authenticity of its miraculous dirt, colorful images, and credulous Nuevomexicano pilgrims. Feature stories that emerged in the 1950s about the Santuario both demonstrate growing public interest in the church and express their Anglo audience's ongoing desires to locate and experience a kind of Hispano folk magic in a romanticized and changeless village tableau. The title from a 1953 feature in the *Saturday Evening Post* is representative of such stories: "They Want No Progress in Chimayo." The article focuses primarily on the handcrafts and traditions of Chimayó's famous weaving industry, but the Santuario and the Santo Niño also make appearances to complete the narrative of a village governed by primitive yet immemorial rhythms. The historian Stephen D. Fox, in his analysis of outsiders and Anglos who have become enamored of New Mexico's Indian and Hispano healing traditions, insightfully moves the nomenclature for these people from "health seekers" to "ethnicity seekers." Encompassing groups from the first wave of artists and writers in the early twentieth century on to the counterculture and spiritually curious of the 1960s, these ethnicity seekers wanted healing and restoration not only for their bodies but, more importantly, for what they regarded as a sick society. The simple, authentic, and spiritually gifted Hispano villagers and their miraculous healing dirt were too spiritually evocative and aesthetically compelling to pass up. Fox suggests that throughout the century, in addition to ongoing Hispanic utilization of their own traditional healing modalities such as Catholic folk devotion, the *pocito*'s dirt, and various kinds of *curanderismo*, Anglo ethnicity seekers entered into "a complex mixture of social criticism, romantic generalization, true insight and personal projection."[23]

On the one hand, the rising touristic interest in the Santuario and its tales of miracles provides us with several published accounts of the place and its people. On the other hand, interpretation of these accounts is troubled by their exoticizing tone; the view of the past that these feature stories and touristic accounts affords us is always filtered through the racial assumptions of the (mostly) Anglo authors. Moreover, the purpose of these stories is to entertain and promote tourism. The Nuevomexicano population is not only reduced to the picturesque but, more problematically, depicted as a window onto a more innocent and magical past. A 1955 piece by a writer named Charles A. Wood exemplifies this kind of writing about the Santuario. After Wood enjoyed the art and atmosphere of the place and meditated on its role as a site of pilgrimage, he gave the dirt a try to cure a headache, which, to his surprise, was alleviated. This motivated him to find some local color to testify to the powers of the shrine. He found a willing storyteller in Mrs. Vigil after looking for a few days, "handicapped by my inability to converse in the dialect of the Spanish-speaking community." Mrs. Vigil had suffered from a chronic paralysis in her legs and had tried a variety of medicines and treatments before making her way to the *pocito*. In Wood's recollection of his conversation with Vigil, she almost appears as a caricature of the credulous and premodern villager:

"There isn't much to tell, *Señor*," she replied after a moment's hesitation. "I had become desperate. I thought I would never walk again; my time was soon to come. Then I remembered the sick and the crippled who had gone into *El Santuario* and had been cured. *If Santo Niño had done it for them*, I asked myself, *why would he not do it for me?* I had always worshipped him."

The dirt, applied over a period of time to her legs, gradually healed her of all pain, and she regained the ability to walk and work. Vigil's tale, however, is not just testimony; it is held out as a tantalizing opportunity for the Anglo tourist to experience the authentic and enchanted past. Wood concludes that "even in a skeptical, you've-got-to-show-me day, *the age of miracles is not past!*"[24] Readers were thus encouraged to follow the Hispano pilgrims to their adobe church, to see their legendary Holy Child, and to feel the power of tradition and simple faith for themselves.

The next chapter covers in detail the physical improvements to the Santuario and to the site's infrastructure that were achieved by Father Casimiro Roca in the 1950s and 1960s. Those improvements, combined with ongoing press coverage and touristic promotion, allowed the pilgrimage to continue to grow in size and popularity through the middle decades of the twentieth century. By the 1970s, the Good Friday pilgrimage had become a well-known, significant regional event. A 1975 photo spread and feature story in the Sunday magazine of the *Denver Post* reported that in 1973, thirty thousand visitors came to the Santuario, three thousand of them on Good Friday alone. These estimates were drawn from visitor registry pads located in the church, which also documented that the majority of visitors arrived from Colorado, Texas, New Mexico, Utah, Arizona, and California. One of the priests reported that, through the course of the year, about half of the visitors to the Santuario were Anglo.[25] While no breakdown was made in the article between tourists and pilgrims by ethnicity, other sources indicate that the majority of the Holy Week pilgrims at this time period—as today—were Hispanic, which suggests that white visitors were coming at other times of the year as tourists and perhaps also for devotional purposes. By the end of the decade, news reports and the testimony of Father Roca were putting the Good Friday crowds between ten and twelve thousand pilgrims, with most of the pilgrims being Nuevomexicano Catholics. The size and permanence of the pilgrimage led the Archdiocese of Santa Fe to list the Santuario as an "official pilgrimage site" in 1979.[26]

In line with the modern pilgrimage's genesis with the veterans of Bataan, other "special interest" pilgrimages also began to be held around this time. In the 1970s, the Archdiocese of Santa Fe initiated an annual pilgrimage for vocations in which faithful Catholics from all over the state converge on the Santuario after a week-long walk of a hundred miles or more. Focused less on the miraculous nature of the place and more on its prominence in the New Mexican psyche as a site of pilgrimage, the stated purpose of these pilgrimages is to pray for people who may be considering entrée to the priesthood or other ordained service in the Catholic Church, but participants also report the feelings of communitas, rejuvenation, and recommitment to their faith typical of many Christian pilgrimages. The pilgrimages for vocations continue today, and many pilgrims can boast of participating multiple times, effectively having walked hundreds of miles in their lives toward Chimayó.[27] Another pilgrimage associated with the Santuario that emerged in this period was the Prayer Pilgrimage for Peace, begun in 1982 by Catholic peace activists to mark the fortieth anniversary of the atomic bomb. The pilgrimage featured walkers and runners carrying dirt from the *pocito* as well as a symbolic flame of peace between the Santuario and the famous nuclear research facilities at Los Alamos, New Mexico. With a distinctive commitment to social justice and to end nuclear armament, the participants in the pilgrimage, once in Los Alamos, gathered around a community pond where they floated a "raft of life" carrying various symbolic items such as "homemade bread, tulips, apple blossoms, forsythia, juniper branches, balloons, and woven blankets." In contrast to the Good Friday pilgrimage and the pilgrimage for vocations, the Prayer Pilgrimage for Peace was determinedly interfaith and ecumenical, with participation of various Christian denominations, Jews, Muslims, Buddhists, Sikhs, Hindus, Baha'is, and members of metaphysical religious movements.[28] The Archdiocese of Santa Fe maintained an organizational role in this pilgrimage through the mid-1990s, but according to a Santuario administrator, the Peace Pilgrimage has been defunct for a number of years.[29]

Another type of pilgrimage in Chimayó that has played off of the perceived spiritual power and community heritage of the Santuario has to do with the statistically high numbers of drug offenses and abuses in the Chimayó and Española area. Chimayó became known in the 1990s as the "heroin capital" of Río Arriba County, and the rate of overdose deaths there was more than three times the national average. The incidence of crime in the village had skyrocketed as addicts carried out thefts and sometimes violent assaults to sustain their habits. In response to the situation, an ecumenical group of community activists organized a march in 1999 after appealing to local Penitente chapters to get involved and step forward as the ancestral leaders of the community. Eventually 150 Penitente brothers led over 300 marchers from Santa Cruz to the

Santuario. The march heightened the visibility of the drug problem and was one of the factors that led to greater law enforcement action and a major drug bust. Chimayó and the whole Española Valley continue to suffer from higher-than-average rates of drug abuse, but special pilgrimages to the Santuario as well as the annual Holy Week festivities have kept greater attention on the problem, and various community-centered projects have arisen that, in some way, draw on the Santuario as a symbolic source of tradition and healing.[30]

The Holy Week pilgrimage has kept on growing, and the number of annual visitors to the church also continues to rise. The hundreds of thousands of tourists and pilgrims who today visit the Santuario, often as part of bus line tours of northern New Mexico, have inspired criticism that the site has become too commodified, or that the crowds of tourists have marred the spiritual nature of the place. Chris Quintana, an editorialist for the University of New Mexico's student newspaper, made the Good Friday pilgrimage in 2012 and found that he had mixed feelings about the experience. On the one hand, he appreciated the kindness of those who handed out water and snacks to the walkers and the sincerity of fellow pilgrims, but he was turned off by other aspects of the pilgrimage: "It's not my place to say where capitalists are and aren't, but their presence seemed to bastardize the journey. After all, I found it hard to consider any sort of God while a man hawked snow cones, hot dogs and fried pork skins."[31] In what follows, I examine tourism at the Santuario and how discourse about tourism and commodification often serves as yet another way to claim ownership on the devotions and material spaces of the church.

Spiritual Tourists and Touristy Pilgrims

Despite complaints from pilgrims and former pilgrims that Chimayó has become too commercial and full of tourists, it is facile and reductive to categorize tourists and pilgrims as two completely separate kinds of visitors to the Santuario. People's motivations, feelings, and multiple purposes for traveling to the Santuario are complex; the tourist who arrives on a tour bus may spend time in prayer and carry away a baggie of dirt that fulfills various roles as a quaint souvenir and a potentially powerful connection to narratives of miraculous healing. Likewise, the pilgrim who walks hours on Good Friday may also spend time taking photographs and perusing the gift shops. This is not to say that pilgrimage and tourism are identical, but as many scholars have pointed out, they have a great deal in common. In what follows, I examine the overlapping realms of tourism and pilgrimage at the Santuario.

Even if one could isolate the authentic intentions of every visitor to the Santuario—an impossible task—it would still be exceedingly difficult to find the person who is either pure pilgrim or pure tourist. And from the vantage point of the external observer, the actions of the one often look remarkably like those of the other. Scholars of tourism have noted that tourism in its contemporary forms often meets "individuals' periodic needs for spiritual renewal." The anthropologist Nelson Graburn holds this view and further suggests that modern tourism is a kind of "secular ritual" that stands in opposition to everyday life. He insightfully proposes that the bulk of middle-class tourists may be the ones most in need of a little simplicity or authenticity in their lives, even if these experiences are manufactured and commodified.[32] This process is at play for many of the tourists who visit the Santuario as part of a tour package or itinerary during a vacation to the "Land of Enchantment." They come to relax and enjoy the scenery, but they also come to encounter the Spanish and Indian heritage of the place. One tour package advertises the kind of experience on offer at the Santuario: "It is a spiritual place—and has been for hundreds of years for both the Native American, who once inhabited the land, and for the descendants of the Spanish settlers who still live there. Visit the Santuario de Chimayo and the Santo Nino Chapel, spiritual sites steeped in mystical and magical stories of healing."[33] The tourist who reads this advertisement knows what to expect and can look forward to his or her own experience: Chimayó is a "spiritual place," and it is on the tour.

One of the leading scholars of tourism, Dean MacCannell, describes this kind of touristic encounter as "staged authenticity." In this type of scenario, the tourist is invited to get "in with the natives" through what MacCannell, using a stage metaphor, calls the "front" and the "back." The visitor, in his or her quest to have an authentic experience, or to be exposed to an authentic space, moves incrementally into more and more intimate levels of engagement with the proffered authenticity. The trouble with this movement into staged authenticity is that it never arrives. "It is only when a person makes an effort to penetrate into the real life of the areas he visits that he ends up in places especially designed to generate feelings of intimacy and experiences that can be talked about as 'participation.'" Thus participating, "tourists have entered touristic space, [and] there is no way out for them as long as they press their search for authenticity." The conundrum that arises from seeking authentic experiences is precisely that the search itself is part of the touristic field of activities.[34] In Chimayó, this kind of "staged authenticity" is present in a number of ways, including through the sale of locally crafted artworks and foodstuffs, opportunities to arrange special tours of the site with official staff of the church as well as with enterprising local guides, and a slew of ways to collect and experience the Santuario's famous holy dirt. The various church-owned and private gift shops at the site all provide containers for sale in which to gather and save earth from the *pocito*, and brochures and placards inform visitors about the history and contemporary use of the dirt.

MacCannell's insights about "staged authenticity" certainly ring true for many touristic venues in New Mexico, including Chimayó, but at the Santuario it is not possible to neatly divide the insiders from those who are merely dropping in to participate in the lives of others. After all, despite its many unique qualities, the Santuario has been an official location of the Catholic Church for many years and thus a place on which Catholics, and even other kinds of Christians, may make some level of claim and involvement. My hours of observation of and conversations with visitors to the Santuario, including those who would self-identify as tourists, have shown to me that some tourists make their own connections to the Santuario. In fact, many of the tourists come to pray, rehearse the physical movements of their Catholicism (such as genuflecting, crossing oneself, and touching the holy water), or encounter the emotional and physical sensations that they associate with church buildings in general. Of course, these objectives can and often do overlap with the kinds of interactions with "staged authenticity" that MacCannell identifies. Nonetheless, I suggest that at the Santuario, something more than the mere purchase of an "authentic experience" is at play for many tourists. The explicitly religious nature of the Santuario, its history, its miraculous claims, and its key events (namely, the Holy Week pilgrimage) differentiate it in some ways from other tourist destinations.

Therefore, it is necessary to continue to nuance our understanding of how tourism and religion overlap at the Santuario by turning to other theories while still appreciating the theoretical usefulness of "staged authenticity" in Chimayó.

In his study of the Spanish missions located in San Antonio, Texas, the religious studies scholar Thomas Bremer identifies four features of what he calls "the borderlands of religion and tourism." Not surprisingly, many of the examples he uses to illustrate these four features relate to pilgrimage sites and are thus quite instructive in helping us understand the role of tourism to Chimayó. First, Bremer notes that tourists and religious adherents have a deep regard and attachment for "special places." Moreover, that which sets apart a special place as either a religious or a touristic destination is often slippery; for instance, the Santuario appeals to both kinds of visitors often for the same reasons, such as its air of spirituality, the holy dirt, or its history. Bremer notes that this results in a "simultaneity of places" wherein the touristic and the religious can shift rapidly between uses and meanings.[35]

A second feature flows from the first: both tourism and religious travel involve "an articulation of identities." Tourists as well as religious visitors to sites go to special places to define, explore, and perform their various identities. Again, to turn to the Santuario for examples, the day after the Good Friday pilgrimage in 2015, a large Aztec dance troupe converged on Chimayó to dance for hours beside the church in their ornate and colorful costumes. A participant in his thirties explained to me in English that almost all the dancers came from Albuquerque and had come to Chimayó to share their skills. Aztec dance troupes often explicitly understand their practice as one of cultural reclamation of indigenous heritage over and against the terrors and erasures of Spanish colonialism.[36] Although the young dancer did not say as much, I wondered whether the dancers' choice to dance at the Santuario during the Christian Holy Week represented an act of remembrance and reclamation of the indigenous heritage of the site. But other interpretations of why the dancers were there were also on hand. Pilgrims stopped and watched the dancers and snapped photos. I asked an older Hispanic woman what she made of the dancers with their drums and their Aztec costumes. She replied, "They're from Old Mexico." She explained to me that they were there to commemorate the apparition of the Virgin of

Guadalupe outside Mexico City. "Lots of people from Old Mexico come to the Santuario," she said. The palimpsest of meanings and identities that have accrued at the Santuario made possible these varying performances and explanations of identity. Where the Aztec dancers dance to reclaim the indigenous bona fides of the holy place, the Hispanic woman understood them as welcome guests from far away who were likely projecting an apparition story from their homeland on this special and celebratory place.[37]

The third feature that conceptually unites both religious practice and tourism for Bremer is the importance of aesthetics and the aestheticization of experience. Tourists seek out beautiful and uplifting vistas and encounters in a way that is not dissimilar to the religious search for the sublime. In both cases—religious and touristic—one of the most desirable aesthetics is that of authenticity. Tourists, especially those engaged in cultural or heritage tourism, but even those at the beach or hiking in the woods, seek out the "real," the sometimes ineffable sense that one is having a true experience. As MacCannell notes, in touristic settings, this kind of authenticity is often staged, perhaps in a way that we could fruitfully compare to the stagings of religious ritual that occur on a continuum from the quotidian of daily Mass to the exceptional such as a Passion play. Embodied performance is part of both tourism and religious practice. Chimayó is such an obvious example of these overlapping valences that Bremer points to the Santuario to make his point: "Whether or not they believe in (or are in need of) its miraculous curative powers, nearly everyone who comes to the shrine seeks to claim a bit of Chimayó's dirt to rub on their bodies and to take with them when they return home." He continues, "Without the authentic dirt right from the pit, their visits to the *santuario* would seem less than complete and might leave them feeling a bit unfulfilled." Of course, a visitor to the Santuario who is not a tourist behaves in much the same way; the routine of a visit to the Santuario is an aesthetic performance that is shared, on some levels, between tourist and nontourist alike.[38]

The fourth point at the intersection of religion and tourism that Bremer identifies is familiar to anyone who has visited religious sites that double as tourism destinations: commercialization. As we saw in chapter 4, Bernardo Abeyta used the Santuario for trade since its inception, and the site has been continuously tied to commerce from the beginning. Today, everything from goods to food to souvenirs are sold in Chimayó in conjunction with the Santuario. One of the most popular stops for tourists and devotees alike, known for its supply of unique artwork, jewelry, and Chimayó's famous chile, is El Potrero Trading Post. Owned by the Vigil and Bal families, the gift shop and store has been in operation since 1921 to serve the needs of pilgrims and tourists alike. One story that highlights the mutual relationship between the Santuario and the store claims that "the Vigil Store [El Potrero Trading Post] once housed an unusual number of soda machines, which the owner said were needed by pilgrims who ingested the holy dirt on site and started choking."[39] In addition to this shop, the Holy Family Parish, the official Catholic administrator of the Santuario, operates no fewer than three gift shops in close proximity to each other and the Santuario. A former manager of the Santuario, Joanne Dupont Sandoval, explains, "We have three gift shops, but these allow us to exist."[40] Besides goods and keepsakes, Chimayó, like other religious/touristic destinations, also trades in experiences and benefits from the sightseeing packages and motor coach tours that include stops at the Santuario. Given the many points of contact and overlap, it is often futile, suggests Bremer, to attempt to define clear boundaries between the act of visiting religious sites and tourist destinations. The meanings, behaviors, and actions of tourists, pilgrims, and other devotional visitors, while not identical, have been and are entangled.[41]

All of these overlapping features of tourist and religious destinations as well as the commonalities of practice between tourists and religious devotees lead to the observation that religious travel, especially pilgrimage, is related in important ways to tourism, and vice versa. They overlap and interrelate so much that it is often appropriate to talk about "religious tourism." Scholars of religion and tourism debate whether, on the one hand, the visitor's motivation or, on the other, the religious content of the destination or trip is more important to defining religious tourism. For those who focus on the religious motivations of travelers, the kind of religious tourism that occurs can often be defined as pilgrimage or some other kind of specific religious gathering such as a commemoration or celebration. On the other side of the definitional debate, those who lift up the religious content of touristic sites are more likely to add tours to particular religious locales as another kind of religious tourism. Both these kinds of religious tourism occur at the Santuario: the pilgrimage and the visit by a tourist who intentionally seeks out religious sites as part of tourism. In the latter case—the tourist who is interested in visiting religious sites—religious tourism can overlap significantly with another kind of leisure travel: heritage tourism. This, too, is part of Chimayó's explicit appeal in that many tourists *and* pilgrims go to the Santuario to connect or reconnect with Nuevomexicano village life and religious practice. Moreover, tour packages that include Chimayó often focus more on New Mexican heritage than on the spiritual or religious aspects of the tour.[42]

Ultimately, we must conclude that tourists and pilgrims do not belong to discrete groups. The intentions that bring individuals to the Santuario may vary. Some may come unreflectively as part of a regular family activity. Others may come to enjoy a ride in northern New Mexico and to see the sights. But most come with an orientation, if not toward the miraculous power of the place, at least toward the narrative mystique and aesthetic sacredness of this storied church and its environs. For longtime pilgrims, the traditional movements and observations of the pilgrimage guide their way along with individual petitions, promises, and desires. For first-timers, members of tour groups, and the curious, the Santuario's story and significance help make sense, and even meaning, from the natural movements one makes through the front doors of the church, down the nave, and into the sacristy and the room with the *pocito*.

So, does this overlap in movement and meaning making signify that the Santuario "belongs" to all who visit? One response, of course, is no. The place "belongs" to its heirs, the Hispano communities of northern New Mexico that built the church, nurtured it, were nurtured by it, and who still account for the largest population of people who attend daily Mass, visit during the year, and arrive en masse during the Holy Week pilgrimage. But tens of thousands of others also visit the Santuario every year, people who, as suggested above, are not merely tourists. Many of these visitors, in contrast to the Nuevomexicano pilgrims who so often go to the Santuario in multigenerational family units, come alone, or at least involved in a personal journey of sorts. One scholar who has studied the Santuario and its pilgrimage notes that "many first generation pilgrims and spiritual seekers" understand that the "pilgrimage to Chimayo is a journey one takes for oneself, to find oneself; an event whose meanings

are inherently relativistic. . . . Self-help and personal development movements of the second half of the twentieth century helped foster the sense
of one's pursuit of spirituality centers as a journey of self-discovery."[43]
While this fragmentation and focus on the personal may be the experience of some, I have argued here that longtime pilgrims along with occasional tourists and other visitors find more in common than the image
of the lone spiritual seeker may first suggest. Rather, the well-known narratives of miraculous healing, the centrality of the *pocito* and the holy
dirt, and the redolence of Christian imagery expressed in the idioms of
the *santeros* make the experience of visiting the Santuario relatively similar for ancestral Nuevomexicanos, other Catholic pilgrims, tourists, New
Age practitioners, and even historians and ethnographers. The semiotician Larry Russell found in his study of pilgrims and other visitors to the
Santuario that the symbols, material objects, and visual culture of the
Santuario provided a compelling framework for a pastiche-like construction of healing-centered rituals.[44] It is not so much that the Santuario is
the same in meaning and practice to all its visitors, but it affords visitors
the resources and impetus each needs to find his or her own place of
healing. That resonating experience moves many to lay claim to the Santuario as a place that is unique and special to them while simultaneously
being shared by many, many others.

* * *

On Holy Thursday (the day before Good Friday), my traveling companion and I spent most of the day at the Santuario to observe and take
part in the activities preceding the biggest day of pilgrimage. Early in
the afternoon, we crossed the road that runs in front of the church and
ascended a small hill that faces the Santuario from the south. At the top
of the little hill, someone has planted a large white cross, and at least
one of the legends about Bernardo Abeyta claims that he was on this
hill when he looked down and saw a light glinting in the dirt far below,
the light that would turn out to be the Esquipulas crucifix emerging
from the *pocito*. From this vantage point, a few hundred feet above the
pasture and Santa Cruz River that abut the Santuario, we could gather
in the entire site, the Santo Niño Chapel, the Santuario itself, the gift
shops, and plaza and other open spaces in miniature surrounded by tiny
milling pilgrims and tourists. To the northeast, even higher than us, we

saw the rising mass of Tsi Mayoh. Far to the west and east were the even higher peaks of the Jemez and Sangre de Cristo ranges. Away to the south, we could see the scrubby land all the way to New Mexico's main population centers. What impressed us the most from this view was the sense that the Santuario was, indeed, a navel of the earth, a connecting place at the center. The knowledge that the next day would bring tens of thousands of walkers heightened this feeling that we stood right above a gathering place *par excellence.*

We descended back to the people below, where I encountered a group of four pilgrims, three men and a woman. One of the men was weeping as the other three surrounded him. They had just arrived at the San-tuario after a twenty-one-mile walking pilgrimage from Tesuque, just north of Santa Fe. The weeping man explained that he made this pil-grimage every year to remember and honor his brother, who had been killed years ago after being hit by a car while making the Chimayó pil-grimage. Exhausted from their journey, emotions were running high—a mixture of euphoria, grief, and love for each other. The discomfort that I often feel during fieldwork, which comes from asking personal ques-tions during moments of religious importance, was erased in this case by the warmth of the grieving brother's story. He was gratified to tell me about his brother and about the vow he has kept. The Santuario, and the miles on the road approaching it, were healing to him, and his compan-ions hugged him and smiled proudly at him as he told me about their pilgrimage. To tell the story, not just to his fellow pilgrims but to me, helped complete both of our experiences at the Santuario that day. I, not exactly a tourist and not exactly a pilgrim, found myself swept into the gravitational field of the Santuario and its power to gather and to heal.

The Holy Family and the Santuario Today

In an obituary that came out at the time of his death in 2015, Father Casimiro Roca is quoted as having said, "The Santuario is my salvation."[1] In some ways, the opposite could also be said, that Roca saved the Santuario. In his decades-long tenure as a pastor and priest, Roca oversaw the mid-twentieth-century development of the place from a regionally important, structurally decaying church into a national and international site of pilgrimage. It was under his guidance that the Santuario achieved the status of an official U.S. National Historic Landmark, and Roca worked to maintain its historical integrity. By one measure, without Roca's intervention on behalf of the Catholic Church, the Santuario could well have become too decrepit to use. The priest's organizational prowess and long-term care ensured the soundness of the building— including the room with the famous *pocito*—and its ongoing viability as a site of pilgrimage. By other measures, perhaps despite Roca, the patrimony of the Santuario passed out of local hands and into a more nebulous semi-public, semi-ecclesiastical space. By the time of his death at the age of ninety-seven, Roca had stepped down long ago from the day-to-day pastoral leadership of the Santuario, but he lived to see other members of his order carry on his ministry in ways that enhanced the development of the shrine as a sacred center for hundreds of thousands of annual visitors.

After the Spanish Colonial Arts Society purchased the Santuario in 1929 and turned the property over to the Archdiocese of Santa Fe, it took several years for the Catholic Church to undertake a new era in the life of the shrine. But by the middle of the century, the Santuario received regular pastoral leadership and administration for the first time in its history. In this chapter, I look at official Catholic ownership and oversight of the Santuario and examine how the "new management" brought changes to the site. The chapter also considers ongoing contestations among the growing number of constituencies laying claim to the Santuario in the contemporary period. The massive increase in the number of visitors, the attendant rise in public prominence, the ongoing—perhaps even growing—faith in the miraculous power of the dirt, and the cementing of the Santuario as a permanent fixture in New Mexico's heritage tourism industry all have affected how the chapel is perceived and used. Between the Catholic Church's renewed role in the church's life and its increasing fame, the contemporary Santuario is an exceedingly complex site of both competing and cooperating desires. To begin, we turn to arguably the most important person, other than Bernardo Abeyta, in the entire history of the Santuario de Chimayó: Father Casimiro Roca.

Father Roca

The parish of Santa Cruz de la Cañada, one of the oldest in New Mexico, administered the area of Chimayó since the time of de Vargas's reconquest of the region until well into the twentieth century. The Franciscans oversaw Santa Cruz parish for most of its history until a member of the diocesan clergy finally took the reins in 1834.[2] After the U.S. takeover and the formation of the Diocese—and later Archdiocese—of Santa Fe, various priests ministered to the geographically extensive parish until 1920, when a Catalonian Spanish congregation of priests, the Sons of the Holy Family, settled in the area. When the Santuario was purchased in 1929, it had long been an outlying post of the Santa Cruz parish, and it continued as such. At that point, Father Salvador Gené, one of the Sons of the Holy Family, pastored the enormous parish with its many missions, which included Los Alamos, San Ildefonso, Nambé, Pojoaque, Española, Truchas, Cordova, Ojo Sarco, and Las Trampas, as well as several chapels in the village of Chimayó. As he did before the sale, Gené or another priest celebrated Mass in the Santuario only once a month, but this practice did not last long. Physical deterioration in the Santuario made the building unsafe to use, and at some point in the 1930s or 1940s, even this limited usage of the Santuario was curtailed, and the Mass was moved to the adjacent Medina Chapel.[3]

Although several priests worked from Santa Cruz, the parish was so large that many of the Catholics in the region did not interact regularly with a member of the clergy. It was clear to Gené that more personnel were needed, and so, after first working in Colorado and California, a thirty-six-year-old Casimiro Roca arrived in New Mexico in 1954 to assist the growing needs of Hispanic Catholics in the greater Santa Cruz area. As an immigrant priest, Roca understood himself and his vocation as a missionary to underserved Spanish-speaking Catholics in the American Southwest. One of his first efforts in New Mexico was a preaching mission to the rarely visited churches of the eastern section of the parish. Community leaders, known as *mayordomos*, of the various chapels and churches in the scattered villages organized the communities to welcome Roca, hear his preaching, receive the sacraments, and gather for congregational fellowship. Before long, Roca had renewed weekly Mass at the Santuario as well as in the decrepit church in Truchas (nine miles east of Chimayó on the high road to Taos).[4]

From the beginning of what would become his life's work in the region, Roca was committed to building up New Mexico's Hispanic Catholic community in the area east of Española. In his autobiography, Roca recalled his initial feelings about the region and worried about how it had suffered from Catholic neglect and Protestant advances, especially by the Presbyterians, who had established a number of schools in the area.

> Little by little, a good number of the families were leaving behind their traditional Catholicism. When I arrived, the attendance at Mass was meager, the church building was in bad shape and without electricity, and there was very little space next to the building. It saddened me that these families were losing the religious heritage of their ancestors. . . . What made the situation more difficult is that the Catholic families who decided for a Protestant education could be excommunicated according to Church law at that time. This would mean being prohibited from receiving the sacraments and not being allowed a Catholic burial.[5]

Roca's answer to this problem, especially after the archbishop made him the pastor of a new parish in Truchas, was to build. Roca's commitment to infrastructure improvements and building projects would carry him through much of the rest of his ministry and would save the Santuario from crumbling to the ground.

On a shoestring budget, and with only dubious support from the archbishop, Roca and his parishioners, largely through their own labor and donated materials, managed to construct a new church building in Truchas within a year of his arrival. The energetic priest's methods consisted of relying on volunteer labor (volunteers made and placed ten thousand adobe bricks for the church) and cajoling free assistance from expert craftspeople when necessary. In some cases, he drew on the deep-seated Catholic allegiance of local workers to persuade them to donate labor to his building causes. For instance, at Truchas, he convinced a nearby woodcarver and lapsed Catholic to produce a cross for the church façade by asking him "if he wanted to save his soul." The cross was donated, and the man returned to the church. In the months following the dedication of the new structure, Roca's impulse to strengthen infrastructure took hold and led to building repairs at many of the chapels in his new parish.[6]

It was also at Truchas that Roca began to learn how to work in concert with the long traditions of lay leadership that had developed in the absence of priests, lessons that he would later carry to his work at the Santuario. Various orders of the Penitente Brotherhood among the villages of the new parish had long led community religious observance in the region. During his first Holy Week at Truchas, Roca discovered that the parish schedule he had devised coincided with Penitente ceremonies, resulting in a low level of participation at the church. "That experience taught me it's not a good idea to compete with popular religiosity." By the next year, the priest coordinated festivities at the church with the local leader of the Penitentes and noticed an uptick in attendance. Even with this synchronized approach to Catholic observance in the isolated mountain villages, Roca was not immediately able to build up a strong parish community in Truchas and soon found himself making frequent preaching jaunts to Oklahoma, Texas, Nebraska, and Kansas to expand outreach to poorly served Hispanic Catholics.[7] The historical record is not clear as to why church attendance at Roca's new building flagged, but possible explanations include long traditions of lay leadership combined with a changing economy that meant that many people were relocating out of the villages to larger urban job centers. Nevertheless, even as he continued to search for the best outlets for his ministry away from northern New Mexico, Roca remained tied to the Archdiocese of Santa Fe and to his parish duties in Truchas and the other villages.

In 1959 Archbishop Edwin Byrne, apparently impressed both by Roca's efforts in Truchas and by the needs of Hispanic Catholics east of

Santa Cruz, wrote, "I have decided to separate the valley of Chimayó from the parish of Santa Cruz and join it to the territory covered by Our Lady of the Rosary Parish in Truchas. But Chimayó will be the seat of the parish, and I want Father Casimiro Roca to be in charge and to move his residence there." Chimayó, then as now, was less of a cohesive town than a series of population centers gathered around various chapels. These included chapels dedicated to Nuestra Señora de Dolores and Nuestra Señora del Carmen, the oratory of Saint Bonaventure on the Plaza del Cerro in the center of town, and, of course, the Santuario and El Santo Niño (Medina) Chapel in the part of the village known as El Potrero. Of these, the Santuario was easily the most prominent; a priest from Santa Cruz was celebrating Mass there every Sunday by the time of the restructuring of the parish under Roca.[8] By Roca's own account, the Catholic life of the village was at that point still overseen by a well-ordered cadre of Penitentes who yet maintained some of the same offices, namely that of *hermano rezador* (prayer leader) and *hermano enfermero* (an expert in home remedies and caring for the sick), that had appeared in a Penitente constitution first framed by Bernardo Abeyta over a hundred years before Roca's arrival.[9]

The priest, burnishing his already established credentials as a builder, found a new and lasting project in the decrepit shrine. "When I came," remembered Roca, "the Santuario was almost falling down. The walls were cracking, there was no plaster on the walls. Only the four walls were standing." The site suffered from other problems as well. "I noticed that even animals were inside the building. Pigeons and bats would fly in and out of cracks in the walls. The doors were dilapidated and the steep steps made [the] entryway dangerous." By 1960, a year after his installation as priest of the new, expanded parish, Roca had dedicated himself to a major restoration of the Santuario.[10] Erosion of the soil behind the building, where the land slopes gently down to the Santa Cruz River, presented the most serious threat to the Santuario. The weather had taken its toll over the decades, wearing away the sandy ground near the holy dirt of the *pocito*, and collapse of the whole structure was a real possibility. Roca happened upon two local contractors, Norberto Atencio and Ray "Cabrita" Quintana, and asked them, "Do you have faith?" Calling to mind the Gospel passage where Jesus exhorts his followers that faith can move mountains, Roca explained the Santuario's plight to the two men, who, at first, were nonplussed. But several days later, a caravan of trucks and machinery arrived at the church and, over the next few days, unloaded approximately 150,000 tons of fill dirt to stop the erosion and provide much-needed stability to the property. With glee, Roca reported that the men took no payment for the job. "*We know you don't have a red cent on you. But we didn't do it for you. We did it for the Lord!*"[11] Over time, the priest spearheaded efforts to build a cement retaining wall to further guard against erosion, cleaned and repaired walls and flooring, rehung doors, and added an additional foot of earth to the four main walls to provide extra support.

Over the course of his decades of ministry at the Santuario, Roca took steps to ensure the ongoing maintenance of the church so that it would not fall again into disrepair. One major step he and others took in this regard was to apply for and receive official National Historic Landmark status for the Santuario in 1970, and in 1990 the national importance of the site was further recognized under the rubric of the National Register of Historic Places.[12] Roca also organized regular replastering of the building, touch-ups to the paint, and maintenance of the grounds. It was in 1980, twenty years after his first charge at Chimayó began, that the priest decided to pave the dirt floor of the church and the surrounding grounds. Shortly afterward, he also arranged purchase of a small house adjacent to the Santuario to open the first church-operated gift shop, which would supply a source of ongoing funding to maintain the property.[13] Both the floor and the shop were in response to ever-growing numbers of pilgrims and tourists; Roca's impulse to build and improve for the sake of Catholic outreach to New Mexico's Hispanic population most certainly saved the Santuario from decay even as it provided the infrastructure for the transformation of the Santuario from a locally important pilgrimage site to an internationally recognized center of religious and heritage tourism as well as health seeking.

Ambivalent Responses to Tourism and Commercial Ventures

Pilgrimage's relationship to tourism at the Santuario—and in general—is covered in the previous chapter; here, as I examine the most recent history of the shrine, the focus is how the current ecclesiastical administration of the Santuario has operated amidst the frequent tension involved in managing a site that is both a Catholic church and a significant tourist attraction. In many ways, the Santuario's allure as a tourism destination grew naturally along with New Mexico's tourism industry in the twentieth century. On the scenic high road to Taos, Chimayó is a convenient stop for sightseers who can pause, quickly tour the church, and perhaps have lunch at the nearby and well-known Rancho de Chimayó restaurant before climbing back in their cars and heading on their way. But the Santuario is a draw all by itself, especially for the sectors of New Mexico's tourist market that focus on Hispano heritage or the plethora of alternative healing centers in the state. The Santuario, as it always has, fulfills various community and economic needs despite its official status as a Catholic church. The Sons of the Holy Family, Roca's congregation of priests, continues their oversight of the place, and they have both promoted tourism and critiqued what they perceive as the occasional excesses and superficiality of the tourist trade.

Don Usner, a historian and photographer with family roots in Chimayó, has spent many years in and around northern New Mexico, and like many locals, has a long memory of the Good Friday pilgrimage. However, despite the unquestionable numerical growth in the number of pilgrims and tourists to the Santuario, especially during Holy Week, Usner, whose views are representative of many Chimayó residents, is ambivalent at best about the crowds. Making his way through fields and back ways to the Santuario on Easter Sunday, he notes, with nostalgia, "Gone are the throngs of pilgrims who made their way to the Santuario two days ago on Good Friday—a day when we generally avoid visiting Chimayó. The carnival atmosphere of the pilgrimage contrasts dramatically with the way it used to be, the way we liked it."[14] He evokes days gone by, when the crowds were more manageable, before the clusters of gift shops were built. And Usner is not alone in his feeling that the growth in both tourists and pilgrims has not been healthy for Chimayó, or even for the authentic performance of Catholicism in the town. Usner recounts an entertaining story in which a crowd of pilgrims is walking east through Chimayó on Good Friday to arrive at the Santuario. A faithful member of the Holy Family Catholic Church in Chimayó (also administered by the Sons of the Holy Family) chases beside the pilgrims on the road, hectoring them, asking them why they are walking away from the parish church since that was where the sacraments were.

The implication is that the "real" church is the parish church, where the locals worship, while the Santuario is a sideshow for tourists and outsiders.[15]

In short, and as Usner's observations reveal, the two groups who have felt most ambivalent about the rise in the number of visitors to the Santuario have been local residents and official representatives of the Catholic Church. And, arguably, the issue continues to be religious ownership. Local residents, for whom tourist and pilgrim dollars are essential keys to the economy, nonetheless often complain that the values and authenticity of Chimayó are being permanently marred by the constant flow of visitors in and out of the area. For instance, in 1990 lifelong Chimayó resident Paul Medina shared his frustration with a reporter. "'Europeans are pouring in,' he says. 'They come to my house asking where the place is that the lame come out walking.'" Medina was specifically disgruntled with the amount of publicity that, to his mind, had reached too many people in far-flung locations. Even local employees of the Santuario can become tired of the influx. Frances Chavez, a former caretaker of the Santuario, protested that the hordes of tourists made her job more difficult: "Some people take a whole lot of dirt from the hole. . . . Some Sundays I have to put in six pails of dirt."[16] The priests of the Sons of the Holy Family, in similar fashion, both benefit from the crowds and occasionally grouse about them. Roca celebrated the growth at the Santuario, especially in relation to the pilgrimage, but he was less enthusiastic about mere sightseers. In his memoirs, he recalled that during Holy Week festivities there were often "many who milled around the grounds for nothing more than curiosity." He acknowledged that tourism "has its proper value and tourists are always welcome at the Santuario" as long as they did not detract from "the spiritual sense" of the place.[17] In other words, both local residents and clergy, although desirous of the benefits of tourism, yet worry that casual visitors, and even pilgrims, will alter their own sense of what the Santuario and its environs ought to be.

Over the years, dozens of feature stories in both state and national newspapers have appeared about the Santuario, especially around Holy Week and the annual pilgrimage. During the decades of his service, Roca was interviewed on many occasions for these stories, and one can broadly trace his changing attitude over time toward the crowds of visitors. Ever a pastor, he rarely has harsh words, but his initial recognition that not all visitors come to the Santuario with the same doctrinal orthodoxy that he or other clergy might like slowly evolves over time to frustration and even exasperation. "Roca said," reports a 1979 story, that "until 1970, 100 percent of the persons who visited El Santuario did so for religious purposes." But by the time of the article, nine years later, his estimate was that a mere 75 percent were there for what he considered religious motivations.[18] At least from Roca's point of view, larger and larger numbers of tourists were arriving at the Santuario simply to see the sights rather than out of a sense of religious devotion.

Roca may have included in this group those who came just for the miraculous dirt without an attendant faith in God's healing power. The Sons of the Holy Family have been clear since the days of Roca's ministry that the dirt has no special powers, and they have made several efforts to disabuse the credulous. In 1996 Roca told a reporter that he had taken to avoiding the Santuario during Holy Week because he was so irritated by the "hysteria over the dirt." He affirmed his belief in miracles at the site but insisted that it is "religious faith, the faith in God and Jesus Christ that heals."[19] Over a decade later, a retired Roca held the same line with a reporter from the *New York Times*: "'It's not the dirt that makes the miracles!' the Rev. Casimiro Roca said with exasperation."[20] The current ecclesiastical administrators of the shrine, in line with their colleague Roca, have continued to interpret the dirt for the visiting public. In one of the glossy publications available for sale in the gift shops, the current priests write, "In itself, the dirt does not have any curative powers." However, they do acknowledge that the dirt of Chimayó can serve as a conduit for effective prayer and contemplation: "The thing to consider is that people come to El Santuario not only when they want something, but also to pray, in thanksgiving, and to worship God. Something about this place helps people to experience their God."[21] Roca's tone of exasperation, in this more recent statement from other Sons of the Holy Family, is replaced by a reminder that, in the theology of the Catholic Church, it is the power of God that answers prayers of supplication and thanksgiving. Visitors are thereby nudged away from a magical engagement with the dirt itself, divorced in some way from devotion to God.

A brochure that is posted in several locations around the Santuario provides precise instructions on how to properly use the dirt for healing and also an interpretation of what makes the dirt holy. Although many pilgrims associate the holy dirt with the Santo Niño (see chapter 4), this brochure, along with other publications by the Sons of the Holy Family, attempts to return attribution to the Lord of Esquipulas.[22] Bold type admonishes the reader: "The Holy dirt is not to be eaten or drunk." Instead, a six-point ritual of prayer and healing is suggested wherein the supplicant stills his or her heart, acknowledges weakness and sin, makes a petition for healing with the caveat that God's will be done, and, finally, rubs "the holy dirt over the part of your body in need of healing while you invoke the name of Jesus as your Lord and Savior."[23] Photographs on the brochure juxtapose the *pocito* with a close-up shot of the suffering face of Jesus from the Esquipulas crucifix on the Santuario's main altar. The message is somewhat less plain than Roca's earlier insistence that the dirt itself is not miraculous. At various points, the text of the brochure acknowledges that the dirt is indeed "holy," but this holiness has everything to do with the faith of the supplicant in the crucified Christ, especially as he is known in the image of the Lord of Esquipulas. It is that association that makes the dirt miraculous as well as the well-publicized fact that a priest blesses all the dirt before it is placed in the *pocito*.

Try as they might, the clergy and other Catholic administrators of the shrine have not always been able to control how others use the dirt or interpret the Santuario. Nonetheless, when challenged, the priests and other official spokespeople for the archdiocese have occasionally demanded that their ownership of the church be recognized in such a way that they be accorded unique rights to the place, its attendant rituals, and the inherent value it holds. Two examples from the early 1990s illustrate this. First, in 1992, the New Mexico Department of Tourism ran a full-page advertisement in several national tourism magazines, including *Condé Nast Traveler*, *Sunset*, *National Geographic Traveler*, and *Travel and Leisure*, promoting the Easter pilgrimage to the Santuario. The ad specifically mentioned the "healing earth" as a particular attraction that tourists would not want to miss. The *Chicago Tribune* reported, "In response to howls of dismay from the Archdiocese of Santa Fe that such ads are a sacrilege, state officials have agreed not to do it again."[24] The archdiocese chastised the Department of Tourism for not consulting with it prior to running the spots, implying that this kind of marketing to tourists should and could not occur without the Catholic Church's express permission. Others, including an editorialist for the *Albuquerque Tribune*, felt that access to the Santuario, its dirt, and the pilgrimage ought to be explicitly shared between various stakeholders, including "tourist officials, media representatives, church leaders and pilgrims."[25] In this incident, tourism promoters had assumed that the sights of New Mexico, including the Santuario, were a public good that was theirs to sell to tourist consumers. Church officials vigorously opposed this stance, claiming that the Santuario was theirs and that the church, its ostensibly miraculous dirt, and its central event—the Holy Week pilgrimage—ought to be excluded from the mammon-motivated world of secular tourism.

The second example, which also unfolded in 1992, involved an even more acute case of commercialization of Chimayó's dirt. A New Age-inflected mail-order company based in Los Angeles began selling a product known as a "Miracle Cross of Chimayó." As the name suggests, these were small crosses that contained a small quantity of dirt from the Chimayó area. A brochure that accompanied the crosses conveniently noted that "now you don't have to travel to Chimayo to experience the benefits of its blessed earth." With a money-back guarantee, the crosses also promised that "your money problems will fade as your savings grow." Father Miguel Mateo, the priest in charge of the Santuario at the time, sent several letters in protest to the company, specifically voicing displeasure concerning the crass dollar values that the "Miracle Crosses" assigned to Chimayó's dirt. Burton Usen, the owner of the distribution company, claimed that the dirt in the crosses did not come from inside the church but rather from the Chimayó vicinity, and he promised to inform consumers that his product was in no way connected to the Santuario. Mateo, echoing his predecessor, Father Roca, insisted that "The dirt becomes a symbol and expression of faith. . . . Everyone knows it is the faith of the person that is important. It is the power of God that heals." In other words, the dirt should not be bought and sold as a free-standing commodity of healing power—it only works, so to speak, in the context of faith and in the symbolic space of the Santuario itself. "We do not have an answer," said Mateo, "why this happens here [in Chimayó] and not in Los Angeles." Despite Mateo's protests about Usen's commercialization of the dirt, the priest did note that running the Santuario was an expensive undertaking, and he mentioned that they were raising money to build a parking lot and that they would need an additional $26,000 to clean the inside of the church.[26] Eventually, the priests' complaints were joined by objections of local people in the Chimayó area, and Usen agreed to stop marketing his crosses.[27] It is doubtful that the discontinuation of Usen's venture led to any increase in revenues at the Santuario, but the priests were able to demonstrate that their objectives concerning the Santuario and its dirt, while certainly not devoid of financial considerations, remained focused on promoting faith in God's power rather than in some intrinsic power of the dirt itself.

The modern history of the Santuario, however, suggests that tourists as well as non-Hispano health seekers, with their desires and their dollars, have had an influence not only on organizations like New Mexico's Department of Tourism but also on the Catholic Church. Early in the 1960s, Casimiro Roca had his mind on what tourists could do for the Santuario and the rest of Holy Family Parish. In his memoirs, he recalls how he and his parishioners in Chimayó decided to revive the nearly defunct tradition of celebrating the Fiesta del Señor Santiago on July 25. Santiago is the patron saint of the Spanish Conquest, and religious folk dramas concerning the establishment of Catholicism in New Mexico had long been part of his feast day celebration; it also provided another reason for visitors to come to Chimayó. "We had an idea of seizing the opportunity of the occasion," wrote Roca, "to give the fiesta some appeal to tourists, which might at the same time help us raise some funds." The revived event would feature "presentations of the dramatic re-enactment of *Moros y Cristianos* and the folk dance *Los Matachines*."[28] Tourism only increased from that point forward, and the Sons of the Holy Family in recent years have worked to improve infrastructure at the site for large numbers of visitors, including expanded parking lots, permanent bathroom facilities, tidy picnic areas, a visitors' center, and several gift shops. As in Roca's era, the stated purpose of these tourist accommodations is not mere profit but rather the ability to continue to maintain the Santuario as a holy place for all. A recent site administrator explains, "We have three gift shops, but these allow us to exist."[29] In brief, Catholic clergy and leaders in Chimayó have promoted tourism that meets their financial and religious priorities for the shrine even while they have been generally critical of others' efforts to promote and profit from the Santuario.

Healing and the Holy Dirt Today

Even as the Catholic Church has tried to control interpretation as well as commerce related to Chimayó's holy dirt, devotees and visitors from many walks of life continue to seek out the dirt for its purported miraculous power. Interviews with people who claim to have been healed by the dirt confirm that for many, the miraculous emerges out of the combination of a devout faith in the healing power of God and the physical experience of visiting the Santuario and gathering the dirt. Bonnie Trujillo is from the Chimayó area and is related to the Medina family that once owned the Santo Niño Chapel. When she was younger, she was diagnosed with a terminal form of cancer; although she underwent chemotherapy, her doctors predicted that she had only months to live. Throughout her ordeal, she maintained an active prayer life, went to Mass, gathered dirt from the Santuario, and was especially buoyed by the helpful accompaniment of Father Roca and other priests of the Chimayó parish. Despite all odds, she went into remission: "When my doctor called me into his office, he even started to cry. He said, 'You are my miracle.'" Trujillo reports that she has faith in the holy dirt but faith in God first. She explains that the dirt itself is representative of the "holy ground" the shrine is on. "I tell people to think of the dirt as similar to holy water, to think of it as sacramental."[30]

In addition to faith and the substance of the dirt, others add a third element to the miraculousness of the Santuario: the shared act of going to Chimayó together with loved ones. Esther and Alberto live south of Albuquerque now but grew up coming with their families to visit Chimayó. When Esther was diagnosed with a lung disease that required the transplant of both lungs, she and her family prepared for the worst. However, in Esther's memory, miracles abound. First, she just made it on to an airplane to get to her surgery right before a blizzard closed the airport. Second, on both occasions when she flat-lined in the hospital, a doctor was present in her room and was able to revive her, once through a harrowing maneuver that required the doctor to stop her bleeding with his bare hand. The day I talked with them, Esther and Alberto were visiting the Santuario with a few other family members to give thanks for Esther's improbable recovery. The Santuario played a role in Esther's illness, mostly as a reminder of her community. "My sickness made me glad to be Catholic, and glad, really, to be Hispanic. I have so many people with me to take care of me. We stick together."[31]

The Catholic Church has, so far, never made an official investigation of the ostensible miracles at Chimayó. But the lack of ecclesiastical research does not indicate that the Church denies that miracles occur. On the contrary, the current pastor of the Santuario, Father Julio González, is fond of linking Chimayó with other international Catholic pilgrimage and healing centers such as the famous Lourdes in France. Recent publications put out by the Sons of the Holy Family feature testimonies that people have shared in email and letters. For example, a woman from Chicago writes that a loved one anticipated radiation treatments for throat cancer. After he rubbed the dirt on his neck and throat, the cancer seemed to disappear. "With all our hearts, we know it was the healing dirt." Another testimony claims that a young girl who had been dying from cancer was completely healed and required no additional surgery because of the holy dirt. An additional testimony, not atypical, reports that while the dirt did not bring a physical cure, emotional well-being was achieved: "Peace of mind is sometimes better."[32] The priests, by sharing and highlighting these testimonies, communicate that healing, whether it be of the body or of the spirit, is important not only to visitors and pilgrims but also to the priests themselves in their understanding of the shrine.

In fact, while no formal investigations have been made by Church officials into allegations of miracles at the Santuario, the priests have been informally collecting written testimonies of healing and other miracles for several years. I was able to examine a subset of these testimonies for which Santuario staff have been able to obtain permission to publicize and share. Of course, this sample of stories is not completely representative of all the visitors to the Santuario; only a few take the time to write to the priests concerning their experiences, and an even smaller fraction later provide permission to record and share their stories. Nonetheless, these testimonies provide a unique window onto the claims that devotees are making about their interactions with the Santuario, the Santo Niño de Esquipulas, and the famous dirt. As in the published examples cited above, a great deal of the collected testimonies have to do with the healing of cancer. In my unscientific review of the letters, roughly one-fourth of all the stories have to do with the cessation or easing of various forms

Figure 7.1. The *pocito* of holy earth. Author's photo.

of cancer. Some of the cancer miracles concern the letter writer himself or herself. For instance, a woman writes that she rubbed the dirt on her breasts and was cured from stage 3 breast cancer.[33] More common, however, are letters from loved ones who shared the dirt with people with cancer; they write to report that their intercession, accompanied by the dirt, led to healing. A moving example comes from a father whose four-year-old son was in remission after receiving the dirt.[34] Other letters in this vein report that even their doctors were amazed by the healing power of the Santuario's holy earth. An eleven-year-old girl from Colorado got over Ewing's Sarcoma after only one chemotherapy treatment plus administration of the dirt. Her doctors called it a miracle.[35] Another twist on this story is that medical professionals are doubtful of miraculous healing, but that the patients attribute their cure to the dirt. For example, a woman from Texas rejoices that the dirt, along with chemo and radiation, healed her from lymphoma, and healed her friend from anal cancer. She writes, "As doctors, they are convinced that it was their treatments that cured us. I feel that it was the hand of God that saved us."[36]

After cancer, the next most-mentioned set of miracles has to do with fertility. These letters, unlike the ones concerning the healing of cancers, always focus on the experiences of the letter writer herself (it is always women in these cases) rather than referring to a friend or family member to whom dirt was given. A typical account comes from a couple in Seattle, who, with little detail, give thanks and attribute their ability to have a child to the holy dirt.[37] It is obvious from several of these notes of thanksgiving that the miracle of a son or daughter's birth has led to a long-term sense of gratitude and devotion; in these testimonies, the child is already a teenager, and the mother is looking back on the role of the Santuario in the child's birth. In a letter that provides more detail than most, a woman writes that she and her husband had been diagnosed as infertile and had undergone treatment at a prestigious fertility clinic at a prominent research university hospital, but to no avail. They came to visit the Santuario on vacation, and two days later in Taos were delighted to have a positive pregnancy test. The letter exudes joy and gratitude for their daughter, who at the time the letter was written had just turned eighteen.[38] Given the central role of the Santo Niño de Atocha at the Santuario and his special care and regard for children, it is perhaps not surprising that so many couples have found their prayers answered concerning the birth of children after visiting the church.

The remainder of the letters in the Santuario's files are more difficult to classify into discrete groups, but a large number have to do with the miraculous cessation of various chronic conditions and pains. Several of these testimonies, in addition to mention of the dirt, point to the power of the Santo Niño as a particular source of their healing. (It is notable that, despite the priests' emphasis on the crucifix of Our Lord of Esquipulas, he is not once cited as the source of the miraculous in the testimonial letters.) A longtime visitor to the Santuario writes that he was healed of chronic stomach pain. "I have faith in Our Miraculous Child of Atocha," he writes.[39] A similar testimony comes from a California man who attributed his recovery from a health crisis and coma to the Niño.[40] Other letters evidence an overwhelming faith in the efficacy of the holy dirt, so much so that it becomes a kind of cure-all for entire families. For instance, a suffering woman in Texas was healed of a progressive muscle disorder, hearing loss, hypoglycemia, and insomnia; she also testifies that other members of her family, after using the dirt, have been healed of smoking, alcoholism, and eczema.[41] Another family

Figure 7.2. People leave thousands of photos of their loved ones at the Santuario every year. Author's photo.

stockpiled some of the dirt in 1995 and now use it in small quantities for all complaints, "and are cured every time."[42] These letters, both the ones that feature the Santo Niño and those that focus on the holy dirt, certainly demonstrate faith, and often mention the power of God to heal. However, they also exhibit a popular commitment to the material and narrative features of the shrine that the priests have attempted to downplay. This does not so much create a tension with the clergy (who also acknowledge the miraculousness of the place) as demonstrate an ongoing disconnect in the attribution of the miracles. After all, the priests would not feel the need to continue to instruct that the dirt is not itself miraculous if they did not frequently observe a belief to the contrary.

Not all of the testimonials, however, deviate from the interpretive framework for the miraculous that the clergy have promoted. As we have seen, brochures, priests' statements, and signage at the Santuario all attempt to remind the visitors—both pilgrims and tourists—that miracles come from a faithful relationship with God. This is not to say that such miracles may not be mediated through particular devotions such as the

Santo Niño de Atocha, the Lord of Esquipulas, or the dirt in the *pocito*. But over and over again, Roca and his successors have maintained that the holy dirt, by its own, has no inherent healing properties. It works, so to speak, only through faith in God's power and love. In fact, healing in this context becomes less about miraculous cessation of physical symptoms and more about the peace and solace that come from a closeness to God. Some of the letters accentuate this very point, especially those testimonies that come from people who did not experience a physical cure of their maladies. Such letters sometimes come from devotees who are suffering from a chronic condition, such as muscular sclerosis (MS) or lupus. For instance, a woman with MS wrote, "I can't explain how powerful and what a feeling I had during the time we were all in the room [with the *pocito*] praying to God for what we need in life." These prayers led to a new perspective for the woman concerning God's care for her.[43] Others testify that a visit to the Santuario was just what they needed to overcome feelings of grief or depression. A moving example comes from a woman with pain in her ankles as well as suicidal feelings. She rubbed dirt on her ankles and "Immediately I felt a warmth and tingling on my ankles and feet." This led to spiritual if not physical healing, and also helped her decide not to commit suicide.[44]

Several miracles in the testimonial letters defy categorization into particular types of petitions or answers to specific diseases but instead suggest an almost magical approach to the dirt's power; in these letters the precinct of the Santuario becomes a kind of center of mysterious and benevolent power. Not surprisingly, some of these testimonies depart considerably from Catholic orthodoxy. One such letter suggests that the dirt is just as salutary for pets as it is for their human owners. A standard poodle, liberally treated with the dirt, lived three years longer than its veterinarian had diagnosed.[45] Another letter opens the possibility that not only the dirt is holy at the Santuario but, by virtue of association, even the items for sale in the gift shops have miraculous properties. Thus, one writer testifies that a visor clip (for the sun visor in an automobile) bought at the Santuario protected the writer's family from injury in an accident.[46] And in a miracle reminiscent of Jesus's feeding of the five thousand or Elijah and the widow of Zarephath, an ecstatic woman writes that, while on a family vacation to New Mexico, she and her family planned to travel to the Santuario by car. On the way, her husband, who was driving, realized that they were about to run out of gas. However, the gas tank was miraculously filled to one quarter of a tank, and the family was able to complete their journey to Chimayó. Moreover, writes the woman, the whole family, and especially her husband, were cured of anxiety.[47] These kinds of letters, while entertaining to read, underscore an important point about the miraculousness of the Santuario for many people: it is not limited by priestly narratives but rather thrives and evolves to meet the desires of those who come.

An International Pilgrimage Site and Its Discontents

The Santuario de Chimayó, by any measure, is a major attraction. Hundreds of thousands of visitors make their way to the church and its grounds annually, and there is every indication that the numbers will continue to grow. The question of religious ownership, in this context, is a high-stakes one: Who ultimately gets to set the agenda for how the Santuario will evolve to meet the needs of the throngs of pilgrims and tourists? The most obvious answer is the Catholic Church, the legal owners of the Santuario and much of the surrounding property. Since the tenure of Father Roca, the Sons of the Holy Family have made it their mission to maintain and develop the site for large numbers of visitors. Roca, the consummate builder, made relatively modest changes to the site's infrastructure, but his successors have expanded on his initial vision. However, other stakeholders in the Santuario also have ideas for its future that sometimes put them at loggerheads with the Catholic Church. As we have seen, New Mexico's tourism industry, which overlaps with the state's identity as a center for complementary and alternative medicine and healing, has attempted to promote the Santuario, but not without engendering the ire of the archdiocese. Another group that lays claim to the Santuario and Chimayó itself are local residents—and their more widely dispersed relatives and descendants—who often argue for maintaining a particular vision of the church that, to them, is more authentic and in synch with traditional usage patterns. This latter constituency is the one most likely to despair of new developments and building around the Santuario lest the tenor of life, community religious observance, and the basic aesthetic of the village be permanently altered.

Father Julio González is the current pastor of Holy Family Parish in Chimayó, a post that includes oversight of the Santuario. When González began this position shortly after the turn of the century, the grounds around the church were quite simple, with no buildings other than the gift shop Roca had opened and public bathrooms to the immediate west of the Santuario. Under his direction, the environment around the Santuario has changed considerably. At the time of the publication of this book, González had organized the construction of several "prayer portals," either new or renovated outbuildings that contain places to reflect, to pray, and to display the many photographs, baby shoes, and other items that devotees leave at the shrine. He has also included a couple of areas that nod to the Native American heritage of the region. At the entrance to the grounds from the main parking lot is the Three Cultures Monument, which features a statue of a conquistador, a friar, and a (somewhat out-of-place) Plains Indian man with a feathery headdress. Additionally, there is a Native American Cenacle, which features a painting of American Indians seated around the table of Jesus's Last Supper. The cenacle lies in the corner of the extensive Madonna Gardens, a large area between the Santuario and the Santa Cruz River that contains several images of Mary from around the world, including Our Lady of Guadalupe, the Vietnamese Our Lady of La Vang, Our Lady of Sorrows, and a few others. The Madonna Gardens abut an outdoor prayer area and picnic grounds. Farther away from the parking lot, adjacent to the Santo Niño Chapel, are a monument to the Nativity and the Holy Family Barn, yet another area to reflect, pray, and inspect relatively new religious statuary. González also expanded the number of buildings dedicated to sales, with three new gift shops in addition to the earlier one built by Father Roca. One of these new gift shops is housed in the Bernardo Abeyta Welcome Center. Besides offering gifts for sale, the welcome center also features an art display, various interpretive plaques, and a topographic map of the Santuario grounds, with details about plans for future buildings.

Of course, this kind of development indicates a particular vision for the Santuario on the part of González, and by association, the Archdiocese of Santa Fe. The theological agenda, not surprisingly, is to increase traditional Catholic devotions, including Mass attendance; intercessory prayers often mediated through saints, Mary, or particular images of Christ; and adherence to Church doctrine with a minimum of messy or syncretic folk religious practices. Part of González's mission, therefore, has been to refocus devotion on the crucified Christ represented most miraculously at the Santuario in the crucifix of Esquipulas. The Santo Niño, as a more popular figure, but significantly less doctrinaire in terms of Catholic Christology, has been relegated as much as possible to the colorfully decorated and remodeled Santo Niño Chapel. As one Santuario employee put it, González's theological vision is that the Santuario itself is about the death and resurrection of Jesus while the Santo Niño Chapel is about the Christ Child; the clergy have attempted to promote the entire site—including both the Santuario and the Santo Niño Chapel—as a kind of pilgrimage campus that features these "parallel spiritualities" expressed in Jesus's various life stages.[48] The proliferation of Marian images at the Santuario, the building up of the grounds, and the collection of healing testimonies all suggest that González and the archdiocese imagine the Santuario's future as an international pilgrimage destination on par with Lourdes in France or Compostela in Spain.

These innovations have offended some residents and others who have long memories of the Santuario as it was before the changes. Alicia Baca, a local business owner who makes her living from tourism, explained to me that she was upset both by the aesthetics of the new construction and the process by which the new development was implemented. She claims that the Church erected many new buildings without proper permits, and she is unhappy that pasture land was destroyed to install all the new Madonnas that "have nothing to do with the Santuario." Like many others, she is especially appalled by what she considers to be the garish and kitschy updates to the Medina Chapel, saying that it now resembles something one would encounter at Disneyland. She complained that all these things are not true to the "essence" of the place. I asked what she meant by essence, and she responded, "The essence of the Santuario and Chimayó is one of simplicity, quaintness, the town that time forgot." For Baca and others, there is a value in this folksy version of Chimayó, even if it does not fully capture all the realities of an economically depressed, scruffy northern New Mexico town. The Church's desire to reconfigure the Santuario as an internationally famous pilgrimage center, which also ignores much of the troubled realities of the modern Española valley, likewise does not reflect Baca's vision of the place. She worries that Father González is padding his legacy at the expense of community concerns to maintain at least some control over the tourism that both blesses and distresses Chimayó's residents.[49]

Some of the sharpest community criticism stems from González's radical redecorating of the former Medina family chapel into the colorful and sometimes cartoonish Santo Niño Chapel. Writing for the newsletter of the New Mexico Hispanic Culture Preservation League, Pauline Anaya reacts to the changes:

> Never could I have imagined [that] such profound and complete destruction of this very simple rural and humble chapel would have happened. This place that held an essence, an emphasis of life experienced by its early Spanish founders. For me it was a small connection to my past. The rural, Spanish Provincial historic traditions were once felt here. . . . I am still perplexed at how what is in its place seems like a "mockery" to what had been and is now. Does everything have to be about commerce? At minimum, I still feel insulted.[50]

The historian Don Usner expresses similar reservations: "The beloved Santo Niño chapel, across the plaza from the Santuario, has been transformed into a kitschy shrine to bad taste." Usner laments as well the proliferation of new buildings and a colorful map that is posted around the Santuario's campus: "Take a look at the map, and be afraid. It brings Disneyland to Chimayó."[51] Both Usner and Anaya signal that their concern lies both in the aesthetic changes that have occurred at the Santuario and also in what they see as the crass marketing of the Santuario to an imagined crowd of lowbrow, entertainment-seeking tourists.

A group of concerned residents and business owners has come together to oppose further development. The group, called Chimayó Citizens for Community Planning (CCCP), echoes the criticisms about the rapid development. The CCCP's objective is to preserve historic sites in Chimayó as well as the area's natural resources, landscape, and traditional industry and agriculture.[52] In 2012 the group applied to place the

Santuario and the surrounding El Potrero area of Chimayó on a list of New Mexico's most endangered places; in their application, the group's members wrote,

> In the past seven years El Potrero has been degraded by hasty piecemeal constructions and renovations on property owned by the Church around the Santuario and the Santo Niño chapel. These include: enlargement of the parking lot which is located in former pasture lands and orchards close to the Santa Cruz River; building of oversized Stations of the Cross and other structures which block the view corridor of the river and the pastures beyond it; clichéd renovations of the facades of two buildings next to Santo Niño chapel itself; unnecessary paving of paths and construction of walls all out of keeping with local architectural style and with the simplicity of the Santuario itself; and numerous pieces of pop statuary and two-dimensional art which are totally alien to Hispanic New Mexico traditions and serve to trivialize the spiritual ambience and purpose of the Santuario. None of these innovations have been subject to planning or serious review, and the result has been to turn this part of El Potrero into a kind of religious theme park.[53]

The citizens' group is particularly worried about further development in the form of a retreat center, which would include a museum in Bernardo Abeyta's ancestral home. The renovations and new construction would be carried out by Los Niños Foundation, a group that has received some support from the Archdiocese of Santa Fe.[54] But the residents have exerted enough pressure that the project is moving slowly and is increasingly attentive to community input. Raymond Bal, a leader in the CCCP and co-owner of El Potrero Trading Post—a gift shop now almost completely surrounded by properties of the Catholic Church—explains that he is not averse to all change but that he would like Chimayó's future to be an extension of the past.[55]

To be sure, not all local Nuevomexicano devotees are averse to the Church's leadership or plans for the Santuario. This even includes members of a group that historically has often been at odds with the Catholic hierarchy, the Fraternidad Piadosa de Nuestro Padre Jesús, or the Penitentes. Early in the 2000s, Father González had invited various Penitente chapters back to the Santuario to help celebrate Holy Week. During the Holy Week festivities in 2015, I observed various rituals, rosaries, and processions that included Penitentes from the towns of Arroyo Seco, Cordoba, and Chimayó itself. Johnny García, a Penitente leader, agreed to speak to me about his relationship to the Santuario and the archdiocese. He joined the Brotherhood in 1977, and since that time has not made the Good Friday pilgrimage since he is busy at his *morada*, but he spends a lot of time during the year at the Santuario, and it is clearly a very important place for him and his family. At the time of our conversation, the archbishop of Santa Fe, Michael Sheehan, had recently announced plans to retire. I asked García how he felt about Sheehan. García responded, "Look, I'm not going to criticize the Archbishop. They are our leaders." He added, "I'm a committed Catholic. We have to follow the rules." In words similar to the rhetoric about the holy dirt that the clergy promote, García said that the dirt works in conjunction with prayer and faith. He told a story about an acquaintance of his—"a Hispanic, a Catholic!"—who got angry when he found out that the *pocito* did not replenish itself miraculously. "He should know better. The holy water container doesn't refill itself either!" observed García. For García, being a faithful Penitente includes being a faithful Catholic, which, in turn, means respecting the structures of authority of the Church as well as the teachings of both local clergy and ecclesiastical doctrine. While not all local residents agree with García, he and others like him are basically content to support the Church's decisions concerning the Santuario.[56]

In some ways, the clash over the future direction of the Santuario is remarkably similar to past conflicts at the storied church. At the heart of the current discord are competing (although sometimes overlapping) claims about who should have the power to define what the Santuario is, what it looks like, how it ought to be experienced, what functions it plays, and who can access it. Of course, these questions, which today are crystallized so clearly at the Santuario, have defined and structured the religious and social life of northern New Mexicans for generations. The Chimayó Rebellion of 1837 was sparked when Catholic Nuevomexicanos found their social structures, religious rituals, and economic well-being threatened. The perceived threats came from the expanding but feeble Mexican state and the changing authority of the Catholic Church, whose

Franciscan representatives were being steadily replaced by diocesan clergy. Local residents, governmental authorities, and Catholic priests could all make claims on the patterns of daily life, economic arrangements, and ultimate loyalties of the people. In 1837 these claims came to a violent head with the semi-theocratic declarations of the rebels that they would live as they saw fit under the guidance of God in the faith of Jesus Christ. Despite the citizens' resolve, the state and the Church recaptured control, but these more powerful forces could not obliterate the people's taste for self-determination. Rather, it was economic hardship and the inevitable arrival of a new state—the United States—that led to a new but familiar rearrangement of religious and social life in the region. The sale of the Santuario in 1929 provides us with another example of competing claims on the meaning, the aesthetics, and the actual property of Hispano Catholics. This time there was no rebellion for self-determination, but rather a desperate sale of the Santuario in hard times to Anglo buyers who had an agenda to control the site and its interpretation. Anglo artists wanted the place as a canvas for their imaginings of Hispano folk life; Anglo church authorities wanted the place almost as a legal acknowledgment of what they already claimed: the Catholic churches of New Mexico. In 1929 the desires of the Nuevomexicano people for authority over their own religious practice and social relationships were most clearly expressed in a tenacious continuation of devotion and of pilgrimage.

Today, we have another chapter in this new, but again familiar, contest between economies of control, interpretations of God's power and care, and access to holy spaces—what I have referred to throughout this book as religious ownership. Father González represents one type of ownership, in that he acts as the official voice of the Catholic Church at the Santuario. González regards the Santuario as a truly miraculous place that has the power to communicate God's grace, healing, and love to ever larger numbers of visitors. Under his stewardship, the Santuario could well find itself as another Lourdes, a place that has grown out of its local and historical context to become an international Catholic destination. The chorus of Hispano Catholics and other locals who worry that this will turn their hallowed and miraculous retreat into a kind of religious Disneyland articulate a different vision for the place based on their own claims of ownership: the Santuario is a part of their past, of their culture. And the thousands of tourists also have their say in the form of the ownership that is bought dollar by dollar in shops, restaurants, tour packages, and hotels. If there is any peace to be had in these contests of meaning and desire, in these competing claims at the Santuario, perhaps it is that the history of the place is full of such turbulence. The Santuario, its images, and its holy dirt continue to beckon despite—or maybe because of—the many parties who want to make the place their own.

Conclusion

Rare is the visitor to the Santuario de Chimayó who returns home without taking a piece of the place back, most often a small sample of the holy dirt. For some, these baggies and canisters of sandy earth are merely souvenirs. But for many others, they are a tangible connection to the Santuario; in a very real sense, thousands of people possess a little bit of the ostensibly sacred and miraculous ground from which the two-hundred-year-old church rises. Throughout this book, we have drawn on the metaphor of "religious ownership" to try to better understand the competing claims that people make on religious sites, rituals, narratives, and experiences. In broad strokes, the two kinds of religious ownership we have explored are possessing and belonging. Possession includes, at the most basic level, legal ownership. In this regard, Bernardo Abeyta and his descendants were the first owners of the Santuario until 1929, when the Spanish Colonial Arts Society purchased the church and deeded it to the Archdiocese of Santa Fe, which remains its legal owner today. But this kind of possession can also be predicated not on legal deeds but rather on claims of authentic and ancestral connection. Here, local residents of Chimayó as well as longtime Nuevomexicano pilgrims and devotees (despite the Catholic Church's legal claims to the Santuario) are the owners of the ritual life and legendary origin stories that motivate their lifelong commitments and attachments to the place. Likewise, though not as prominent, Tewa people may also remind other users of their original presence on the land, and its importance in their own stories of healing and divine activity. More recently, the tourist, the alternative or spiritual health seeker, and the non-Hispano pilgrim may also claim the Santuario as a place with a universal patrimony, open for the consumption of all who choose to make the journey to gaze on its beautiful adobe walls, rustic art, pleasant grounds, and close sacristy with its cast-off crutches, intercessory photos, and low-slung entryway into the tiny room that houses the *pocito* of holy earth. Like the citizens who own the treasures of a public museum, hundreds of thousands of such visitors come to admire and to share its history, its aesthetic environment, and its goods and services. Of course, sometimes all these claims on the Santuario peacefully overlap and even complement one another, while in other circumstances disputes arise, and competing parties vie for both legal control and authentic connection.

The other type of religious ownership is less about the claims that individuals or groups make on a religious site and more about the feelings of belonging that one experiences when one is literally or figuratively "at home." Here, what matters are sensations of connection, windows onto the ineffable, wisps of familiarity or recollection, and, above all, a common and repeated narrative that a place is special, holy, and even elemental. In a 1987 interview, Father Roca described the Santuario as such a special location. The reporter asked the priest, "What is it about this place that can cause dramatic physical and emotional changes in people?" Roca responded, "At the *santuario* people feel that God listens to them." The reporter agreed and mused that "There is a sense that the divine touches the human plane at that spot in a special way. It is a feeling, more than anything tangible, that the area is grounded in grace."[1] Indeed, for some who visit the Santuario, it is not just the adobe church alone but the whole interaction of history, aesthetics, and the particular environment that has been nurtured by various groups throughout New Mexico. As one commentator puts it, "The Land of Enchantment has become a land of awakening spirituality, and a host of seekers attest to its power as a sacred location. Though they may not be able to verbalize its attraction, many people—many more every day—find in New Mexico the soul-nurturing 'something' conducive to a life of spiritual searching."[2]

The social geographer Dydia DeLyser, in her study of tourism to Hispanic sites in southern California, suggests that "social memories," which emerge from the shared experiences of people who visit special places, help create meaning from these locations. She explains that tourists (and, I would add, pilgrims) are especially good at recognizing, creating, and experiencing such places:

[A]t tourist sites in particular, the factual and the fictional often freely interpenetrate; neither necessarily has priority in the framing of a given site. And this is not because tourists are unable to differentiate the real from the false, but because they (we) are eager to engage both the factual *and* the fictional as they (we) actively create meaning at given sites, linking in different ways the more public narratives to their (our) own personal lives and experiences.[3]

At the Santuario, this creative process is at play for Nuevomexicano Catholics as well as for outside tourists as all, to some extent, engage the legends of Bernardo Abeyta and the miraculous Esquipulas crucifix, the Santo Niño's nightly jaunts of mercy, and the movement of literally tons of sandy dirt of Chimayó's hills into the homes of people around the world. These stories interweave and overlap, and as DeLyser notes, link up with each one of our personal experiences in a vast story that we tell together about this special place. To be sure, religious places are some of the most likely locations onto which we come together to remember, formulate, and reemphasize our social memories and our shared meanings. Landscapes of special places like the Santuario, notes DeLyser, are made up not just of "hills and dales, streams and coastlines," but also of the cultural traces that people have constructed and crafted all over our world. These traces, at the Santuario, are the paintings and *bultos* of the *santeros*, the interpretive plaques in the visitors' center, the bins full of empty plastic receptacles in the gift shops awaiting to be purchased and filled with holy dirt, and the person-to-person remembrances of past visits and prayers answered. The Santuario, thus, is a place where diverse people make and share social memories; as such it is a "cultural and landscape phenomenon," a place where shared stories lead to shared memories, which in turn spark the sense of common belonging.[4]

Of course, the Santuario de Chimayó, in a legal sense at least, belongs to the Catholic Church. This remains true no matter how many people make competing claims on the place or feel like they belong there in a special way. Even when Bernardo Abeyta began to build the place in 1813, he did so with the official blessing of Catholic officials so that the church could be a place wherein the Mass was celebrated. The central artifact on the main *retablo*, the Cristo de Esquipulas, although linked visually and historically with indigenous peoples, is nonetheless a depiction of Jesus, the Christian Savior. The other images and statues that line the walls are, likewise, Catholic saints and symbols. The catholicity of the Catholic Church is such that all Catholics—and to some extent, all Christians—can make reasonable claims on any Catholic church and its ritual life. In one interpretation, this would mean that an Anglo Catholic from Des Moines has as much right to the Santuario as a lifelong Chimayó resident.

However, as this book has argued, religious ownership is constantly and irretrievably interwoven with ethnic identity, history, commerce, and personal and group feelings. We have examined these kinds of claims in the history of the Río Arriba region, in the aesthetic colonialism of Mary Austin and her ilk, in the Sons of the Holy Family and their administration of the Santuario, and in the ever-swelling wave of tourists and health seekers who flock to New Mexico. And so, simultaneously, the Santuario is a Catholic church, a relic of northern New Mexican religiosity, a site of miracles and healing, and a tourist destination. Ultimately, what this means is that the notion of religious ownership as an interpretive tool is not meant to be determinative, somehow weighing claims against each other to figure out who the "real" owner or claimant is. Rather, the Santuario is an ideal site to examine how competing and overlapping claims are made on a place, on stories, on heritage, and even on the power of God.

The various ways of thinking about religious ownership that I have applied to the Santuario de Chimayó may be fruitfully applied to other contested, multivalent religious sites, especially those that appeal significantly to tourists. National churches and shrines such as the Washington National Cathedral and the Basilica of the National Shrine of the Immaculate Conception are obvious examples of Christian churches that must answer the needs of various and sometimes competing constituencies.[5] Special places that people visit for recreation but also for spiritual renewal such as national parks, battlefields, and national historic sites would also benefit from an analysis that focused on discourses of ownership and belonging.[6] The set of questions that accompanies this interpretive lens is ideally suited to other sites in the American West and Southwest because of the sizable Native American populations, the history of Spanish colonialism and the Mexican-American War, the role of robust Latin American and Asian immigration to the region, and the variety of religious groups that have thrived in the area, such as Mormons, various New Age and other metaphysical communities, and Christian

Evangelicals and Pentecostals. Study of the Santuario's history can help to point the way for similar explorations of other sites that exist at nexuses of colonial contact, migration, and competing religious, ethnic, and cultural narratives.

Changing Demographics and the History and Future of U.S. Catholicism

Despite the fact that the Santuario de Chimayó is arguably the largest Catholic pilgrimage destination in the United States, it remains relatively little-known and under-studied. In fact, the present work is the first book-length treatment of this unique and superlative church. What can account for this silence? Why is this place that is so precious to hundreds of thousands of people not more recognized for the incomparable historic and religious site that it is? Trends in the writing of history have likely played a role; as others have noted, the study of the history of American Catholics has not been as robust as it deserves to be, given the fact that Catholics have been the largest single religious group in the United States since the middle of the nineteenth century. One of the foremost historians of Catholicism, Robert Orsi, has commented that understanding Catholics is crucial for understanding U.S. history in general:

> Catholics have always been in the mix and have always been different, and carefully exploring this difference is key to understanding U.S. Catholic history.
>
> But it is also key to understanding U.S. history: we have come to the point now where we can turn around and see that looking at the history of the United States through the lens of the study of U.S. Catholics and Catholicism and from the perspective of the Catholic imaginary challenges many of the old, taken-for-granted narratives of American civilization, raises new questions, and demands some theoretical and historiographical creativity and innovation.[7]

Exploring the history of the Santuario de Chimayó and its pilgrimage thus becomes an important part of telling American history. The stories and experiences of northern New Mexican Catholics deserve their place in our national narrative and reveal truths about ourselves as a people that were formerly obscured by historiographical silence.

Within the story of American Catholicism, the practices and unique observances of Latino/a Catholics require particular attention, as these devotions have not only been ignored by academics, but also have sometimes been actively criticized by Catholic authorities. The story of Nuevomexicano Catholicism contains examples of this kind of suppression. Archbishop Lamy and his immediate successors clearly had little love for the Penitente brothers who practiced their faith in and around the Río Arriba area. An even earlier bishop, located in Durango, Mexico, was even more hostile, referring to the rites of the Penitentes as nothing more than "butchery."[8] Although much less condemnatory in tone, even the beloved Father Roca often voiced his exasperation with what he considered to be misuse or folk superstition regarding the *pocito*'s dirt. Despite these occasional proscriptions from the Church itself, and a regrettable lack of historical attention, Hispanic Catholic devotional life is gaining traction as an important field of research.[9] In light of these efforts to tell and interpret the practices and experiences of Latino/a Catholics and integrate them into the larger narratives of Catholic history, study of the holy dirt of Chimayó, devotion to the Santo Niño and the Cristo de Esquipulas, and the massive walking pilgrimage represents a significant contribution to our understanding of not only Hispanic devotionalism but of U.S. Catholicism in general.[10]

For the Catholic Church in the United States, very few topics are more important today than the contributions of its Latino/a members. Various recent studies have profiled the demographics of the U.S. Catholic Church, and its future is going to be tied more than ever before to its Hispanic constituents. In the early 2000s, three of the leading researchers in Latino/a religion, Gastón Espinosa, Virgilio Elizondo, and Jesse Miranda, carried out a large survey entitled *Hispanic Churches in American Public Life*. They reported, first of all, that Latinos in the new millennium were the nation's largest minority group, with especially significant populations in the American West and Southwest, Florida, and the Northeast. Not surprisingly, 93 percent of Latinos self-identified as Christian, but significantly—and despite solid gains by Protestant churches—"the overall percentage of Latino Catholics has remained above the 70 percent mark." The researchers attributed this figure to an ongoing wave of immigration from Latin America, especially from Mexico, a country with one of the highest percentages of Catholicism in the hemisphere.[11] This influx of new Catholics has been absolutely vital for the U.S. Catholic Church. The political scientists Robert Putnam and David Campbell report that "An appreciation of the Latino factor within American Catholicism begins with simple arithmetic." They explain, "Without the inflow of Latinos to shore up the numbers of Catholics in the United States, the American Catholic population would have experienced a catastrophic collapse."[12]

In 2010, when Putnam and Campbell published the results of their own survey of religion in American public life, Latinos already made up 35 percent of all American Catholics. But the more striking datum is that, of Catholics under the age of thirty-five, a staggering 58 percent are Latinos. Given the fact that young Latinos are more likely to attend Mass than their older, Anglo counterparts, then young Catholics who are actually active in Catholic churches are 70 percent Latino/a.[13] More recent survey data corroborate the findings of the earlier studies, and note that there is an "ongoing ethnic transformation of the Catholic Church." Already, the western part of the country, even without counting the enormous generational shift toward young Hispanic Catholics, has a Latino/a Catholic majority of 59 percent. Specifically, "Hispanic Catholics now make up the majority of the Catholic population in five states: Texas (74%), California (70%), New Mexico (70%), Arizona (59%), and Nevada (59%)." In each of these states, Latinos also count for at least one-fourth of the overall population, meaning that Latinos in those areas have "large Catholic footprints."[14]

In other words, Latino/a Catholics are the present and the future of the U.S. Catholic Church. In such a context, it is more important than ever for us to understand the historical processes and the devotional practices of Hispanic Catholics, not to mention the cultural, religious, and political impacts that Latinos have made and continue to make on the United States. The long traditions of lay piety and organization, the undisputed and growing popularity of the Holy Week pilgrimage, the aesthetic honesty and appeal of its adobe architecture and *santero*-made artwork, and the direct and material access to the power of God and the saints in the dirt of the *pocito* are all aspects of the Santuario de Chimayó that merit our attention. These expressions of Nuevomexicano Catholicism, through their own intrinsic value and the demographic transformation of American Catholicism, have become the shapes and contours of faith both for local Hispanos and for many thousands of others. Of course, not all of the visitors to the Santuario are Catholic or Hispanic, but that is precisely the point. The Santuario, along with so many other sites of Latino/a Catholic and popular devotions, despite its lack of coverage in American or Catholic history books, has an influence that demands our attention and analysis.

Indeed, thousands of people have made the Santuario a part of their lives, a window onto the deepest of their loves, a quiet corner of their spirits. The Santuario is a special place in a special land, where ancient soil brings together diverse stories and yearnings. Many have made claim to it, to its rhythms and to its miraculous power, and while these claims have sometimes led to conflict, very few have been willing to relinquish their connection to the church at the end of the journey. The Santuario, after all, is a place of healing.

NOTES

ABBREVIATIONS

AASF: Archives of the Archdiocese of Santa Fe
ASCA: Archives of the Spanish Colonial Arts Society, Santa Fe
CSWR: Center for Southwest Research, University of New Mexico, Albuquerque
FAC: Fray Angélico Chávez History Library, Santa Fe
NMSA: New Mexico State Records Center and Archives, Santa Fe

INTRODUCTION

1 *Pocito* is the diminutive form of the Spanish word *pozo*, which means "well, hole, or shaft."
2 Various origin stories for the Santuario and its holy dirt are covered in detail in chapter 2.
3 Orsi, *Between Heaven and Earth*, 2.
4 A beautiful collection of photos with a historical sketch does exist: Howarth and Lamadrid, *Pilgrimage to Chimayó*. Two other books that spend considerable time on the Santuario are Kay, *Chimayo Valley Traditions*; and Usner, *Sabino's Map*. The Santuario has also been the subject of at least two doctoral dissertations: Seagraves, "A Bit about Dirt"; and Russell, "Finding the Way Home."
5 Borhegyi and Boyd, *El Santuario de Chimayo*, 32.
6 U.S. Census Bureau, 2010 Census, search term "Espanola city, New Mexico," http://factfinder.census.gov, accessed April 5, 2016.
7 This *dicho* is one of many collected by a son of Chimayó, Don J. Usner, in his book *Chasing Dichos through Chimayó*, 217.

CHAPTER 1. CATHOLIC SETTLEMENT OF RÍO ARRIBA

1 Borhegyi, "The Evolution of a Landscape," 25–26.
2 Schroeder, "The Tewa Indians of the Rio Grande," 284.
3 An early and influential historical account of the Oñate expedition was written in 1610 in laudatory verse by one of Oñate's own men: Gaspar Pérez de Villagrá, in Villagrá et al., *Historia de la Nueva México*.
4 Hammond and Rey, *Don Juan de Oñate*, 393, 734.
5 Lange, Lange, and Riley, *Southwest Journals of Adolph F. Bandelier*, vol. 2, 74.

6 Kessell, *Pueblos, Spaniards, and the Kingdom of New Mexico*, 32.
7 Ibid., 34–40. Sánchez, Spude, and Gómez, *New Mexico*, 36–41. The Battle of Acoma also constitutes a significant topic of Villagrá's 1610 epic.
8 Sanchez, Spude, and Gómez, *New Mexico*, 22–32.
9 Bunting, *Early Architecture in New Mexico*, 3–4.
10 "Act of Obedience and Vassalage by the Indians of San Juan Bautista," in Hammond and Rey, *Don Juan de Oñate*, 344. See also Almaráz, "Transplanting 'Deep, Living Roots,'" 14. For information about the Patronato Real and the *Requerimiento*, see Schwaller, *The History of the Catholic Church in Latin America*, 39–48.
11 Benavides is quoted in Sandoval, *On the Move*, 14–15.
12 Ibid., 109.
13 Schroeder, "The Tewa Indians of the Rio Grande," 285.
14 Sandoval, *On the Move*, 109.
15 Schroeder, "The Tewa Indians of the Rio Grande," 285; Sandoval, *On the Move*, 17.
16 Gutiérrez, *When Jesus Came, the Corn Mothers Went Away*, 120–31.
17 Kessell, *Pueblos, Spaniards, and the Kingdom of New Mexico*, 9; and Spicer, *Cycles of Conquest*, 162.
18 Schroeder, "The Tewa Indians of the Rio Grande," 285; Spicer, *Cycles of Conquest*, 162–63; and Brooks, *Captives and Cousins*, 52–53.
19 "Letter from the Governor and Captain-General, Don Antonio de Otermín, from New Mexico [1680]," and "List and Memorial of the Religious Whom the Indians of New Mexico Killed [1680]," in Spicer, *Cycles of Conquest*, 163; Hackett, *Historical Documents Relating to New Mexico*, vol. 3, 327–39. For more on religious causes of the revolt, see Bowden, "Spanish Missions," 217–28; and Knaut, *The Pueblo Revolt of 1680*, esp. chaps. 3 and 4.
20 "Historia 26," *Archivo General de la Nación de México*, vol. 26, pt. 3, n.p., CSWR.
21 Spicer, *Cycles of Conquest*, 164; Adams and Chávez, *The Missions of New Mexico*, 215, n. 1.
22 Sánchez, Spude and Gómez, *New Mexico*, 57–58.
23 Twitchell, *The Spanish Archives of New Mexico*, vol. 1, 241–57.
24 Spicer, *Cycles of Conquest*, 165–66.
25 Adams and Chávez, *The Missions of New Mexico*, 72–84.
26 Spicer, *Cycles of Conquest*, 164–65.
27 Twitchell, *The Spanish Archives of New Mexico*, 241–57; "Land Grant to Luis Lopez," Borrego-Ortega Family Papers, NMSR. Marriage *diligencia* for Josepha Lujan and Clemente Montoya, 1701, AASF.
28 Borhegyi, "The Evolution of a Landscape," 27–28; Simmons, "Settlement Patterns and Village Plans in Colonial New Mexico," 105. This settlement pattern, lacking central organization, defied Spanish codes that required orderly development plans for the proper observance of civil and ecclesiastical authorities. For more on the Spanish ideal as codified in the Laws of the Indies, see Stilgoe, *Common*

Landscape of America, 34–39. See also Carson, "Interaction between Culture and Architecture in a Hispanic Plaza," 39–50.

29 Usner, *Sabino's Map*, 61–66.

30 The exact date of construction of the *oratorio* in the plaza is unknown. It may have originated with the plaza itself in the 1730s, or perhaps it was added later. Larcombe, "Plaza del Cerro," 173; and Usner, *Sabino's Map*, 187.

31 Brooks, *Captives and Cousins*, 123–25.

32 Hendrickson, *Border Medicine*, 19–28.

33 The story of these fascinating witchcraft trials is told in Ebright and Hendricks, *The Witches of Abiquiu*. Chimayó connections are sprinkled throughout the book, but specific mention of Chimayosos implicated in the trials can be found on pp. 225 and 266–67.

34 Ibid., 241, 251. See also Spicer, *Cycles of Conquest*, 166–67.

35 Adams and Chávez, *The Missions of New Mexico*, 75–77.

36 Carroll, *The Penitente Brotherhood*, 107; Brooks, *Captives and Cousins*, 216–17.

37 Spicer, *Cycles of Conquest*; Sandoval, *On the Move*, 19; Chávez, *But Time and Chance*, 20; and Schwaller, *The History of the Catholic Church in Latin America*, 107–8.

38 Weigle, *Brothers of Light, Brothers of Blood*, 21–23.

39 The English translation of Zubiría's statement comes from López Pulido, *The Sacred World of the Penitentes*, 41. A clear transcription of the full Spanish text can be found in appendix 1 of Weigle, *Brothers of Light, Brothers of Blood*.

40 Some of the most explicit descriptions of Penitente activity come from Anglo observers near the turn of the last century. These descriptions, while not always strictly condemnatory, are yet imbued with a sense of ethnocentric detachment, looking upon the rites with a superior and bemused fascination with the exotic and atavistic. See, for example, Henderson, *Brothers of Light*; and Lummis, *The Land of Poco Tiempo*, 56–80.

41 The constitution in question was gathered by Alex M. Darley, a Protestant missionary and vocal critic of the Penitentes. Nevertheless, Darley's writings indicate that he had achieved considerable access to their activities. See Darley, *The Passionists of the Southwest*, 14–22.

42 Weigle, *Brothers of Light, Brothers of Blood*, 151–52.

43 Martinez, "Apologia of Presbyter Antonio Jose Martinez," 339; Ahlborn, "The Penitente Moradas of Abiquiú," 126.

44 Chávez, *But Time and Chance*, 35–36.

45 A representative example of the point concerning the Penitentes as a response to the secularization of the missions is found in Ahlborn, "The Penitente Moradas of Abiquiú," 126.

46 Taylor, "Penitentes of New Mexico," 501.

47 Lummis, *The Land of Poco Tiempo*, 61.

48 Weigle, *Brothers of Light, Brothers of Blood*, 27–29.

49 Ebright and Hendricks, *The Witches of Abiquiu*, 256. Religious studies scholars have made a case for religious exchange in complex contexts of cultural and colonial contact. For examples, see Tweed, *Retelling U.S. Religious History*, 17; and Albanese, *A Republic of Mind and Spirit*, 17–18.

50 Adams and Chávez, *The Missions of New Mexico*, 84; and Carroll, *The Penitente Brotherhood*, 4–5.

CHAPTER 2. THE ORIGIN OF THE SANTUARIO

1 Read, "El Santuario de Chimayo," 81.

2 This account of the origin of Chimayó is not so much a composite as an overlapping display of almost identical accounts that are likely drawn from oral traditions. See especially Borhegyi and Boyd, *El Santuario de Chimayo*, 32; and González, *The Santuario de Chimayo in New Mexico*, 11.

3 For one clear articulation of this idea, oft-repeated throughout the work, see Durkheim, *The Elementary Forms of the Religious Life*, 56. For an analysis of Durkheim's ideas of how religions create unity even while enforcing social divisions, see Masuzawa, *In Search of Dreamtime*, 40.

4 Durkheim's statements here are taken from Halbwachs, *Sources of Religious Sentiment*, 90, 104.

5 As discussed in chapter 1, the Santa Cruz de la Cañada area has been variously inhabited by Tewa and Tano people even since the Spanish colonization of the region, but large settlements in the locations of Chimayó and the Santuario most likely ceased by approximately 1400 C.E. For more information, see Borhegyi, "The Evolution of a Landscape," 24–30.

6 Ortiz, *The Tewa World*, 18–22, 122, 141–42.

7 Lange, Lange, and Riley, *Southwest Journals of Adolph F. Bandelier*, vol. 2, 74.

8 Harrington, *The Ethnogeography of the Tewa Indians*, 341–42.

9 Edgar L. Hewett, *American Museum Journal* 12, no. 1 (January 1912): 33, quoted in Harrington, *The Ethnogeography of the Tewa Indians*, 342.

10 For some of the biographical information about Harrington, Hewett, and Bandelier, I am indebted to Laura Holt, the librarian and archivist at the School for Advanced Research in Santa Fe.

11 Lummis, *The Land of Poco Tiempo*, 19.

12 Usner, *Sabino's Map*, 16. Tony Chavarria, the curator of ethnology at the Laboratory of Anthropology in Santa Fe, confirms that many Pueblo stories maintain that much of New Mexico is connected through underground passages; these stories relate to various Pueblo origin myths, which generally feature an emergence of the people from under the ground into the present world.

13 Howarth and Lamadrid, *Pilgrimage to Chimayó*, 10. Chavarria provides the related detail that the Zunis, another Pueblo people, have lava beds in their territory that they identify as the dried blood of giants.

14 Harrington, *The Ethnogeography of the Tewa Indians*, 568; Ortiz, *The Tewa World*, 19.

15 Gutiérrez, "El Santuario de Chimayo," 74; Turner and Turner, *Image and Pilgrimage in Christian Culture*, 33.

16 According to a century-old academic report about the Tewas, "The Pueblo Indians guard with great tenacity the secrets of their shrines. Even when the locations have been found, they will deny their existence, plead ignorance of their meaning, or refuse to discuss the subject in any form" (344). The report further explains that Tewa shrines are hard to locate in any case since they often blend into the surrounding landscape. See Douglas, "Notes on the Shrines of the Tewa and Other Pueblo Indians."

17 See Bunting, *Early Architecture in New Mexico*, 54. Bunting finds that almost all buildings of note in the colonial period were mission churches.

18 The town in Guatemala is spelled "Esquipulas," without an accent and with stress on the penultimate syllable. The anthropologist Stephan de Borhegyi introduced a misspelling of the word as "Esquípulas," a mistake that has been reproduced many times throughout the scholarly literature. I have elected to correct the error throughout the present work. I have not changed other misspellings or more significant modifications of the name.

19 Other sources suggest that Esquipulas is a Hispanicization of a Maya name, perhaps Eskip'urha. See, for instance, John Sinclair, "The Earth—The Faith—The Blessing," 7, John Sinclair Papers, box 10, folder 3, CSWR. One author creatively but probably mistakenly posits that Esquipulas is a corruption of Aesculapius, a Roman god of healing: Carrillo, "Our Lord of Esquipulas in New Mexico," 54.

20 Borhegyi, "The Cult of Our Lord of Esquipulas," 389.

21 Ibid., 391–95. Borhegyi's conclusions are confirmed in Kay, *Chimayo Valley Traditions*, 30–32.

22 Borhegyi, "The Cult of Our Lord of Esquipulas," 390.

23 For example, see Howarth and Lamadrid, *Pilgrimage to Chimayó*, 19. For a contemporary ethnography on the role of crosses, trees, and other similar images in Maya religion, see Aguilera, *The Maya World of Communicating Objects*.

24 For a minority report on the differences between the two images, one that claims that "little connects the two crucifixes visually" (63), see DeLoach, "Image and Identity at El Santuario de Chimayo."

25 Wall placards, El Rincón de Don Bernardo Abeyta Welcome Center, Chimayó, NM, viewed June 29, 2014. The quoted material on the placard has no attribution.

26 The Church's analysis, rather surprisingly, echoes that of the historian of religions Mircea Eliade, who endeavored to find shared religious meanings behind the ritual facades appreciated by actual religious practitioners. For a discussion of the axis mundi and this universalizing project, see Eliade, *The Sacred and the Profane*, 32–42. For an example of an Eliadean scholar applying this theoretical paradigm to a New Mexico Hispano context, see Carrasco, "A Perspective for a Study of Religious Dimensions in Chicano Experience," esp. 201–3.

27 Gavin, Mauldin, and Lucero, *History and Iconography of the Architecture and Art at Nuestro Señor de Esquipulas Church*, 3, 10, 17, 18, 68, ASCA.

28 Carrillo, "Our Lord of Esquipulas in New Mexico," 51–53.
29 Microfilm records of Spanish documents, AASF. My access to the Archives of the Archdiocese was quite limited, and I am unable to provide additional information about the microfilms that the staff allowed me to see.
30 Chávez, *But Time and Chance*, 47; Chávez, *Archives of the Archdiocese of Santa Fe*, 120.
31 Bernardo Abeyta's letter to Fray Sebastián Álvarez, November 15, 1813, document 1, Churches in New Mexico Collection, folder 17, NMSA. My translation.
32 Fray Sebastián Álvarez's letter to the Lord Provisor and Capitular Vicar of the Diocese of Durango, November 19, 1813, document 2, Churches in New Mexico Collection, folder 17, NMSA. My translation.
33 Howarth and Lamadrid, *Pilgrimage to Chimayó*, 18; Kay, *Chimayo Valley Traditions*, 35.
34 Borhegyi, "The Cult of Our Lord of Esquipulas," 395; Gutiérrez, "El Santuario de Chimayo," 73–74.
35 "Popular Legends Surround Building of Santuario." *People of God* is the official newspaper of the Archdiocese of Santa Fe. The article is unsigned but claims to be based on a 1982 brochure published by the Sons of the Holy Family, the order that has administered the Santuario since the 1950s. I have not been able to locate a copy of this brochure.
36 Borhegyi and Boyd, *El Santuario de Chimayo*, 17–18. The story is reproduced in Weigle and White, *The Lore of New Mexico*, 41–42. Benigna Chávez, an older resident of Chimayó, recounted the same story with minor variations in 1995. In her version, Abeyta does not bring the crucifix to Santa Cruz but instead keeps it in his home, and the people of Chimayó are given more credit in Chávez's telling for helping build and plaster the Santuario. Usner, *Sabino's Map*, 86–87.
37 Price, "On the Road to Chimayó," 30.
38 This version first appears in print in DeHuff, "The Santuario at Chimayo," 16–17. DeHuff's account is reproduced in Kaplan, "The Church Where Faith Heals," 10, and is slightly modified in Howarth and Lamadrid, *Pilgrimage to Chimayó*, where it is not the unrecognized "San Esquipulas" but rather the Esquipulas Christ who appears to Abeyta.
39 Weigle and White, *The Lore of New Mexico*, 43.
40 Jaramillo, *Shadows of the Past*, 107.
41 Walter, "A New Mexico Lourdes," 3. Walter's account is lauded by an important Hispano polemicist, historian, and legislator from the turn of the last century, Benjamin Read. See Read, "El Santuario de Chimayo," 82.
42 "Tradition from the Pen of Padre Martinez of Taos," trans. J. M. Whittock, 1900. Accompanying letter from Ruth Barber to Martha E. Vigil, 1972, Churches in New Mexico Collection, NMSA.
43 Prince, *Spanish Mission Churches in New Mexico*, 317.
44 Usner, *Sabino's Map*, 88.
45 Wright-Rios, *Revolutions in Mexican Catholicism*, 30–31.

46 Wall placards, El Rincón de Don Bernardo Abetya Welcome Center, Chimayó, NM, viewed June 29, 2014.

47 Kay, *Chimayo Valley Traditions*, 42–43.

48 Vicente de la Fuente quoted in Turner and Turner, *Image and Pilgrimage in Christian Culture*, 41.

49 Carroll, *The Penitente Brotherhood*, 51–56. Carroll's overall argument has to do with the novel nature of the Penitentes, an argument he supports elsewhere in his book. However, to make his case he sometimes ignores the Santuario de Chimayó, as it often represents continuity rather than innovation. In one particularly flagrant case, he writes that "despite New Mexico's distance from the centers of ecclesiastical control; and despite the isolation that was a defining feature of Hispano settlement patterns, Hispano settlers simply did not have visionary experiences" (56). This statement obviously begs the question of the many versions of the apparition stories around Chimayó.

CHAPTER 3. NEW MEXICAN CATHOLICISM IN TRANSITION

1 Simmons, "In the Shadow of the Miter," 207, 210, 213.

2 The quoted archbishop was Francisco Javier de Lizana y Beaumont, who also served briefly as the viceroy of New Spain. Lynch, *New Worlds*, 109, 115.

3 Schwaller, *The History of the Catholic Church in Latin America*, 118.

4 Chávez and Chávez, *Wake for a Fat Vicar*, 25.

5 Wright, "How Many Are a 'Few'?," 237–38.

6 Chávez and Chávez, *Wake for a Fat Vicar*, 22; Martínez, "Apologia of Presbyter Antonio Jose Martinez," 335.

7 Chávez, *But Time and Chance*; Aragon, *Padre Martinez and Bishop Lamy*; Martínez, "Apologia of Presbyter Antonio Jose Martinez," 325–46. It is worth mentioning that negative perceptions of Martínez's position in New Mexico stem only in part from Martínez's own complex personality; many come from the damning caricature of him made in Willa Cather's novel *Death Comes for the Archbishop*, in which the civilized and heroic French bishop Father Latour (obviously Lamy) is pitted against the superstitious and conniving Father Martínez (who is not provided with a pseudonym).

8 Aragon, *Padre Martinez and Bishop Lamy*, 17, 20, 57. Martínez also imported the first printing press to New Mexico and began publishing his own newspaper in 1835. See Defouri, *Historical Sketch of the Catholic Church in New Mexico*, 28.

9 Chávez and Chávez, *Wake for a Fat Vicar*, 29; López Pulido, *The Sacred World of the Penitentes*, 40.

10 Campbell, "American Catholicism in Northern New Mexico," 51.

11 Churches in New Mexico Collection, folder 17, NMSA.

12 "Visita . . . a la Capilla y Ayuda de Parroquia del Sor. de Esquipulas," 1818, and another inventory from July 27, 1826, microfilm documents, AASF. Santuario inventory, April 4, 1821, Chimayó file, ASCA.

13 Gutiérrez, "El Santuario de Chimayo," 75. Joanne Dupont Sandoval, retired co-manager of the Santuario, confirms that Abeyta sold items to pilgrims and other customers from within the Santuario. Interview, July 2, 2014. Confirming Gutiérrez's findings is Carson, "Interaction between Culture and Architecture in a Hispanic Plaza," 41.

14 Carroll, *The Penitente Brotherhood*, 117–19. See also Bator, "Authority and Community in Nineteenth-Century American Catholicism," 85–86; and Darley, *The Passionists of the Southwest*, 14.

15 Letter from Sebastián Álvarez to the bishop of Durango, November 16, 1813, Churches in New Mexico Collection, folder 17, NMSA. My translation. It is interesting to note that Fray Álvarez not only served as the pastor of the Santa Cruz parish but was also the Custodio, a spokesperson and regional leader, of the Franciscan order in New Mexico at the time of Mexican independence. His loyalties to the Franciscans' claim to New Mexico and to its local Catholic traditions soon led to his denunciation by diocesan representatives in New Mexico who had been charged with secularizing the remaining Franciscan outposts. In this sense, Álvarez's support of Abeyta and the Santuario could be interpreted as one of the Franciscans' final acts of church formation in their longtime mission field. For more, see Pacheco Rojas, "El proceso de formación del Obispado de Nuevo México," 68–69.

16 Eighteenth-century Chimayó is treated in detail in chapter 1. See also Ebright and Hendricks, *The Witches of Abiquiu*, 225.

17 David J. Weber, "El gobierno territorial de Nuevo México—la exposición del padre Martínez de 1831," Tomas Atencio Papers, box 11, folder 49, CSWR. My translation.

18 Sánchez, Spude, and Gómez, *New Mexico*, 84–87.

19 The manuscript can be found, with notes by Benjamin M. Read, in the Charles and Jacqueline Meketa Papers, box 2, folder 13, CSWR. The English translation used here appears in Lecompte, *Rebellion in Río Arriba*, 94.

20 Benjamin M. Read Collection, folder 16, NMSA. My translation. The third objective about the plan of the department refers to Mexico's reorganization of the territory of New Mexico into an official department, a move that troubled the rebels because of the associated increase in oversight and taxation.

21 Sánchez, Spude, and Gómez, *New Mexico*, 89–90.

22 Brooks reports in *Captives and Cousins*, 278, that González's father was a *genízaro* and his mother was an Indian of Taos Pueblo. González married three times: once in Taos Pueblo, again in Picurís Pueblo, and finally into a Spanish family in La Cañada.

23 Bator, "Authority and Community in Nineteenth-Century American Catholicism," 93. At various times in his ministry, Martínez himself took pride that he had at one time been named the "delegate minister" to at least the Penitentes in Taos, a role he seems to have expanded to other places at times. See Martínez, "Apologia of Presbyter Antonio Jose Martinez," 339. For more on Abeyta's and the Penitentes'

involvement in the rebellion, see Kraemer, *An Alternative View of New Mexico's 1837 Rebellion*, esp. 21–22. Kraemer argues, "On demographic grounds alone, the involvement of the Penitentes in the Rebellion seems almost certain" (22).

24 Chacón is quoted in Brooks, *Captives and Cousins*, 278.

25 This exchange between Gonzales and Armijo was recorded by an anonymous author who interviewed Teodoro Benavides on May 8, 1904. At that date, Benavides was eighty-four years old, meaning that he would have been seventeen during the 1837 Chimayó Rebellion. Mauro Montoya Collection, FAC.

26 Brooks, *Captives and Cousins*, 280. For a Marxist analysis of the rebellion that argues that northern villagers and Pueblos enjoyed a class solidarity that led to economic autonomy in the region, see Dunbar-Ortiz, *Roots of Resistance*, 95–96. To be sure, economic considerations were at the forefront of reestablishing peace; of special concern was to maintain the growing trade with American business interests. One fascinating document from the period is a letter written by "Citizens of the United States Merchants" sent to the American legation in Mexico City that describes the "Chimayo Revolution." The merchants who authored the letter had lent money to several of the Mexican officials who had been assassinated during the revolt, and they were keen to discover how Mexico would fulfill the debt obligations of the dead men. In an ironic twist, the U.S. businessmen, in their appeals to Mexican authorities for greater accountability and open commerce with New Mexico, very likely benefited from the concessions made to them after the 1837 Rebellion. Of course, the U.S. takeover of the region was less than ten years away. This letter is located in the Benjamin M. Read Papers, folder 8, NMSA.

27 Chávez, *But Time and Chance*, 53.

28 Ibid., 55–56.

29 Martínez's letters to Zubiría are dated September 25, 1837, and January 31, 1838, Tomas Atencio Papers, CSWR. My italics.

30 Martínez's letter to Zubiría is quoted in Romero, "Begetting the Mexican American," 348; see also 352.

31 Dunbar-Ortiz, *Roots of Resistance*, 96; Sánchez, Spude, and Gómez, *New Mexico*, 109–10.

32 Chávez, *But Time and Chance*, 53.

33 Kearny is quoted in an unsigned booklet, *The Old Faith and Old Glory*.

34 A small sampling includes the hagiographical and popular *Lamy of Santa Fe*, by Paul Horgan, and the far more critical *Padre Martinez and Bishop Lamy*, by Aragon. The latter highlights a common thread of Lamy's story: his battles with Antonio José Martínez, a feud that perhaps gets more attention than it deserves because of Willa Cather's famous novel *Death Comes for the Archbishop*. In addition to these, nearly every history of New Mexico recounts Lamy's role as the first American Catholic leader (though he was French) and his administration of the new archdiocese.

35 Boyd, *Popular Arts of the Spanish New Mexico*, 450–51.

36 Sandoval, *On the Move*, 30–31.

37 Butler, Engh, and Spalding, *The Frontiers and Catholic Identities*, 199–201; López Pulido, *The Sacred World of the Penitentes*, 42–43; Weigle, *Brothers of Light, Brothers of Blood*, 53–54.

38 A full reproduction of the 1852 Christmas Pastoral is found in Chávez and Chávez, *Wake for a Fat Vicar*, 131–34. The material quoted here is on p. 133 and is my translation. Lamy's instructions for tithing—and threat of excommunication—would be repeated in later pastorals as well. See, for example, "Circular del Il.mo Señor Don Juan Lamy, Obispo de Santa Fe," Catron Papers, box 1, folder 5, CSWR.

39 Steele, *Archbishop Lamy*, 68–69.

40 Hanks, *Lamy's Legion*, xiii.

41 Campbell, "American Catholicism in Northern New Mexico," 97.

42 Bator, "Authority and Community in Nineteenth-Century American Catholicism," 230.

43 Weigle, *Brothers of Light, Brothers of Blood*, 58, 59–60.

44 Prince, *Spanish Mission Churches in New Mexico*, 320–21.

45 Read, "El Santuario de Chimayo," 84.

46 Ibid., 82.

47 "Consecrated Ground: Description of an Interesting Spot a Few Miles out of Santa Fe," *Santa Fe New Mexican*, October 3, 1885, AASF.

48 Marriott, *María: The Potter of San Ildefonso*, 31.

49 Ibid., 36–37.

50 Ibid., 37–38, 43.

CHAPTER 4. THE SANTO NIÑO DE ATOCHA

1 Sinclair, "The Earth—The Faith—The Blessing," 15–16. John Sinclair Papers, box 10 folder 3, CSWR.

2 Pescador, *Crossing Borders with the Santo Niño de Atocha*, 5–21. Pescador's work on the Santo Niño in the United States is the best and most thorough to date, and I am indebted to him for his careful and suggestive research, which has considerably influenced my own thinking.

3 Frankfurter, "A Gathering of Children," 34.

4 Pescador, *Crossing Borders with the Santo Niño de Atocha*, 45, 55, 60.

5 Ibid., 62, 66.

6 Frankfurter, "A Gathering of Children," 34, 36.

7 Boyd, *Saints and Saint Makers of New Mexico*, 126–27. See also Lange, "Santo Niño de Atocha," 5.

8 Pescador, *Crossing Borders with the Santo Niño de Atocha*, 81, 86–91.

9 Ibid., 91.

10 Frankfurter, "A Gathering of Children," 36, 38.

11 Kay, *Chimayo Valley Traditions*, 49.

12 Boyd, *Popular Arts of the Spanish New Mexico*, 69–76. Boyd helpfully includes transcriptions of the original Spanish inventories. Microfilms of the original documents from May 8, 1818, and July 27, 1826, are available in the Archives of the Archdiocese of Santa Fe. It should be noted that neither of these inventories

mentions the Santo Niño de Atocha. This is not incontrovertible proof that his devotion had not arrived to New Mexico by 1826, but a strong suggestion that it had not. Joanne Dupont Sandoval, a retired co-manager of the Santuario, confirms that Abeyta used the front rooms of the Santuario for sales; interview with Joanne Dupont Sandoval, July 2, 2014.

13 The story comes from Boyd, *Saints and Saint Makers of New Mexico*, 131.

14 The notion of religious competition in a religious economy grows out of rational choice approaches to religious devotion. For examples, see Chesnut, *Competitive Spirits*; and Finke and Stark, *The Churching of America*.

15 Borhegyi and Boyd, *El Santuario de Chimayo*, 21–22.

16 Otero-Warren, *Old Spain in Our Southwest*, 149–50; Pescador, *Crossing Borders with the Santo Niño de Atocha*, 108.

17 DeHuff, *Say the Bells of Old Missions*, 66–67; Borhegyi and Boyd, *El Santuario de Chimayo*, 21–22. Borhegyi's explanation is reproduced in Kay, *Chimayo Valley Traditions*, 49, and is also the source for Gutiérrez, "El Santuario de Chimayo," 79–80. Apart from Pescador, Lamadrid is unique in recent accounts of the Santo Niño's move from the Medina Chapel to the Santuario in that he does not rely on an argument of religious competition; see Howarth and Lamadrid, *Pilgrimage to Chimayó*, 21–22.

18 Pescador, *Crossing Borders with the Santo Niño de Atocha*, 103–4; Marriott, *María: The Potter of San Ildefonso*, 42–43. This example is the weakest part of Pescador's argument, for two reasons. First, Martínez's childhood memory, recounted to an anthropologist many decades later, may not be the most reliable. Second, the building she describes, which Pescador identifies as the Medina Chapel, does not sound exactly like it either in aspect or location. She describes a building on a hill in front of an arroyo that has a cross in front of it. The Medina Chapel is on level ground near the Santuario and has a notable bell tower rather than a cross. Nonetheless, Pescador's point that Martínez does not visit the Santo Niño in the Medina Chapel is suggestive and supportive of his viewpoint.

19 Pescador, *Crossing Borders with the Santo Niño de Atocha*, 105; Walter, "A New Mexico Lourdes," 7.

20 Pescador, *Crossing Borders with the Santo Niño de Atocha*, 105–6; Woodward, "The Penitentes of New Mexico," 334–37.

21 Fundación "Corazón Inmaculado de María," *La Señora Santa María*; Edmonds and Gonzalez, *Caribbean Religious History*, 53.

22 Hughes's analysis challenges the ongoing scholarly vogue for studying images of the Virgin that neglect more common crucifixion images. Hughes, *Biography of a Mexican Crucifix*, 5.

23 Carroll, *The Penitente Brotherhood*, 90, 96.

24 Lamy's sermons tended to downplay the suffering of the Passion and instead focused on the interior piety of Mary and her son. See Campbell, "American Catholicism in Northern New Mexico," 223. On the importance of Mary and the

rosary in nineteenth-century American Catholicism, see Mitchell, *The Mystery of the Rosary*, esp. 205–18.

25 Carroll, *The Penitente Brotherhood*, 119.

26 Frankfurter, "A Gathering of Children," 33.

27 Lange, "Santo Niño de Atocha," 5.

28 Chauvenet, *John Gaw Meem*, 65.

29 Pescador, *Crossing Borders with the Santo Niño de Atocha*, 85.

30 There is a considerable literature about borderlands folk saints. For an introduction, see Griffith, *Folk Saints of the Borderlands*, 175; and Hendrickson, *Border Medicine*, 64–75.

31 Ramón Gutiérrez, the prominent historian of Southwestern religions, with a nod to the legend concerning the Moorish jail in Spain, has insisted that the Santo Niño is a stand-alone miraculous figure not to be confused with the Christ Child. I argue here that this is a historically incorrect etiology, but I agree with Gutiérrez that the Santo Niño acts more like a saint than an image of Christ. Gutiérrez, "El Santuario de Chimayo," 85, n. 16.

32 Graziano, *Cultures of Devotion*, 12; Hughes, *Biography of a Mexican Crucifix*.

33 Vanderwood, *Juan Soldado*, 226.

34 Ibid., 239; Griffith, *Folk Saints of the Borderlands*, 152.

35 Anonymous woman in her sixties, interviewed in January 2000, quoted in Russell, "Finding the Way Home," 216.

36 Ibid., 215.

37 Roca, *The Holy Child of Atocha*, 13.

38 González and Suntum, *El Santuario de Chimayo*; González, *The Santuario de Chimayo in New Mexico*.

CHAPTER 5. SELLING THE SANTUARIO

1 This romanticization of New Mexico's Spanish colonial past coheres well with Carey McWilliams's famous phrase for similar Anglo reconceptualizations of southern California in this period: "fantasy heritage." See McWilliams, *North from Mexico*, 15–25.

2 Prince, *Spanish Mission Churches in New Mexico*, 316.

3 Santa Fe Transportation Company Courier Instructional Bulletins, FAC.

4 Usner, *Sabino's Map*, 192–93.

5 Ibid., 79.

6 Forrest, *The Preservation of the Village*, 30.

7 "Historical and Beautiful Sanctuario at Chimayo Being Sold."

8 Pearce, *Mary Hunter Austin*, 50.

9 Austin, *Earth Horizon*, 336.

10 Montgomery, *The Spanish Redemption*, 169.

11 State Corporation Commission of New Mexico, from Certificate of Incorporation No. 15923, October 29, 1929, quoted in Weigle, "The First Twenty-Five Years of the Spanish Colonial Arts Society," 181.

12 Austin, *Earth Horizon*, 359.

13 Meem is well-known for his design of the University of New Mexico's Zimmerman Library and other signature buildings on that campus. Among many other projects, he also designed the Laboratory of Anthropology in Santa Fe and served on that city's planning commission. See La Farge, *Santa Fe*, 309, 374.

14 Bellmore, "John Gaw Meem: Zimmerman Architect."

15 Weigle, "The First Twenty-Five Years of the Spanish Colonial Arts Society," 184.

16 Henderson, "E. Dana Johnson," 123.

17 "Historical and Beautiful Sanctuario at Chimayo Being Sold."

18 Weigle, "The First Twenty-Five Years of the Spanish Colonial Arts Society," 185; "Nameless Donor Buys Chapel of Santuario."

19 Scott, "The Still Young Sunlight," 134.

20 "Nameless Donor Buys Chapel of Santuario."

21 Applegate, letter to Mary Austin, February 20, 1929, ASCA.

22 Ibid.; Weigle, "The First Twenty-Five Years of the Spanish Colonial Arts Society," 185.

23 Although I was granted some access to the Archives of the Archdiocese of Santa Fe for the preparation of this book, all of my subsequent communications to the archives, including questions about Daeger, have gone unacknowledged and unanswered.

24 Austin, *Earth Horizon*, 359.

25 Warranty deed from Jose Chavez and Dorotea M. de Chavez to Archbishop Albert T. Daeger and the Archdiocese of Santa Fe, October 15, 1929, Chimayo Vertical File, FAC.

26 U.S. Department of the Interior, SR-188, El Santuario de Chimayó, section 7, p. 5, and section 8, p. 18.

27 Chimayó File, ASCA.

28 Stone, "History, Hope and Holiness Surround Santuario," 11.

29 Austin, *Earth Horizon*, 358.

30 Forrest, *The Preservation of the Village*, 48.

31 Nieto-Phillips, *The Language of Blood*, 135.

32 Grimes, *The Craft of Ritual Studies*, 154.

33 Regarding the colonial implications of how New Mexico's history has been told, Chris Wilson writes,

    three manifestations of historical amnesia (the omission of violent repression, the denial of racial and cultural mixing, and the suppression of evidence of the modern world) interfere with the public understanding of the origins of contemporary social, economic, and political structures. Members of the *mexicano*-Chicano working class are missing from tourist imagery and political rhetoric, for instance, which long made it easier to ignore their needs. Wilson, *The Myth of Santa Fe*, 313.

34 *Official Catholic Directory* (New York: P. J. Kennedy and Sons, 1915–1955).

35 Toppino, "Chapel of the Holy Mud," 1.

CHAPTER 6. THE PILGRIMS AND PILGRIMAGE

1 Interview with Joanne Dupont Sandoval, July 2, 2014. The figure of 500,000 visitors is the highest I have encountered. A more conservative recent estimate is 300,000. See Levine, "A Little Church in New Mexico."

2 Howarth and Lamadrid, *Pilgrimage to Chimayó*, 24.

3 Turner and Turner, *Image and Pilgrimage in Christian Culture*, 34.

4 Gonzales, "Los Peregrinos."

5 Russell, "Finding the Way Home," 89–90.

6 Turner and Turner, *Image and Pilgrimage in Christian Culture*, 18–19.

7 Ibid., 27–32.

8 Holmes-Rodman, "'They Told What Happened on the Road,'" 44.

9 Fabre, "Feasts and Celebrations," 6.

10 Eade and Sallnow, *Contesting the Sacred*, 2.

11 Ibid., 137.

12 Coleman, "Pilgrimage to 'England's Nazareth,'" 65–66.

13 Fray Sebastián Álvarez's letter to the Lord Provisor and Capitular Vicar of the Diocese of Durango, November 19, 1813, document 2, Churches in New Mexico Collection, folder 17, NMSA. My translation.

14 Usner, *Sabino's Map*, 70.

15 Carson, "Interaction between Culture and Architecture in a Hispanic Plaza," 41.

16 Usner, *Sabino's Map*, 185.

17 Marriott, *María: The Potter of San Ildefonso*, 31.

18 Usner, *Sabino's Map*, 187.

19 Howarth and Lamadrid, *Pilgrimage to Chimayó*. The Archdiocese of Santa Fe acknowledges the Bataan survivors as the first organizers of the modern Chimayó pilgrimage; see *People of God* 29, no. 3 (April 2011). The historian Michael Carroll also makes this observation in his book *American Catholics in the Protestant Imagination*, 121–26. Carroll's insistent revisionism pushes him to conclude—incorrectly—that the Santuario was not a particularly popular site of Hispanic devotion until the advent of the massive walking pilgrimage post–World War II because the Santuario enjoyed little coverage in the early twentieth-century Anglo press, was not mentioned in official church documents by French clerics, and had no special event associated with Good Friday. Of course, none of these observations provides proof that Hispanic New Mexicans did not make pilgrimage to the Santuario in the nineteenth century. However, there is ample evidence, much of it presented in the present work, that Nuevomexicanos in that period did make pilgrimage to the Santuario for devotions to the Santo Niño and Esquipulas, and to seek divine intervention in the form of miraculous healing.

20 New Mexico National Guard Museum, "New Mexico National Guard's Involvement in the Bataan Death March."

21 The story appeared on the front page of the *Santa Fe New Mexican* on April 29, 1946, and is quoted in Carroll, *American Catholics in the Protestant Imagination*, 124.

22 McNulty, "Chimayo Pilgrims Pass Halfway Mark"; Boyd, *Saints and Saint Makers of New Mexico*, 127. One of the features of the Bataan commemoration, despite its terminus in a Catholic church, was its ecumenical nature, which likely contributed to the number of original pilgrims in 1946; see Seagraves, "A Bit about Dirt," 118–19. While the contemporary Holy Week pilgrimage got its start in 1946, there is evidence that New Mexican soldiers from earlier wars, including World War I, also went to Chimayó after returning home to seek healing; see Russell, "Finding the Way Home," 217.

23 Clark, "They Want No Progress in Chimayo," 38; Fox, "Healing, Imagination, and New Mexico," 227.

24 Wood, "Miracles at Chimayo," 41. All italics in the original.

25 Kaplan, "The Church Where Faith Heals," 10–11.

26 King, "Pilgrimage to a Hallowed Place," 27.

27 Seagraves, "A Bit about Dirt," 120–21; Holmes-Rodman, "'They Told What Happened on the Road,'" 24–51.

28 Fox, "Sacred Pedestrians," 48–49; Seagraves, "A Bit about Dirt," 121–22.

29 Interview with Joanne DuPont Sandoval, June 2, 2014.

30 Tobar, "Beautiful Land, Ugly Addictions"; Glendinning, *Chiva: A Village Takes on the Global Heroin Trade*, 87, 207.

31 Quintana, "Pondering the Chimayó Pilgrimage."

32 Badone and Roseman, "Approaches to the Anthropology of Pilgrimage and Tourism," 5; Graburn, "Secular Ritual," 42, 49.

33 Santa Fe Walkabouts, "Taste of New Mexico—Chimayo and the Pueblos," www.santafewalkabouts.com, accessed April 10, 2016.

34 MacCannell, *The Tourist*, 105–6.

35 Bremer, *Blessed with Tourists*, 3–4.

36 These movements often insist that reclaiming precolonial cultural forms is a form of healing: *La cultura cura* (Culture cures). Studies of Aztec dance and reclamation include Huerta, "Embodied Recuperations"; and Hernández-Ávila, "La Mesa del Santo Niño de Atocha."

37 Bremer, *Blessed with Tourists*, 4–5.

38 Ibid., 6.

39 Vikan, *From the Holy Land to Graceland*, 72.

40 Interview with Joanne Dupont Sandoval, July 2, 2014.

41 Bremer, *Blessed with Tourists*, 6–7.

42 Stausberg, *Religion and Tourism*, 13–14. Stausberg draws on Vukonić, *Tourism and Religion*.

43 Seagraves, "A Bit about Dirt," 127–28.

44 Russell, "Finding the Way Home," 127.

CHAPTER 7. THE HOLY FAMILY AND THE SANTUARIO TODAY

1 Matlock, "Longtime Priest at Santuario de Chimayó Dies."

2 Wright, "How Many Are a 'Few'?," 237.

3 González and Suntum, *El Santuario de Chimayo*, 16–17.
4 Roca, *A Long Journey for Two Short Legs*, 98–99.
5 Ibid., 99.
6 Ibid., 107–11.
7 Ibid., 105, 111, 114.
8 Ibid., 117–19.
9 Darley, *The Passionists of the Southwest*, 14–18.
10 "Priest of Santuario to Mark Anniversaries before Departure."
11 Roca, *A Long Journey for Two Short Legs*, 127–28. Italics in original.
12 González, *The Santuario de Chimayo in New Mexico*; U.S. Department of the Interior, SR-188, El Santuario de Chimayó; U.S. National Park Service, "El Santuario de Chimayo New Mexico."
13 Roca, *A Long Journey for Two Short Legs*, 157.
14 Usner, *Chasing Dichos through Chimayó*, 201.
15 Ibid., 33.
16 Martínez, "Pilgrimage of Faith."
17 Roca, *A Long Journey for Two Short Legs*, 157.
18 "Santuario de Chimayo Visited by Thousands."
19 Ragan, "Priest Irked by Chimayó Clamor."
20 Eckholm, "A Pastor Begs to Differ with Flock on Miracles."
21 González and Suntum, *El Santuario de Chimayo*, 31.
22 Recently, clergy in Chimayó have been trying to reinterpret the Santuario as the home of the Lord of Esquipulas and the former Medina Chapel as the home of the Santo Niño de Atocha. One booklet even implies that the Santuario de Chimayo consists of two chapels, one of the Christ of Esquipulas and one of the Holy Child; these come together as a system of "two chapels, two spiritualities," the former for reverent and penitential devotion to the crucified Christ, the other for childlike joy and hope. See González, *The Santuario de Chimayo in New Mexico*.
23 "Santuario de Chimayo Holy Dirt."
24 Coates, "Easter Passion Pilgrims Suffer in Tourism's Glare."
25 Price, "We Can Learn from the Chimayó Incident."
26 Colker, "A Dust-Up over Mail-Order 'Miracle Mud.'"
27 Sharpe, "Company Cancels Sale."
28 Roca, *A Long Journey for Two Short Legs*, 128.
29 Interview with Joanne Dupont Sandoval, July 2, 2014.
30 Interview with Bonnie Trujillo (pseudonym), June 5, 2014.
31 Interview with Esther and Alberto (pseudonyms), July 5, 2014.
32 González and Suntum, *El Santuario de Chimayo*, 29–31.
33 Testimonial Files, Santuario de Chimayó, letter from January 2, 2013. As a condition of my access to these files, I agreed to keep all names confidential.
34 Letter from January 6, 2014.
35 Letter from July 19, 2012.

36 Letter from April 11, 2012.
37 Letter from December 10, 2008.
38 Letter from September 14, 2013.
39 Letter from July 4, 2011.
40 Letter from April 30, 2011.
41 Letter from February 21, 2012.
42 Letter from September 29, 2011.
43 Letter from June 29, 2013.
44 Letter from May 6, 2010.
45 Letter from October 11, 2013.
46 Letter from March 27, 2010.
47 Letter from 2010, no specific date given.
48 Interview with Joanne Dupont Sandoval, July 2, 2014.
49 Interview with Alicia Baca (pseudonym), July 2, 2014.
50 Anaya, "La Capella [*sic*] de Santo Niño en Chimayo."
51 Usner, "Fear This," 11.
52 Bullington, "New Mexico Tourism," 54.
53 Nomination form for New Mexico's Most Endangered Places List, 2012, submitted by Chimayó Citizens for Community Planning, ASCA.
54 "Santuario de Chimayó Planning Retreat."
55 Interview with Raymond Bal, April 2, 2015.
56 Interview with Johnny García (pseudonym), March 31, 2015.

CONCLUSION

1 Dispenza, "Hallowed Ground," 49.
2 Ibid., 46.
3 DeLyser, *Ramona Memories*, 183–84.
4 Ibid., xv–xvi.
5 Quinn, *A House of Prayer for all People*; Tweed, *America's Church*.
6 For examples, see Bremer, *Blessed with Tourists*; and Mitchell, *Spirituality and the State*.
7 Orsi, "U.S. Catholics between Memory and Modernity," 41–42.
8 Bishop Zubiría used this term in his pastoral letter of 1833. See Weigle, *Brothers of Light, Brothers of Blood*, 201–4.
9 A small but influential sample includes Matovina and Riebe-Estrella, *Horizons of the Sacred*; León, *La Llorona's Children*; Nabhan-Warren, *The Virgin of El Barrio*; and Espinosa and García, *Mexican American Religions*.
10 An excellent historiographical essay on the importance of these kinds of studies is Gutiérrez, "The New Turn in Chicano/Mexicano History."
11 Espinosa, Elizondo, and Miranda, *Hispanic Churches in American Public Life*, 14.
12 Putnam and Campbell, *American Grace*, 299.
13 Ibid., 300.
14 Jones and Cox, *The "Francis Effect"?*, 1–2.

BIBLIOGRAPHY

Adams, Eleanor B., and Fray Angélico Chávez, eds. *The Missions of New Mexico, 1776: A Description by Fray Francisco Anastasio Domínguez*. Albuquerque: University of New Mexico Press, 1956.

Aguilera, Miguel Angel Astor. *The Maya World of Communicating Objects: Quadripartite Crosses, Trees, and Stones*. Albuquerque: University of New Mexico Press, 2010.

Ahlborn, Richard E. "The Penitente Moradas of Abiquiú." In *Contributions from the Museum of History and Technology*, Paper 63, 123–67. Washington, DC: Smithsonian Institution Press, 1968.

Albanese, Catherine L. *A Republic of Mind and Spirit: A Cultural History of American Metaphysical Religion*. New Haven: Yale University Press, 2007.

Almaráz, Félix D., Jr. "Transplanting 'Deep, Living Roots': Franciscan Missionaries and the Colonization of New Mexico—The Fledgling Years, 1598–1616." In *Seeds of Struggle/Harvest of Faith: The Papers of the Archdiocese of Santa Fe Catholic Cuatro Centennial Conference*, edited by Thomas J. Steele, Paul Rhetts, and Barb Awalt, 1–26. Albuquerque: LPD Press, 1998.

Anaya, Pauline. "La Capella [*sic*] de Santo Niño en Chimayo." *New Mexico Hispanic Cultural Preservation League* 13, no. 3 (March 2011).

Aragon, Ray John de. *Padre Martinez and Bishop Lamy*. Las Vegas, NM: Pan-American Publishing, 1978.

Austin, Mary. *Earth Horizon*. New York: Literary Guild, 1932.

Badone, Ellen, and Sharon R. Roseman. "Approaches to the Anthropology of Pilgrimage and Tourism." In *Intersecting Journeys: The Anthropology of Pilgrimage and Tourism*, edited by Ellen Badone and Sharon R. Roseman, 1–23. Urbana: University of Illinois Press, 2004.

Bator, Joseph Andrew. "Authority and Community in Nineteenth-Century American Catholicism: John Baptist Lamy in New Mexico." Ph.D. diss., Northwestern University, 1991.

Bellmore, Audra. "John Gaw Meem: Zimmerman Architect." University of New Mexico, n.d. Accessed January 7, 2015. http://library.unm.edu.

Borhegyi, Stephan F. de. "The Cult of Our Lord of Esquipulas in Middle America and New Mexico." *El Palacio: A Review of Arts and Sciences in the Southwest* 61, no. 12 (December 1954): 387–401.

———. "The Evolution of a Landscape." *Landscape* 4, no. 1 (1954): 24–30.

Borhegyi, Stephan F. de, and E. Boyd. *El Santuario de Chimayo*. Reprint ed. Santa Fe: Ancient City Press, 1982 [1956].

Bowden, Henry Warner. "Spanish Missions, Cultural Conflict and the Pueblo Revolt of 1680." *Church History* 44, no. 2 (June 1975): 217–28.

Boyd, E. *Popular Arts of the Spanish New Mexico*. Santa Fe: Museum of New Mexico Press, 1974.

———. *Saints and Saint Makers of New Mexico*. Santa Fe: Laboratory of Anthropology, 1946.

Bremer, Thomas S. *Blessed with Tourists: The Borderlands of Religion and Tourism in San Antonio*. Chapel Hill: University of North Carolina Press, 2004.

Brooks, James F. *Captives and Cousins: Slavery, Kinship, and Community in the Southwest Borderlands*. Chapel Hill: University of North Carolina Press, 2002.

Bullington, Emily Alyce. "New Mexico Tourism: Conflict and Cooperation in the Land of Enchantment." M.A. thesis, New York University, 2010.

Bunting, Bainbridge. *Early Architecture in New Mexico*. Albuquerque: University of New Mexico Press, 1976.

Butler, Anne M., Michael E. Engh, and Thomas W. Spalding, eds. *The Frontiers and Catholic Identities*. Maryknoll, NY: Orbis, 1999.

Campbell, Frances Margaret. "American Catholicism in Northern New Mexico: A Kaleidoscope of Development, 1840–1885." Ph.D. diss., Graduate Theological Union, 1986.

Carrasco, David. "A Perspective for a Study of Religious Dimensions in Chicano Experience: *Bless Me, Ultima* as a Religious Text." *Aztlán: A Journal of Chicano Studies* 13, nos. 1–2 (1982): 195–221.

Carrillo, Charles. "Our Lord of Esquipulas in New Mexico." *Tradición*, Summer 1999, 50–54.

Carroll, Michael P. *American Catholics in the Protestant Imagination: Rethinking the Academic Study of Religion*. Baltimore: Johns Hopkins University Press, 2007.

———. *The Penitente Brotherhood: Patriarchy and Hispano-Catholicism in New Mexico*. Baltimore: Johns Hopkins University Press, 2002.

Carson, Ann L. "Interaction between Culture and Architecture in a Hispanic Plaza." In *Archaeology, Art, and Anthropology: Papers in Honor of J. J. Brody*, edited by Meliha S. Duran and David T. Kirkpatrick, 39–50. Albuquerque: Archaeology Society of New Mexico, 1992.

Cather, Willa. *Death Comes for the Archbishop*. New York: Knopf, 1927.

Chauvenet, Beatrice. *John Gaw Meem: Pioneer in Historic Preservation*. Santa Fe: Museum of New Mexico Press, 1985.

Chávez, Fray Angélico. *Archives of the Archdiocese of Santa Fe, 1678–1900*. Washington, DC: Academy of American Franciscan History, 1957.

———. *But Time and Chance: The Story of Padre Martínez of Taos, 1793–1867*. Santa Fe: Sunstone, 1981.

Chávez, Fray Angélico, and Thomas E. Chávez. *Wake for a Fat Vicar: Father Juan Felipe Ortiz, Archbishop Lamy, and the New Mexican Catholic Church in the Middle of the Nineteenth Century*. Albuquerque: LPD Press, 2004.

Chesnut, R. Andrew. *Competitive Spirits: Latin America's New Religious Economy*. New York: Oxford University Press, 2003.

Clark, Neil. "They Want No Progress in Chimayo." *Saturday Evening Post*, May 9, 1953, 38–39, 172–76.

Coates, James. "Easter Passion Pilgrims Suffer in Tourism's Glare." *Chicago Tribune*, April 17, 1992.

Coleman, Simon. "Pilgrimage to 'England's Nazareth': Landscapes of Myth and Memory at Walsingham." In *Intersecting Journeys: The Anthropology of Pilgrimage and Tourism*, edited by Ellen Badone and Sharon R. Roseman, 52–67. Urbana: University of Illinois Press, 2004.

Colker, David. "A Dust-Up over Mail-Order 'Miracle Mud.'" *Los Angeles Times*, September 26, 1992.

Darley, Alex M. *The Passionists of the Southwest, or The Holy Brotherhood: A Revelation of the "Penitentes."* Reprint ed. Glorieta, NM: Rio Grande Press, 1968 [1893].

Defouri, James H. *Historical Sketch of the Catholic Church in New Mexico*. San Francisco: McCormick Bros., 1887.

DeHuff, Elizabeth Willis. "The Santuario at Chimayo." *New Mexico Highway Journal*, June 1931, 16–17, 39.

———. *Say the Bells of Old Missions: Legends of Old New Mexico Churches*. St. Louis, MO: B. Herder, 1948.

DeLoach, Dana Engstrom. "Image and Identity at El Santuario de Chimayo in Chimayo, New Mexico." M.A. thesis, University of North Texas, 1999.

DeLyser, Dydia. *Ramona Memories: Tourism and the Shaping of Southern California*. Minneapolis: University of Minnesota Press, 2005.

Dispenza, Joseph. "Hallowed Ground: Spiritual Paths Lead to New Mexico." *New Mexico Magazine*, March 1987, 46–55.

Douglas, William Boone. "Notes on the Shrines of the Tewa and Other Pueblo Indians of New Mexico." Nineteenth International Congress of Americanists, Washington, DC, December 1915.

Dunbar-Ortiz, Roxanne. *Roots of Resistance: A History of Land Tenure in New Mexico*. Norman: University of Oklahoma Press, 2007.

Durkheim, Emile. *The Elementary Forms of the Religious Life*. Translated by Joseph Ward Swain. New York: Free Press, 1965 [1912].

Eade, John, and Michael J. Sallnow, eds. *Contesting the Sacred: The Anthropology of Christian Pilgrimage*. London: Routledge, 1991.

Ebright, Malcolm, and Rick Hendricks. *The Witches of Abiquiu: The Governor, the Priest, the Genízaro Indians, and the Devil*. Albuquerque: University of New Mexico Press, 2006.

Eckholm, Erik. "A Pastor Begs to Differ with Flock on Miracles." *New York Times*, February 20, 2008.

Edmonds, Ennis B., and Michelle A. Gonzalez. *Caribbean Religious History: An Introduction*. New York: New York University Press, 2010.

Eliade, Mircea. *The Sacred and the Profane: The Nature of Religion*. Translated by Willard R. Trask. San Diego: Harcourt, 1957.

Espinosa, Gastón, Virgilio Elizondo, and Jesse Miranda. *Hispanic Churches in American Public Life: Summary of Findings*. Notre Dame, IN: Institute for Latino Studies, University of Notre Dame, 2003.

Espinosa, Gastón, and Mario T. García. *Mexican American Religions: Spirituality, Activism, and Culture*. Durham: Duke University Press, 2008.

Fabre, Geneviève. "Feasts and Celebrations: Introduction." In *Feasts and Celebrations in North American Ethnic Communities*, edited by Ramón A. Gutiérrez and Geneviève Fabre, 1–9. Albuquerque: University of New Mexico Press, 1995.

Finke, Roger, and Rodney Stark. *The Churching of America, 1776–1990: Winners and Losers in Our Religious Economy*. New Brunswick: Rutgers University Press, 1992.

Forrest, Suzanne. *The Preservation of the Village: New Mexico's Hispanics and the New Deal*. New Mexico Land Grant Series. Albuquerque: University of New Mexico Press, 1989.

Fox, Stephen D. "Healing, Imagination, and New Mexico." *New Mexico Historical Review* 58, no. 3 (July 1983): 213–37.

———. "Sacred Pedestrians: The Many Faces of Southwest Pilgrimage." *Journal of the Southwest* 36, no. 1 (1994): 33–53.

Frankfurter, Alexander M. "A Gathering of Children: Holy Infants and the Cult of El Santo Niño de Atocha." *El Palacio: A Review of Arts and Sciences in the Southwest* 94, no. 1 (1988): 30–39.

Fundación "Corazón Inmaculado de María." *La Señora Santa María*. Bogotá: Consejo Episcopal Latinoamericano, 1979.

Gavin, Robin Farwell, Barbara B. Mauldin, and Helen R. Lucero. *History and Iconography of the Architecture and Art at Nuestro Señor de Esquipulas Church (Santuario de Chimayó)*. Santa Fe: Museum of International Folk Art and the Archdiocese of Santa Fe, 1990.

Glendinning, Chellis. *Chiva: A Village Takes on the Global Heroin Trade*. Gabriola Island, BC: New Society Publishers, 2005.

Gonzales, Lou. "Los Peregrinos: They Come by the Thousands." *Colorado Springs Gazette-Telegraph*, April 12, 1998.

González, Julio. *The Santuario de Chimayo in New Mexico: The Shrine of Our Lord of Esquipulas and the Holy Child*. Chimayó, NM: Sons of the Holy Family, 2013.

González, Julio, and Jim Suntum. *El Santuario de Chimayo: The Shrine of Our Lord of Esquipulas*. Chimayó, NM: Santuario de Chimayo, n.d.

Graburn, Nelson H. H. "Secular Ritual: A General Theory of Tourism." In *Hosts and Guests Revisited: Tourism Issues of the 21st Century*, edited by Valene L. Smith and Maryann Brent, 42–50. Elmsford, NY: Cognizant Communication, 2001.

Graziano, Frank. *Cultures of Devotion: Folk Saints of Spanish America*. New York: Oxford University Press, 2006.

Griffith, James S. *Folk Saints of the Borderlands: Victims, Bandits and Healers*. Tucson, AZ: Rio Nuevo, 2003.

Grimes, Ronald L. *The Craft of Ritual Studies*. New York: Oxford University Press, 2014.

Gutiérrez, David G. "The New Turn in Chicano/Mexicano History: Integrating Religious Belief and Practice." In *Catholics in the American Century: Recasting Narratives of U.S. History*, edited by R. Scott Appleby and Kathleen Sprow Cummings, 109–33. Ithaca: Cornell University Press, 2012.

Gutiérrez, Ramón A. "El Santuario de Chimayo: A Syncretic Shrine in New Mexico." In *Feasts and Celebrations in North American Ethnic Communities*, edited by Ramón A. Gutiérrez and Geneviève Fabre, 71–86. Albuquerque: University of New Mexico Press, 1995.

———. *When Jesus Came, the Corn Mothers Went Away: Marriage, Sexuality, and Power in New Mexico, 1540–1846*. Stanford: Stanford University Press, 1991.

Hackett, Charles Wilson, ed. *Historical Documents Relating to New Mexico, Nueva Vizcaya, and Approaches Thereto, to 1773*. Vol. 3. Washington, DC: Carnegie Institution, 1937.

Halbwachs, Maurice. *Sources of Religious Sentiment*. Translated by John A. Spaulding. New York: Free Press of Glencoe, 1962.

Hammond, George P., and Agapito Rey. *Don Juan de Oñate: Colonizer of New Mexico*. Coronado Cuarto Centennial Publications, 1540–1940, edited by George P. Hammond, vols. 5 and 6. Albuquerque: University of New Mexico Press, 1953.

Hanks, Nancy. *Lamy's Legion: The Individual Histories of Secular Clergy Serving in the Archdiocese of Santa Fe from 1850 to 1912*. Santa Fe: HRM Books, 2000.

Harrington, John Peabody. *The Ethnogeography of the Tewa Indians: Twenty-Ninth Annual Report of the Bureau of American Ethnology to the Secretary of the Smithsonian Institution*. Washington, DC: Bureau of American Ethnology, 1916.

Henderson, Alice Corbin. *Brothers of Light: The Penitentes of the Southwest*. New York: Harcourt, Brace, 1937.

———. "E. Dana Johnson." *New Mexico Historical Review* 13 (1938): 120–25.

Hendrickson, Brett. *Border Medicine: A Transcultural History of Mexican American Curanderismo*. New York: New York University Press, 2014.

Hernández-Ávila, Inés. "La Mesa del Santo Niño de Atocha and the Conchero Dance Tradition of México-Tenochtitlán: Religious Healing in Urban Mexico and the United States." In *Religion and Healing in America*, edited by Linda L. Barnes and Susan S. Sered, 359–74. New York: Oxford University Press, 2005.

"Historical and Beautiful Sanctuario at Chimayo Being Sold; Priceless, Storied Relics Peddled as Curios." *Santa Fe New Mexican*, February 9, 1929. Box 3, folder 19, John Gaw Meem Papers, 1914–1992, Center for Southwest Research, University of New Mexico, Albuquerque.

Holmes-Rodman, Paula Elizabeth. "'They Told What Happened on the Road': Narrative and the Construction of Experiential Knowledge on the Pilgrimage to Chimayo, New Mexico." In *Intersecting Journeys: The Anthropology of Pilgrimage and Tourism*, edited by Ellen Badone and Sharon R. Roseman, 24–51. Urbana: University of Illinois Press, 2004.

Horgan, Paul. *Lamy of Santa Fe: His Life and Times*. New York: Farrar, Straus and Giroux, 1975.

Howarth, Sam, and Enrique R. Lamadrid. *Pilgrimage to Chimayó: Contemporary Portrait of a Living Tradition*. Santa Fe: Museum of New Mexico Press, 1999.

Huerta, Elisa Diana. "Embodied Recuperations: Performance, Indigeneity, and *Danza Azteca*." In *Dancing across Borders: Danzas y Bailes Mexicanos*, edited by Olga Nájera-Ramírez, Norma E. Cantú, and Brenda E. Romero, 3–18. Urbana: University of Illinois Press, 2009.

Hughes, Jennifer Scheper. *Biography of a Mexican Crucifix: Lived Religion and Local Faith from the Conquest to the Present*. New York: Oxford University Press, 2010.

Jaramillo, Cleofas M. *Shadows of the Past (Sombras del Pasado)*. Reprint ed. Santa Fe: Ancient City Press, 1972 [1941].

Jones, Robert P., and Daniel Cox. *The "Francis Effect"? U.S. Catholic Attitudes on Pope Francis, the Catholic Church, and American Politics*. Washington, DC: Public Religion Research Institute, 2015.

Kaplan, Howard. "The Church Where Faith Heals." *Empire Magazine*, April 15, 1973, 10–13.

Kay, Elizabeth. *Chimayo Valley Traditions*. Santa Fe: Ancient City Press, 1987.

Kessell, John L. *Pueblos, Spaniards, and the Kingdom of New Mexico*. Norman: University of Oklahoma Press, 2008.

King, Scottie. "Pilgrimage to a Hallowed Place: Good Friday at Chimayo." *New Mexico Magazine*, March 1979, 26–42. File "Chimayo Docs," Archives of the Archdiocese of Santa Fe.

Knaut, Andrew L. *The Pueblo Revolt of 1680: Conquest and Resistance in Seventeenth-Century New Mexico*. Norman: University of Oklahoma Press, 1995.

Kraemer, Paul. *An Alternative View of New Mexico's 1837 Rebellion*. Nutshell Series, no. 2. Los Alamos, NM: Los Alamos Historical Society, 2009. Chimayó Vertical File, Fray Angélico Chávez History Library, Santa Fe.

La Farge, Oliver. *Santa Fe: The Autobiography of a Southwestern Town*. Norman: University of Oklahoma Press, 1959.

Lange, Charles H., Elizabeth M. Lange, and Carroll L. Riley, eds. *Southwest Journals of Adolph F. Bandelier, 1889–1892*. Vol. 2. Albuquerque: University of New Mexico Press, 1966.

Lange, Yvonne. "Santo Niño de Atocha: A Mexican Cult Is Transplanted to Spain." *El Palacio: A Review of Arts and Sciences in the Southwest* 84, no. 4 (Winter 1978): 2–7.

Larcombe, Samuel. "Plaza del Cerro, Chimayó, New Mexico: An Old Place Not Quite on the Highway." In *Hispanic Arts and Ethnohistory in the Southwest: New Papers Inspired by the Work of E. Boyd*, edited by Marta Weigle, 170–80. Santa Fe: Ancient City Press, 1983.

Lecompte, Janet. *Rebellion in Río Arriba, 1837*. Albuquerque: University of New Mexico Press, 1985.

León, Luis D. *La Llorona's Children: Religion, Life, and Death in the U.S.-Mexican Borderlands*. Berkeley: University of California Press, 2004.

Levine, Irene S. "A Little Church in New Mexico with Some Big Healing Power." *Washington Post*, April 10, 2014.

López Pulido, Alberto. *The Sacred World of the Penitentes*. Washington, DC: Smithsonian Institution Press, 2000.

Lummis, Charles F. *The Land of Poco Tiempo*. Albuquerque: University of New Mexico Press, 1952 [1893].

Lynch, John. *New Worlds: A Religious History of Latin America*. New Haven: Yale University Press, 2012.

MacCannell, Dean. *The Tourist: A New Theory of the Leisure Class*. New York: Schocken, 1976.

Manseau, Peter. *One Nation, under Gods*. New York: Little, Brown, 2015.

Marriott, Alice. *María: The Potter of San Ildefonso*. Norman: University of Oklahoma Press, 1948.

Martinez, Antonio Jose. "Apologia of Presbyter Antonio Jose Martinez." *New Mexico Historical Review* 3, no. 4 (October 1928): 325–46.

Martínez, Demetria. "Pilgrimage of Faith." *Albuquerque Journal*, April 7, 1990.

Masuzawa, Tomoko. *In Search of Dreamtime*. Chicago: University of Chicago Press, 1993.

Matlock, Staci. "Longtime Priest at Santuario de Chimayó Dies." *Santa Fe New Mexican*, August 5, 2015.

Matovina, Timothy M., and Gary Riebe-Estrella, eds. *Horizons of the Sacred: Mexican Traditions in U.S. Catholicism*. Cushwa Center Studies of Catholicism in Twentieth-Century America. Ithaca: Cornell University Press, 2002.

McNulty, William. "Chimayo Pilgrims Pass Halfway Mark on Trek to Famous El Santuario." *Santa Fe New Mexican*, April 27, 1946. Fray Angélico Chávez History Library, Santa Fe.

McWilliams, Carey. *North from Mexico: The Spanish-Speaking People of the United States*. 3rd ed. Santa Barbara: Praeger, 2016.

Mitchell, Kerry. *Spirituality and the State: Managing Nature and Experience in America's National Parks*. New York: New York University Press, 2016.

Mitchell, Nathan. *The Mystery of the Rosary: Marian Devotion and the Reinvention of Catholicism*. New York: New York University Press, 2009.

Montgomery, Charles. *The Spanish Redemption: Heritage, Power, and Loss on New Mexico's Upper Rio Grande*. Berkeley: University of California Press, 2002.

Nabhan-Warren, Kristy. *The Virgin of El Barrio: Marian Apparitions, Catholic Evangelizing, and Mexican American Activism*. New York: New York University Press, 2005.

"Nameless Donor Buys Chapel of Santuario, Presents to Church." *Santa Fe New Mexican*, October 15, 1929.

New Mexico National Guard Museum. "New Mexico National Guard's Involvement in the Bataan Death March." N.d. Accessed August 21, 2015. www.bataanmuseum.com.

Nieto-Phillips, John M. *The Language of Blood: The Making of Spanish-American Identity in New Mexico, 1880s–1930s*. Albuquerque: University of New Mexico Press, 2004.

The Old Faith and Old Glory: The Story of the Church in New Mexico since the American Occupation, 1846–1946. Santa Fe: Santa Fe Press, 1946. Sallie Wagner Collection, box 4, folder 41, New Mexico State Records Center and Archives, Santa Fe.

Orsi, Robert A. *Between Heaven and Earth: The Religious Worlds People Make and the Scholars Who Study Them*. Princeton: Princeton University Press, 2005.

———. "U.S. Catholics between Memory and Modernity: How Catholics Are American." In *Catholics in the American Century: Recasting Narratives of U.S. History*, edited by R. Scott Appleby and Kathleen Sprow Cummings, 11–42. Ithaca: Cornell University Press, 2012.

Ortiz, Alfonso. *The Tewa World: Space, Time, Being, and Becoming in a Pueblo Society*. Chicago: University of Chicago Press, 1969.

Otero-Warren, Nina. *Old Spain in Our Southwest*. New York: Harcourt, Brace, 1936.

Pacheco Rojas, José de la Cruz. "El Proceso de Formación del Obispado de Nuevo México," pt. 1. *New Mexico Historical Review* 91, no. 1 (Winter 2016): 57–78.

Pearce, T. M. *Mary Hunter Austin*. New York: Twayne, 1965.

People of God 29, no. 3 (April 2011). Chimayó Vertical File, Center for Southwest Research, University of New Mexico, Albuquerque.

Pescador, Juan Javier. *Crossing Borders with the Santo Niño de Atocha*. Albuquerque: University of New Mexico Press, 2009.

"Popular Legends Surround Building of Santuario." *People of God* 2, no. 2 (April 1984). Chimayó Vertical File, Center for Southwest Research, University of New Mexico, Albuquerque.

Price, Jess. "On the Road to Chimayó." *New Mexico Magazine*, March 1989, 28–35.

Price, V. B. "We Can Learn from the Chimayó Incident." *Albuquerque Tribune*, April 3, 1992.

"Priest of Santuario to Mark Anniversaries before Departure." *People of God* 2, no. 2 (April 1984).

Prince, L. Bradford. *Spanish Mission Churches in New Mexico*. Reprint ed. Glorieta, NM: Rio Grande Press, 1977 [1915].

Putnam, Robert D., and David E. Campbell. *American Grace: How Religion Divides and Unites Us*. New York: Simon and Schuster, 2010.

Quinn, Frederick. *A House of Prayer for All People: A History of Washington National Cathedral*. New York: Morehouse, 2014.

Quintana, Chris. "Pondering the Chimayó Pilgrimage." *New Mexico Daily Lobo*, April 9, 2012.

Ragan, Tom. "Priest Irked by Chimayó Clamor." *Albuquerque Journal*, April 5, 1996.

Read, Benjamin M. "El Santuario de Chimayo." *El Palacio: A Review of Arts and Sciences in the Southwest* 3, no. 4 (August 1916): 81–84.

Roca, Casimiro. *A Long Journey for Two Short Legs: My Album of Memories*. Chimayó, NM: Sons of the Holy Family, 2007.

Roca, Evaristo. *The Holy Child of Atocha, El Santo Niño de Atocha en El Santuario de Chimayo*. Chimayó, NM: Santuario de Chimayo, 2012.

Romero, Juan. "Begetting the Mexican American: Padre Martínez and the 1847 Rebellion." In *Seeds of Struggle/Harvest of Hope: The History of the Catholic Church in New Mexico*, edited by Thomas J. Steele, Paul Rhetts, and Barb Awalt, 345–72. Albuquerque: LPD Press, 1998.

Russell, Larry. "Finding the Way Home: A Performance of Ritual Pilgrimage to a Shrine of Healing." Ph.D. diss., Southern Illinois University, 2001.

Sánchez, Joseph P., Robert L. Spude, and Art Gómez. *New Mexico: A History*. Norman: University of Oklahoma Press, 2013.

Sandoval, Moises. *On the Move: A History of the Hispanic Church in the United States*. Maryknoll, NY: Orbis, 1990.

"Santuario de Chimayo Holy Dirt." Brochure. Santuario de Chimayo, 2009.

"Santuario de Chimayó Planning Retreat." *Albuquerque Journal*, December 3, 2011.

"Santuario de Chimayo Visited by Thousands." *Santa Fe New Mexican*, May 25, 1979.

Schroeder, Albert H. "The Tewa Indians of the Rio Grande and Their Neighbors—A.D. 1450–1680." In *New Mexico Geological Society Guidebook, 35th Field Conference, Rio Grande Rift: Northern New Mexico*, 283–86. Albuquerque: New Mexico Bureau of Geology and Mineral Resources, 1984. Albert T. Schroeder Collection, New Mexico State Records Center and Archives, Santa Fe.

Schwaller, John Frederick. *The History of the Catholic Church in Latin America: From Conquest to Revolution and Beyond*. New York: New York University Press, 2011.

Scott, Winfield Townley. "The Still Young Sunlight." In *A Vanishing America: The Life and Times of the Small Town*, edited by Thomas C. Wheeler, 122–35. New York: Holt, Rinehart, and Winston, 1964.

Seagraves, Laura Roxanne. "A Bit about Dirt: Pilgrimage and Popular Religion at El Santuario de Chimayo." Ph.D. diss., Graduate Theological Union, 2002.

Sharpe, Tom. "Company Cancels Sale of Chimayó Crosses, Dirt." *Albuquerque Journal*, September 30, 1992.

Simmons, Marc. "In the Shadow of the Miter: New Mexico's Quest for Diocesan Status." In *Seeds of Struggle/Harvest of Faith: The History of the Catholic Church in New Mexico*, edited by Thomas J. Steele, Paul Rhetts, and Barb Awalt, 207–18. Albuquerque: LPD Press, 1998.

———. "Settlement Patterns and Village Plans in Colonial New Mexico." In *New Spain's Northern Frontier: Essays on Spain in the American West, 1540–1821*, edited by David J. Weber, 97–115. Albuquerque: University of New Mexico Press, 1979.

Spicer, Edward H. *Cycles of Conquest: The Impact of Spain, Mexico, and the United States on the Indians of the Southwest, 1533–1960*. Tucson: University of Arizona Press, 1962.

Stausberg, Michael. *Religion and Tourism: Crossroads, Destinations, and Encounters*. New York: Routledge, 2011.

Steele, Thomas J., ed. *Archbishop Lamy: In His Own Words*. Albuquerque: LPD Press, 2000.

Stilgoe, John R. *Common Landscape of America, 1580 to 1845*. New Haven: Yale University Press, 1982.

Stone, Marissa. "History, Hope and Holiness Surround Santuario." *Santa Fe New Mexican*, April 11, 2004.

Taylor, Carl. "Penitentes of New Mexico." *Everybody's Magazine*, April 1904, 501–10. Hayden Special Collections, Arizona State University.

Tobar, Hector. "Beautiful Land, Ugly Addictions." *Los Angeles Times*, February 29, 2000.

Toppino, Mickey. "Chapel of the Holy Mud." *New Mexico Magazine*, February 1961, 1, 34–38. Ruth Armstrong Papers, Center for Southwest Research, University of New Mexico, Albuquerque.

Turner, Victor, and Edith Turner. *Image and Pilgrimage in Christian Culture*. New York: Columbia University Press, 1978.

Tweed, Thomas A. *America's Church: The National Shrine and Catholic Presence in the Nation's Capital*. New York: Oxford University Press, 2011.

———. *Retelling U.S. Religious History*. Berkeley: University of California Press, 1997.

Twitchell, Ralph Emerson. *The Spanish Archives of New Mexico*. Vol. 1. Cedar Rapids, IA: Torch Press, 1914.

U.S. Department of the Interior, National Park Service. SR-188, El Santuario de Chimayó and Collections. National Register of Historic Places registration form. 1990.

U.S. National Park Service. "El Santuario de Chimayo New Mexico." N.d. Accessed December 3, 2015. www.nps.gov.

Usner, Don J. *Chasing Dichos through Chimayó*. Albuquerque: University of New Mexico Press, 2014.

———. "Fear This: Proposed Development for the Santuario in Chimayó." *Tradición*, 2012, 11.

———. *Sabino's Map: Life in Chimayó's Old Plaza*. Santa Fe: Museum of New Mexico Press, 1995.

Vanderwood, Paul J. *Juan Soldado: Rapist, Murderer, Martyr, Saint*. Durham: Duke University Press, 2004.

Vikan, Gary. *From the Holy Land to Graceland: Sacred People, Places and Things in Our Lives*. Washington, DC: AAM Press, 2012.

Villagrá, Gaspar Pérez de, Miguel Encinias, Alfred Rodríguez, and Joseph P. Sánchez. *Historia de la Nueva México, 1610*. Albuquerque: University of New Mexico Press, 1992.

Vukonić, Boris. *Tourism and Religion*. New York: Pergamon, 1996.

Walter, Paul A. F. "A New Mexico Lourdes." *El Palacio* 3, no. 2 (January 1916): 3–27.

Weigle, Marta. *Brothers of Light, Brothers of Blood: The Penitentes of the Southwest*. Albuquerque: University of New Mexico Press, 1976.

———. "The First Twenty-Five Years of the Spanish Colonial Arts Society." In *Hispanic Arts and Ethnohistory in the Southwest: New Papers Inspired by the Work of E. Boyd*, edited by Marta Weigle, 181–203. Santa Fe: Ancient City Press, 1983.

Weigle, Marta, and Peter White. *The Lore of New Mexico*. Albuquerque: University of New Mexico Press, 1988.

Wilson, Chris. *The Myth of Santa Fe: Creating a Modern Regional Tradition*. Albuquerque: University of New Mexico Press, 1997.

Wood, Charles J. "Miracles at Chimayo." *New Mexico Magazine*, April 1955. Fray Angélico Chávez History Library, Santa Fe.

Woodward, Dorothy. "The Penitentes of New Mexico." Ph.D. diss., Yale University, 1935.

Wright, Robert E. "How Many Are a 'Few'? Catholic Clergy in Central and Northern New Mexico, 1780–1851." In *Seeds of Struggle/Harvest of Hope: The History of the Catholic Church in New Mexico*, edited by Thomas J. Steele, Paul Rhetts, and Barb Awalt, 219–62. Albuquerque: LPD Press, 1998.

Wright-Rios, Edward. *Revolutions in Mexican Catholicism: Reform and Revelation in Oaxaca, 1887–1934.* Durham: Duke University Press, 2009.

INDEX

Page numbers in *italics* indicate maps and photographs. Numbers followed by n indicate notes.

Abeita, Juan, 57–58

Abeyta, Bernardo: death of, 11; devotional life, 113; as farmer and trader, 75, 164–165; as *hermano mayor*, 10–11, 38, 56–57, 74–76, *124*; house of, 7; and origins of the Santuario, 1–2, 49–56, 62–63, 65, 154, 168–169, 208n36; as owner and steward of the Santuario, 4, 73–77, 80, 86, 106, 195–196, 210n13, 213n12; property, 56

Abeyta, Juan de Esquipulas, 52

Abeyta, Tomás de Jesús Nazareno de Esquipulas, 52, 76

Abeyta family, 43, 123

Abiquiu, 30–31, 36–37, 75–76, 123, 205n33

Abreu, Ramón, 79

Acoma Pueblo, 17–19

adobe, 127, 132

advertising, 178–179

Aesculapius, 207n19

aesthetics, 135–136, 164

agriculture, 75, 124

Aguirre, Calixto, 105

Ahlborn, Richard, 34, 36

Albuquerque, 32

Albuquerque Tribune, 179

Álvarez, Sebastián, 52–56, 74–77, 154, 210n15

Anaya, Pauline, 190

Anglo Americans or Anglos, xi; pilgrims, 2, 141, 156–157; preservationists, 125–129, 131–134

Apaches, 20, 24

apparitions, 209n49; miraculous stories of, 55–62, 63–65, 119–120

Applegate, Frank, 125–126, 129–131, 134

Archdiocese of Santa Fe: administration of the Santuario, 118–119; establishment of, 10–11, 87–88; ownership of the Santuario, 4–7, 11–12, 92–93, 118, 169–198; pilgrimages for vocations, 150–151, 158–159; purchase of the Santuario, 122–138, *130*; real estate holdings, 143; special interest pilgrimages, 158–159

architecture, 123, 127, 132, 135

Arizona, 201

Armijo, Manuel, 81–84

artists, 125

Asia, 2

Atencio, Norberto, 173–174

Atocha, Spain, 102–103

Austin, Mary, 125–129, *130*, 130–136, 198

authenticity, staged, 161–163

autonomy, religious, 87

Aztec dance, 140, 143–144, 163–164, 217n36

Baca, Alicia, 189

Baha'is, 159

Bal, Raymond, 191

Bandelier, Adolph, 16, 42

Barber, Ruth, 60

Barreiro, Antonio, 32–33

Bataan Death March survivors, 12, 155–156, 216n19, 217n22

Baumann, Gustave, 125, 127, 129
bell towers, 111, 132, *133*
Benavides, Alonso de, 19–20, 25
Benavides, Teodoro, 211n25
benditos (tablets), 48
Benedictine monks, 142
Bent, Charles, 86
Bernardo Abeyta Welcome Center, 7, 188
Black Christ of Guatemala. *See* Cristo
   Negro de Esquipulas crucifix
Black Legend *(leyenda negra)*, 46
Bloom, Lansing, 60
borderlands, 163, 214n30
Borhegyi, Stephan F. de, 5, 47–48, 53, 108–
   110, 207n18
Bourbon monarchy, 32
Boyd, E., 106, 156, 212n12
braided hair, 81
Bremer, Thomas, 163
Brooks, James F., 82–83
Brothers of the Pious Fraternity of Our
   Father Jesus the Nazarene. *See* Her-
   manos de la Fraternidad Piadosa de
   Nuestro Padre Jesús Nazareno
Buddhists, 159
building kits, 18
bultos (statues), 38, 74, 109, 125, 197; Christ
   Child, 105–106; Santiago on his horse,
   108–109, 127–128, *128*, 130; wandering,
   57–58
buried treasure stories, 64–65
bus line tours, 160
Byrne, Edwin, 172–173

California, 154, 201
El Camino del Monte Sol (Santa Fe, NM),
   125, 129
campaniles, 111, 132, *133*
Campbell, David, 201
La Cañada. *See* Santa Cruz River valley
cancer, 182–183
Candlemas, 103
Cantón de La Cañada, 79–81, 84

Canyon Road (Santa Fe, NM), 129
Carrillo, Charles, 51
Carroll, Michael, 37–38, 76, 113, 216n19
La Casa Querida, 125
Cataño, Quirio, 47–49
Cather, Willa, 131–132, 209n7, 211n34
Catholic Church, 27; Franco-American
   oversight of, 88; in Mexico, 10–11,
   32, 70–71, 78; in New Mexico, 69–73,
   78, 99–100; in New Spain, 32; official
   rhetoric, 63–64; in United States, 5–7,
   201–202. *See also* Archdiocese of Santa
   Fe
Catholicism: day-to-day, 29; European,
   36; folk, 31–32, 34–35; Hispano, 37–38,
   51, 98–99; Iberian, 17–18; Latino, 200–
   201; Mexican, 35, 201; New Mexican,
   34–35, 68–100, 199–200; Pueblo, 19,
   36–37, 98–99; Spanish, 5–7; Spanish American, 37–38; U.S., 199–202;
   veneration of Jesus, 56–57, 113; veneration of saints, 56–57, 107–108, 116–117,
   214n30; veneration of the Santo Niño
   de Atocha, 3, 96–100, 101, 104–121, *117*,
   137–138, 146, 156, 200, 216n19, 218n22
Catholics, 2, 14–38, 200–201
CCCP (Chimayó Citizens for Community
   Planning), 190–191
Ceiba tree, 49–50
Cenacle, 188
La Centinela, 28
Chacón, Albino, 78–79, 81
Chapel of the Christ of Esquipulas, 119
Chapel of the Holy Child of Atocha. *See*
   Medina Chapel
Chavarria, Tony, 206nn12–13
Chávez family, 11, 43, 108–110, 123–125,
   128–130; 1929 sale of the Santuario,
   129–134, *130*
Chávez, Angélico, 34, 36, 52, 81
Chávez, Benigna, 155, 208n36
Chávez, Carmen, 11, 92–94
Chavez, Frances, 176

Chávez, Francisco, 134
Chávez, Jose, 129
Chávez, Ramón, 155
Chávez, Raymond, 134
Chicago Tribune, 178–179
Children's Chapel. *See* Medina Chapel
children's shoes, 117
Chimayó, 3, 7–9, 8; El Potrero *placita*, 1–2, 28, 38, 52, 56; *genízaros*, 37; gorges, 16, 42; heroin, 159–160; history of, 26, 36–37, 68–69, 123, 154; Mexican period, 80; Our Lady of the Rosary Parish, 172–173; Penitente activity, 75–76; Plaza del Cerro, 7, 27–28; popular religion, 28–31; population, 11–12; Santo Niño de Atocha in, 105–111; Santuario de (*see* Santuario de Chimayó); Spanish settlement, 23, 27; spiritual tourists and touristy pilgrim visitors, 160–167; Tewa origin of, 41–46; trade center, 154; Tsimajo̱o̱ŋwi Pueblo, 42; weaving industry, 75, 154, 156
Chimayó Citizens for Community Planning (CCCP), 190–191
Chimayó pilgrimage, 139–168; Bataan Death March commemoration, 12, 155–156, 216n19, 217n22; changes over time, 153–160, 175–176; discontents, 187–194; Good Friday pilgrimage, 92, 99, 139–147, 142, 145, 158, 160, 168–169; international status, 187–194; María Martínez family, 97; meaning of, 167–169; miraculousness of, 181–182; participants, 2, 160–167; Prayer Pilgrimage for Peace, 159; Santo Niño de Atocha pilgrimage, 114–116, 115; themes of, 118; theories of, 147–153; walks for vocations, 150–151, 158–159; women's pilgrimages, 150–151
Chimayó Rebellion, 79–86, 99, 192–193, 211n26
Chorti Indians, 47–48
Christ Child. *See* Santo Niño de Atocha

Christ Child *bultos* (statues), 105–106
Christianity, 19–20, 31–32
Christianization, 18, 21
Christians, 159
"Christmas Pastoral" letter (Lamy), 89, 212n38
chronic conditions, 184–186
Citizens of the United States Merchants, 211n26
Cochiti, 26–27
cockleshells, 114
cofradías, 31, 33
Coleman, Simon, 152–153
colonial arts, Spanish, 126–127, 131, 135–136
colonialism, 136, 214n1
Comanches, 17–18, 24, 32
commercial ventures, 143, 160, 164–165, 213n12; commodities of devotion, 105–111; gift shops, 7, 12, 165, 174, 180–181; responses to, 174–180
Committee for the Preservation and Restoration of New Mexico Mission Churches, 127, 134–135
compadrazgo, 29
competition, religious, 107–109, 111, 213n14
Condé Nast Traveler, 178
Cordova mission, 170
cosmology, 41–42, 44, 48–49
El Crepúsculo de la Libertad, 77–78
Cristo de Esquipulas. *See* Señor de Esquipulas
Cristo Negro de Esquipulas crucifix, 38, 47–49, 53–55, 197–198
cultic competition, 107–109, 111, 213n14
cult of Esquipulas, 47–48, 52–53
cult of Santo Niño de Atocha, 3, 96–100, 101, 104–120, 117, 120–121, 156, 218n22
cultural mixing, 81, 136
cultural rebuilding, 126–127
cultural reclamation, 217n36
cultural tourism, 123
culture, religious, 90

curanderos, 29–30, 77, 156–157
Cutting, Bronson, 129
Cutting, Olivia Murray, 129

Daeger, Albert T., 129, *130*, 131, 137–138
dance, Aztec, 140, 143–144, 163–164,
    217n36
Darley, Alex M., 205n41
Death Comes for the Archbishop (Cather),
    131–132, 209n7, 211n34
de Fagle, Joan, 27
DeHuff, Elizabeth, 109
DeLyser, Dydia, 196–197
demographics, 9, 24, 199–202
Denver Post, 158
de Vargas, Diego, 24–27, 136
devotion, 31, 200; commodities of devo-
    tion, 105–111; devotion of the rosary,
    113; devotion to Nuestro Padre Jesús
    Nazareno, 56–57, 113; devotion to Santo
    Niño de Atocha, 3, 96–100, 101, 104–
    121, *117*, 137–138, 146, 156, 200, 216n19,
    218n22; devotion to Señor de Esquipu-
    las, 97, 119–120, 200, 216n19, 218n22;
    folk devotion, 156–157; Hispano, 98–
    99; Marian devotion, 112–113
Diocese of Durango, Mexico, 10–11, 32, 71,
    78. *See also* Catholic Church
Diocese of Santa Fe, New Mexico, 10, 87–
    88. *See also* Catholic Church
dirt. *See* healing dirt
Dolores, 28
Domínguez, Francisco Anastasio, 26, 31,
    33, 37–38
Dominicans, 102–103
drug offenses and abuses, 159–160
Durango, Mexico, Diocese of, 10–11, 32
Durkheim, Emile, 40–41

Eade, John, 151–152
earth, healing. *See* healing dirt
earth navels, 41–42, 44
Easter pilgrimage. *See* Chimayó pilgrimage

eating earth (geophagy), 48, 53–55
Ebright, Malcolm, 31, 36
economics, 11–12
economy, 31–32, 124
Eliade, Mircea, 207n26
Elizondo, Virgilio, 200
El Paso, 22–24, 32
employment, 11–12
endangered places, 190–191, 219n53
Escapula *(santu)*, 57–58
Española city, New Mexico, 7–9, *8*, 14, 124,
    159–160
Española mission, 170
Española Valley, 7–9
Espinosa, Gastón, 200
Esquipula (San), 57
Esquipulas, 47–48
Esquipulas, Guatemala. *See* Santiago de
    Esquipulas, Guatemala
Esquipulas crucifix. *See* Señor de Es-
    quipulas
Esquivel, Juan José, 79, 83, 86
Esquivel family, 83
ethnicity seekers, 156–157
ethnic mixing, 81, 201
ethnic terms, x–xi
Europeans, 36, 176

faith, religious, 177
family reunions, 141–142
fantasy heritage, 214n1
farmers, 29–30
Fernández de San Vicente, Agustín, 32
fertility, 183–184
Fiesta del Señor Santiago (July 25), 180–
    181
Flagellantes. *See* Los Hermanos de la
    Fraternidad Piadosa de Nuestro Padre
    Jesús Nazareno
flagellation, 34, 36, 124
folk art(s), 30–31, 38, 88
folklore, 64–65
folk religion, 30–32, 34–37, 156–157, 214n30

folk traditions, 29–30, 200
Forrest, Suzanne, 124, 135–136
Fox, Stephen D., 156–157
Franciscans, 17–18, 69–70, 170, 210n15; decline of, 31–38, 71–72; influence of, 50; missionary efforts, 10, 19–22, 25, 69–70, 210n15; and Tewas, 18–20
Franco-American oversight, 88–91
Francolon, J. B., 92–94
Frankfurter, Alexander, 114
Fraternidad Piadosa de Nuestro Padre Jesús Nazareno. *See* Hermanos de la Fraternidad Piadosa de Nuestro Padre Jesús Nazareno
French priests, 89–90, 92–93
Fresnillo, Mexico, 103
furniture, 126
future directions, 12, 191–193

Galisteo, 24
García, Johnny, 192
Gené, Salvador, 170
genízaros, 29–30, 34–37, 80–81, 210n22
geography, sacred, 41–42
geophagy (eating earth), 48, 53–55
Gerónimo, 23
gift shops, 7, 12, 165, 174, 180–181
Gonzales, José, 80–82, 84, 119
González, Julio, 144, 182, 188–189, 193–194, 210n22
Good Friday observances, 124, 144
Good Friday pilgrimage, 92, 99, 139–140; 2012 walk, 160; 2015 walk, 140–147, *142*, *145*, 168–169; size of, 158. *See also* Chimayó pilgrimage
gorges, 16, 42
Graburn, Nelson, 161
Granillo, Luis, 63
Great Depression, 124–125
Gregory XVI, 71
Grimes, Ronald, 136
Guatemala, 10, 47–49
Gutiérrez, Ramón, 44, 75, 109–110, 214n31

Harrington, John, 42–43
healing, 29–31, 36–37, 77, 156–157
healing dirt, mud, or earth, 98–99, 152–153, 177–179, 200; commercialization of, 179–180; contemporary use of, 181–187; Esquipulas devotion, 48, 53; how to use, 177–178; miracle stories of, 40, 117–120, 123, 157–158, 177, 181–187; Santuario de Chimayó, 1, 39, 42–46, 51, 55, 76–77, 139, 181–187; testimonials of, 182–187; Tewa use of, 154; *tierra santa* (holy dirt), 48, 55, 177–178, 181–187
health seekers, 155–157
Henderson, Alice Corbin, 125, 128–129
Hendricks, Rick, 31, 36
Los Hermanos de la Fraternidad Piadosa de Nuestro Padre Jesús Nazareno (Brothers of the Pious Fraternity of Our Father Jesus the Nazarene, Penitentes): and Chimayó Rebellion, 80–81, 83; contemporary, 191–192; devotion to Esquipulas, 52; devotion to Nuestro Padre Jesús Nazareno, 56–57, 113; Good Friday observances, 144; *hermano celador* (warden), 33–34; *hermanos enfermeros* (nurses), 33–34, 173; *hermanos mayores* (local leaders), 33–35, 76, 83; *hermanos picadores* (bloodletters), 33–34; *hermanos piteros* (flute players), 33–34; *hermanos rezadores* (readers/reciters), 33–34, 173; history of, 10–11, 29–38, 88, 90–91, 113, 137, 172, 200; march against drug abuse, 159–160; Mexican period, 75–76, 80–81, 83; *moradas*, 33–34, 110–111, 192; rituals and processions, 96, 99, 124, 144–145, 192, 205n40; "Rules That Must Be Observed by the Brothers of the Catholic Confraternity of Penitentes" (Lamy), 88
heroin, 159–160
Hewett, Edgar, 42–43
Hidalgo (Father), 70

Hindus, 159

Hispanic Churches in American Public Life, 200

Hispanicization, 37–38

Hispanics, xi, 141, 158, 201

Hispanos, xi, 31, 34–35, 37–38, 65–66, 98–99

Holmes-Rodman, Paula Elizabeth, 150

Holy Child Chapel. *See* Medina Chapel

Holy Child of Atocha. *See* Santo Niño de Atocha

Holy Child of Prague, 115

Holy dirt (*tierra santa*), 48, 55, 177–178, 181–187

Holy Family Catholic Church, 175–176

Holy Family Parish, 165, 169–194

Holy Mother Mary. *See* Mary, devotion to

Holy Week festivities, 34, 139, 191–192

Holy Week pilgrimage. *See* Chimayó pilgrimage

Hondo Arroyo, 58–59

Hopi Pueblos, 27

Hughes, Jennifer Scheper, 113

hymns, 124

Iberian Catholicism, 17–18

iconography, 103–104

immigrant Mexicans, 140

Indian influences, 35–36, 135–136. *See also specific tribes, Pueblos*

indigenous populations, 2, 22, 36–37. *See also specific groups*

interfaith pilgrimages, 159

interpretive plaques, 197

Isleta Pueblo, 22

Istipula (Sant), 57–58

Jaramillo, Cleofas, 58–59

Jemez, Mexico, 17

Jesús, Nuestro Padre Nazareno, 56–57, 113

Jesus images, 107–108; Christ Child *bultos* (statues), 105–106; Santiago on his horse, 108–109, 127–128, *128*, 130. *See also* Santo Niño Cautivo; Santo Niño de Atocha; Señor de Esquipulas

Jews, 159

Johnson, E. Dana, 127–128

José (San), 108–109

Kay, Elizabeth, 64–65

Kearny, Stephen Watts, 85–87

kinship patterns, 86, 96

Lady of Atocha, 102–103, 112–113

Lady of Guadalupe, 188

Lady of La Vang, 188

Lady of Sorrows, 188

Lamadrid, Enrique, 44, 140, 213n17

Lamy, Jean Baptiste, 11, 69, 87–94, 99–100, 200, 209n7, 210n34; "Christmas Pastoral" letter, 89, 212n38; "Rules That Must Be Observed by the Brothers of the Catholic Confraternity of Penitentes," 88; sermons, 213n24

land grants, 27–28

Land of Poco Tiempo (Lummis), 44

land use, 124

Lange, Yvonne, 114

Latin America, 2

Latinos, xi, 5–7, 200–201

lava beds, 206n13

Lawrence, D. H., 125

legal ownership, 67, 90–95, 195–196

leyenda negra (Black Legend), 46

Libradita, Mama, 155

liminoid phenomenon, 147–148

Lizana y Beaumont, Francisco Javier de, 209n2

El Llano, 28

Llano Quemado chapel, 127

"The Log," 60

López, Luis, 27

Lord of Esquipulas. *See* Cristo Negro de Esquipulas; Señor de Esquipulas

Los Alamos, New Mexico, 9, 159

Los Alamos mission, 170

Los Niños Foundation, 191
Lost Child. *See* Santo Niño de Atocha
Luhan, Mabel Dodge, 125
Lujan, Josepha, 27
Lummis, Charles, 35, 43–44
Luxán, Juan, 16
Lynch, John, 70

MacCannell, Dean, 161–162, 164
Machebeuf, Joseph, 88
Madonna Gardens, 188
Manuela de Atocha, 106
Marianism, 102–103, 112–113, 188
marketing, 178–179
Marriott, Alice, 96
Martínez, Antonio José, 34, 60–62, 69, 77–78, 86–89, 209nn7–8, 210n34; and Chimayó Rebellion, 81, 83–85; as delegate minister, 210n23; Taos seminary, 72
Martínez, María, 96–100, 111, 213n18
Martínez family, 98–99
Mary, devotion to, 102–103, 112–113, 188
Los Matachines, 180–181
Mateo, Miguel, 179–180
Maya, 48–50
mayordomos, 171
McWilliams, Carey, 214n1
media coverage, 156, 158
medicine, 29–30
Medina, Paul, 176
Medina, Severiano, 108–111
Medina Chapel (Santo Niño Chapel), 7, 108–111, *109*, 124, 173, 189; devotion to Santo Niño, 118–120, 218n22; Good Friday observances, 144; location of, 213n18; masses, 170; name change, 118–119; ownership of, 118–119; updates and renovations, 119–120, 189–191
Medina family, 7, 109, 118
Meem, John Gaw, 125, 127, 129, *130*, 134–135, 215n13
memory, social, 196–197
Mexican-American War, 11, 68

Mexican Catholicism, 35
Mexican period, 9, 11, 70–71, 73–81, 83–85, 210n20
Mexico: administration of New Mexico, 78, 210n20; Catholic Church, 10–11, 32, 35, 70–71, 78, 201; independence, 10, 68–73; pilgrims, 2; trade with, 154
Miracle Cross of Chimayó, 179–180
miracle stories, 185–186; of Chimayó, 181–187; of healing dirt, 40, 117–120, 123, 157–158, 177, 181–187; of Santo Niño de Atocha, 104–105, 110–111, 116–118, 184–185; of Señor de Esquipulas crucifix, 55–62, 63–65; testimonials of, 182–187
Miranda, Jesse, 200
mission churches, 127, 134–135, 207n17
Molleno, 50
Montgomery, Charles, 126
Montoya, Clemente, 27
Moors, 104
moradas, 33–34, 110–111
Moros y Cristianos, 180–181
Muslims, 159
mythology, 49–50

Nambé, *8*, 9, 170
National Geographic Traveler, 178
National Historic Landmarks, 174
National Register of Historic Places, 174
native priests, 71–72
Navajos, 79, 107–108
Nevada, 201
New Age spiritual seekers, 2, 140
New Mexico, 6; Catholic Church, 69–73, 78; Catholicism, 51, 65–66, 68–100, 199–201; cultural heritage, 136; Department of Tourism, 178; Historic Preservation Division, 132; history of, 10, 87, 215n33; Mexican period, 70–71, 78–79, 210n20; tourism, 175, 187; U.S. annexation, 68, 85–87, 91–100
New Mexico Historical Society, 128
New Mexico National Guard, 155–156

New Spain, 18, 32, 66–67
New York Times, 177
Nuestra Señora de Dolores chapel, 173
Nuestra Señora del Carmen chapel, 173
Nuestra Señora de los Dolores *bulto,* 75
Nuestro Padre Jesús Nazareno: devotion to, 56–57, 113
Nuestro Señor de Esquipula crucifix. *See* Señor de Esquipulas
Nuevomexicanos, xi, 135–136
nuns, 89–90

Ohkay Owingeh Pueblo, *8,* 9, 16
Ojo Sarco mission, 170
O'Keeffe, Georgia, 125
Old Spanish Trail, 154
Oñate, Juan de, 9, 16–19, 21, 69
oral traditions, 58–59
oratorios, 28, 32, 123, 173, 205n30
origin stories, 66–67, 206n12
Orsi, Robert, 3, 199
Ortega, José Vibián, 52
Ortiz, Alfonso, 41–42
Ortiz, Juan Felipe, 72
Our Lady of the Rosary Parish, 172–173
Our Lord of Esquipulas. *See* Cristo Negro de Esquipulas; Señor de Esquipulas
ownership of the Santuario de Chimayó, 134–138, 166–167; legal, 4, 11–12, 67, 90–95, 134–138, 195–198; religious, 4–7, 11–12, 67, 90–95, 118, 132, 169–199

pacification, 24
paganism, 84–85
Parsons, Elsie Clews, 57–58
Patronato Real, 18–19, 69–70
Peace Pilgrimage, 159
Peña, Ramon, 60–62
peninsulares, 70–71
Penitentes. *See* Hermanos de la Fraternidad Piadosa de Nuestro Padre Jesús Nazareno
Peralta, Pedro de, 18

Pérez, Albino, 78–82, 89
Pescador, Juan Javier, 103, 105, 110–111, 212n2
Philippines, 2
Picuris, 9, 26–27, 84–85
pilgrims and pilgrimage, 196–197; antimodern, 149; Bataan Death March commemoration, 12, 155–156, 216n19, 217n22; as liminoid phenomenon, 147–148; march against drug abuse, 159–160; modern, 149; Prayer Pilgrimage for Peace, 159; Spanish pilgrimage, 114; special interest pilgrimages, 158–159; themes of, 118; touristy pilgrims, 160–167; for vocations, 150–151, 158–159. *See also* Chimayó pilgrimage
pilgrim staffs, 141
Pitaval, Jean Baptiste, 94
pitero (flute player), 33–34
placitas, 28
Placitas, 107–108
Plains Indians, 24–25, 28–29, 31–32
"Plan of Rebels," 79–81
Plateros, Mexico, 103
Plaza Abajo, 28
Plaza del Cerro (Chimayó), 7, 124
pocito (hole), 203n1; Santuario de Chimayó, 1–2, 44, 55, 57–58, 76–77, 97–98, 119–120, 178, *183,* 192, 200
pocito room (Santuario de Chimayó), 132, 145–146
Pojoaque, *8,* 9, 170
Popé, 21–23
popular healing, 29–30
popular religion, 28–31, 172
population, 9, 24, 26, 199–202
El Potrero *placita,* 1–2, 28, 38, 52, 56
El Potrero Trading Post, 7, 165, 191
Prayer Pilgrimage for Peace, 159
prayer portals, 188
Presbyterians, 171
preservation, 125–138

priests, 71–73, 89–90, 170. *See also individual priests by name*
Prince, L. Bradford, 63, 92–94, 122
processions, 45, 56, 96, 99, 103, 124, 144–145, 192
Protestants, 85, 140, 142–143, 171
La Puebla, 28
Pueblo Revolt, 7–9, 21–28
Pueblos, 19–22, 29–31, 35–37, 98–99
punched tin, 126
Putnam, Robert, 201

Quemado, 26
Quintana, Chris, 160
Quintana, Ray "Cabrita," 173–174

racism, 35, 130–131, 137–138
Rafael (San), 108–109
railroad, 11–12, 124
ramadas, 7
rancherías, 28
Ranchito, 28
Rancho de Chimayó restaurant, 175
Rasch, David, 132
Read, Benjamin M., 39, 93–95, 208n41
reclamation, cultural, 126–127, 217n36
record keeping, 24–25
religion, 40–41, 177; autonomy of, 87; borderlands of, 163; folk, 30–32, 34–37, 156–157, 214n30; popular, 28–31, 172. *See also* Catholicism
religious competition, 107–111, 213n14
religious culture, 90
religious movements, 159
religious ownership, 4–7, 11–12, 67, 90–95, 118, 132, 169–199
religious tourism, 160–167, 174–180
Republic of Mexico. *See* Mexico
Requerimiento, 18–19
retablos (altarpieces), 38; Santuario de Chimayó screens, 50, 135, 197–198
revisionism, 215n33, 216n19
Río Arriba, 9, 14–38

Río Grande, 7–9, *8*, 21
rites and rituals: Penitente, 96, 124, 205n40; secular, 161
Roca, Casimiro, 12, 158, 169–181, 196, 200
rosary devotion, 113
Ruiz, Juan, 63
"Rules That Must Be Observed by the Brothers of the Catholic Confraternity of Penitentes" (Lamy), 88
Russell, Larry, 118, 168

sacred geography, 41–42
saint veneration, 56–57, 107–108, 116–117, 214n30
Sallnow, Michael, 151–152
Salpointe, Jean Baptiste, 90–91, 93
San Buenaventura de Chimayó (Plaza del Cerro), 28
Sanches Bergara (or Sánchez Vergara), Mariano, 52
San Cristoval, 24–25
Sanctuario of the Santo Niño. *See* Santuario de Chimayó (El Santuario de Nuestro Señor de Esquipulas)
Sandoval, Joanne Dupont, 165, 213n12
San Ildefonso mission, 170
San Ildefonso Pueblo, *8*, 9, 26–27, 96
San Juan, 9, 16, 20–21, 23, 25, 84–85. *See also* Ohkay Owingeh
San Lazaro, 24–26
Santa Clara Pueblo, *8*, 9
Santa Cruz, 7–9, *8*, 25–29, 52, 71, 206n5; Catholic parish, 32–33, 137, 170, 170–171; Franciscans, 10, 17–22, 25, 31–38, 50, 69–72, 170, 210n15; Mexican period, 84–85
Santa Cruz grant, 27–28
Santa Cruz River valley, 7–9, 14, 25, 28–31; Mexican period, 84–85; Pueblo occupation, 14–15, 23; Spanish settlement, 14–20, 24–28
Santa Fe, 9, 18, 22, 32. *See also* Archdiocese of Santa Fe

Santa Fe Fiesta, 136

Santa Fe New Mexican, 125, 127, 129, 131, 134, 216n21

Santa Fe Trail, 154

santeros (carvers of saints' images), 38, 51, 106, 197

Santiago, 180

Santiago de Esquipulas, Guatemala, 39, 47–50, 53–54, 207nn18–19; Cristo Negro de Esquipulas, 47–48; Señor de Esquipulas crucifix, 38, 47–48, 53

Santiago on his horse (*bulto*),108–109, 127–128, *128*, 130

Santo Domingo, 26–27

El Santo Niño, New Mexico, 106

Santo Niño Cautivo (Captive Holy Child), 104, 114–116

Santo Niño Chapel. *See* Medina Chapel

Santo Niño de Atocha, 101–102, 112–113, *115*, 116; devotion to, 3, 96–100, 101, 104–121, *117*, 137–138, 146, 156, 200, 216n19, 218n22; iconography of, 103–104; as miracle worker, 104–105, 110–111, 116–118; origins of, 102–105, 214n31; as pilgrim, 114–116, *115*

Santo Niño *santeros*, 106

santos, 74, 126

Santuario de Chimayó (El Santuario de Nuestro Señor de Esquipulas), *133*, *185*; administration of, 118–119, 169–170, 192; annual visitors, 139–140, 216n1; architecture, 127, 135; artworks, 74–75, 106, 127, 212–213n12; bell towers, 132, *133*; Bernardo Abeyta Welcome Center, 7, 188; buildings and grounds, 7, 188–190; *bultos* (statues), 74, 106, 109, 127–128, *128*, 197; cenacle, 188; Chapel of the Christ of Esquipulas, 119; Christian power, 112–118; commercial ventures, 3, 12, 106–108, 143, 160, 164–165, 174–180, 213n12; construction of, 1–2, 10, 63, 68, 208n36; contemporary use, 9–10, 12–13, 118–119, 169–194; daily rhythms, 137–138; devotion to Cristo de Esquipulas, 97, 119–120, 200, 216n19, 218n22; devotion to the Santo Niño, 96–97, 108–121, *117*, 137–138, 146, 200, 216n19, 218n22; future directions, 12, 191–193; gift shops, 165, 174, 180–181, 188, 197; Good Friday pilgrimage, 92, 99, 139–147, *142*, *145*, 158, 160, 168–169; healing dirt, 1, 39, 42–46, 51, 55, 76–77, 139, 181–187; history of, 2–3, 193–194; Holy Child Chapel (*see* Medina Chapel); Indian hypothesis, 41–46; influence of, 201–202; interpretive plaques, 197; legal ownership of, 4, 11–12, 67, 90–95, 134–138, 195–198; liturgical items and vestments, 74; local use and access, 86, 137; location or site of, 1–2, 7–9, *8*, 14, 39, 168–169; Madonna Gardens, 188; main altar, 98; maintenance of, 174; Marian images, 188–189; as meeting place, 3, 123; Mexican period, 73–77, 80; miracles, 55–62, 63–65, 181–187; as mission outpost, 11, 137; National Historic Landmark status, 174; official inventories, 74–75; origins of, 39–67, 101, 154, 208n36; ownership of, 134–138, 166–167; pastoral leadership and administration of, 169–170; physical deterioration of, 170, 173; physical improvements, 158; as pilgrimage destination, 2–7, 11–12, 39, 42–43, 62, 75–77, 92–98, 106–107, 122, 139–168, 187–194, 200–202, 216n19; *pocito* (hole), 1–2, 44, 55, 57–58, 76–77, 97–98, 119–120, 178, *183*, 192, 200; *pocito* (hole) room, 132, 145–146; popular use and appreciation of, 95–96; prayer portals, 188; priests, 12, 170–171; processions, *45*, 96, 99, 124, 144–145; property, 92–93; religious ownership of, 4–7, 11–12, 67, 90–95, 118, 132, 169–199; religious worship at, 2, 68, 76–77, 100, 163–164; renovation and restoration of, 132, *133*, 137–138, 173–174; *retablos* (altar screens), 50, 135, 197–198;

sale of, 4, 11–12, 122–138, *130*, 193; Santo Niño Chapel (*see* Medina Chapel); *santos*, 74, 106; Señor de Esquipulas crucifix (large), 1–2, 10, 38–39, 46–66, *51*, 76, 119–120, 197–198; Señor de Esquipulas crucifix (small), 50, 54–55; territorial period, 91–99; testimonials, 182–187; Tewa origins, 41–46, 66–67; Three Cultures Monument, 188; tourism, 12, 123, 161–163, 174–180; as U.S. National Historic Landmark, 169; weekly Mass, 170–171, 173

Santurio de Shamno, 57–58

Saturday Evening Post, 156

Schroeder, Albert T., 15, 20

Scott, Winfield Townley, 129

secularization, 69–70

secular rituals, 161

secular tourism, 178–179

self-flagellation, 36, 124

self-reliance, 118

Señor de Esquipulas crucifix (Chimayó) (large), 38, 39, *51*; devotion to, 47–48, 52–53, 76, 97, 119–120; miraculous apparition of, 55–62, 63–65, 119–120; origin stories, 1–2, 10, 46–55, 55–63, 63–66, 76

Señor de Esquipulas crucifix (Chimayó) (small), 50, 54–55

Señor de Esquipulas crucifix (Guatemala), 38, 47–49, 53–55, 197–198

Señor de Plateros crucifix, 103

Señor Santiago, 180–181

shackles, 104, 114–116

Shamnoag, 57–58

Sheehan, Michael, 143–144, 192

shepherd's cycle, 65

Sikhs, 159

silver, 103–104

Sinclair, John L., 101

singing, 124

sipapu, 44–45

slavery, 17, 22, 27, 29

social memory, 196–197

Society for the Preservation of Spanish Antiquities in New Mexico, 126–127

soil, healing. *See* healing dirt

Sons of the Holy Family, 118–119, 170, 175–177, 180–181, 187, 198, 208n35

southern Tewas. *See* Tanos

Spaniards, 17–21, 24–25, 32, 46–48

Spanish Americans, 37–38, 135–136

Spanish and Indian Trading Company, 125

Spanish Catholicism, 5–7, 113

Spanish colonial arts, 126–127, 131, 135–136

Spanish Colonial Arts Society, 5, 11–12, 126–129, 131–132, 134–138, 195–196

Spanish colonialism, 54–55, 136, 214n1

Spanish Empire, 9–10, 15, 204n28

Spanish farmers, 29

Spanish pilgrimage, 114

Spanish Pueblo style, 127

Spanish settlement, 14–20, 23–25, 27–28

special interest pilgrimages, 158–159

spirituality, 160–167, 196

staged authenticity, 161–163

Stations of the Cross, 124

statues (*bultos*), 38, 74, 109, 125, 197; Christ Child, 105–106; Santiago on his horse, 108–109, 127–128, *128*, 130; wandering, 57–58

storytelling: buried treasure stories, 64–65; miraculous apparition stories, 55–62, 63–65, 119–120; origin stories, 66–67; shepherd's cycle, 65. *See also* miracle stories

Sunset, 178

syncretism, 46

Tamarón y Romeral, Pedro, 73

Tanos, 21–22, 24–27, 206n5

Taos, New Mexico, 9, 17–18, 123

Taos Pueblo, 9, 23, 26–27

Taos seminary, 72

taxes, 78–81, 85, 89–90, 99, 210n20

Taylor, Carl, 35

terminology, x–xi

territorial period, 11, 91–99
testimonials, 182–187
Tesuque, 9
Tewas: Catholicism, 37; Christianity, 19–20; early, 2, 9, 14–16, 18–22, 41–46, 154, 195–196, 206n5; shrines, 207n16; southern (see Tanos)
Texas, 201
Third Order Franciscans. See Franciscans
Three Cultures Monument, 188
tierra santa (holy dirt), 48, 55, 177–178, 181–187
tin, punched, 126
tithing, 89–90, 212n38
Tiwa, 9
Toledo, Juan José, 30–31
tourism, 2, 12, 123, 135–138, 156–157, 187, 195–197; promotion of, 178–181; religious, 160–167, 174–180; secular, 178–179; spiritual, 160–167
Towa é, 42
trade, 154
Las Trampas mission, 170
Travel and Leisure, 178
Tree of Knowledge of Good and Evil, 49–50
Tree of Life, 48–50, 54–55
tree trunks, 60–61
Truchas, 8, 26, 170–173
Trujillo, Bonnie, 181
Trujillo, Juan de Jesús, 72, 86
Tsimajoòŋwi Pueblo, 42
Tsimajopokwi pool, 42
Tsi Mayoh hill, 2, 7, 15, 42–45, 45, 154, 168–169
Turner, Edith, 44–45, 65, 147–150
Turner, Victor, 44–45, 65, 147–151
Tzimayo, 27

underground passages, 206n12
underworld, 44
United States: Catholicism, 199–202; takeover of New Mexico, 85–87, 99–100
University of New Mexico, 160
U.S. Catholic Church, 201–202

Usen, Burton, 179–180
Usner, Don, 44, 63, 175–176, 190

Vanderwood, Paul, 116–117
Vargas, Diego de, 7
Vatican, 11, 70–71
Vélez Capuchín, Tomás, 30–31
veneration of Jesus, Nuestro Padre Jesús Nazareno, 56–57, 113
veneration of saints, 56–57, 107–108, 116–117, 214n30
veneration of the Santo Niño de Atocha, 3, 96–100, 101, 104–121, 117, 137–138, 146, 156, 200, 216n19, 218n22
veterans, 12, 155–156, 216n19, 217n22
Vietnam, 2
Vigil, Juan, 106
Vigil, Martha E., 60
Vigil Store. See El Potrero Trading Post
village crafts, 126
village life, 34–35, 90, 122–123
Villa Nueva de Santa Cruz de la Cañada, 7, 25
Virgin Mother Mary. See Mary
visions. See apparitions
visor clips, 186
vocations, pilgrimages for, 150–151, 158–159

walking sticks, 141
weaving, 75, 81
Weigle, Marta, 35–36
Wilson, Chris, 215n33
witchcraft, 30–31, 36–37, 77, 205n33
women's pilgrimages, 150–151
Wood, Charles A., 157
Woodward, Dorothy, 111
World War I veterans, 217n22

Zacatecas, Mexico, 14, 103
Zaldívar, Vicente de, 17
Zimayo, 23
Zubiría y Escalante, José Antonio Laureano de, 33, 71–73, 84–86, 88, 219n8
Zuni, 17, 206n13

ABOUT THE AUTHOR

Brett Hendrickson is Associate Professor of Religious Studies at Lafayette College in Easton, Pennsylvania. His first book, *Border Medicine: A Transcultural History of Mexican American Curanderismo*, was also published by New York University Press.

CPSIA information can be obtained
at www.ICGtesting.com
Printed in the USA
FSHW02n1953011018
52679FS